RESEARCH
AND THE FUTURE OF AMERICA

Ten Breakthrough Actions Vital to Our Nation's Prosperity and Security

Committee on Research Universities

Board on Higher Education and Workforce

Policy and Global Affairs

NATIONAL RESEARCH COUNCIL
OF THE NATIONAL ACADEMIES

THE NATIONAL ACADEMIES PRESS
Washington, D.C.
www.nap.edu

THE NATIONAL ACADEMIES PRESS   500 Fifth Street, NW   Washington, DC 20001

NOTICE: The project that is the subject of this report was approved by the Governing Board of the National Research Council, whose members are drawn from the councils of the National Academy of Sciences, the National Academy of Engineering, and the Institute of Medicine. The members of the committee responsible for the report were chosen for their special competences and with regard for appropriate balance.

This study was supported by Grant No. 2010-3-04 between the National Academy of Sciences and the Alfred P. Sloan Foundation, Grant No. 10-96822-000-HCD with the John D. and Catherine T. MacArthur Foundation, and Grant No. OIA-1048372 with the National Science Foundation and the U.S. Department of Energy. Any opinions, findings, conclusions, or recommendations expressed in this publication are those of the authors and do not necessarily reflect the views of the organizations or agencies that provided support for the project.

International Standard Book Number-13:   978-0-309-25639-1
International Standard Book Number-10:   0-309-25639-9
Library of Congress Control Number: 2012939571

Additional copies of this report are available from the National Academies Press, 500 Fifth Street, NW, Keck 360, Washington, DC 20001; (800) 624-6242 or (202) 334-3313; *http://www.nap.edu*.

Printed in the United States of America

THE NATIONAL ACADEMIES
Advisers to the Nation on Science, Engineering, and Medicine

The **National Academy of Sciences** is a private, nonprofit, self-perpetuating society of distinguished scholars engaged in scientific and engineering research, dedicated to the furtherance of science and technology and to their use for the general welfare. Upon the authority of the charter granted to it by the Congress in 1863, the Academy has a mandate that requires it to advise the federal government on scientific and technical matters. Dr. Ralph J. Cicerone is president of the National Academy of Sciences.

The **National Academy of Engineering** was established in 1964, under the charter of the National Academy of Sciences, as a parallel organization of outstanding engineers. It is autonomous in its administration and in the selection of its members, sharing with the National Academy of Sciences the responsibility for advising the federal government. The National Academy of Engineering also sponsors engineering programs aimed at meeting national needs, encourages education and research, and recognizes the superior achievements of engineers. Dr. Charles M. Vest is president of the National Academy of Engineering.

The **Institute of Medicine** was established in 1970 by the National Academy of Sciences to secure the services of eminent members of appropriate professions in the examination of policy matters pertaining to the health of the public. The Institute acts under the responsibility given to the National Academy of Sciences by its congressional charter to be an adviser to the federal government and, upon its own initiative, to identify issues of medical care, research, and education. Dr. Harvey V. Fineberg is president of the Institute of Medicine.

The **National Research Council** was organized by the National Academy of Sciences in 1916 to associate the broad community of science and technology with the Academy's purposes of furthering knowledge and advising the federal government. Functioning in accordance with general policies determined by the Academy, the Council has become the principal operating agency of both the National Academy of Sciences and the National Academy of Engineering in providing services to the government, the public, and the scientific and engineering communities. The Council is administered jointly by both Academies and the Institute of Medicine. Dr. Ralph J. Cicerone and Dr. Charles M. Vest are chair and vice chair, respectively, of the National Research Council.

www.national-academies.org

Hunter Rawlings, President Emeritus and Professor of Classical History, Cornell University*

John Reed, Chairman of the MIT Corporation and Chairman and CEO, Citigroup (retired)

Teresa Sullivan, President, University of Virginia

Sidney Taurel, Chairman and CEO, Eli Lilly & Company (retired)

Lee T. Todd, Jr., President, University of Kentucky

Laura D'Andrea Tyson, S. K. and Angela Chan Chair in Global Management, Haas School of Business, University of California Berkeley

Padmasree Warrior, Chief Technology Officer, Cisco Systems

Staff

Peter H. Henderson, Study Director

James Voytuk, Senior Program Officer

Tom Arrison, Senior Program Officer

Mark Regets, Senior Program Officer (until January 31, 2011)

Michelle Crosby-Nagy, Research Associate (until January 14, 2011)

Laura DeFeo, Christine Mirzayan Science and Technology Policy Fellow

Paola Giusti-Rodriguez, Christine Mirzayan Science and Technology Policy Fellow

Amy Hein, Christine Mirzayan Science and Technology Policy Fellow

Michelle Tangredi, Christine Mirzayan Science and Technology Policy Fellow

Sabrina Hall, Program Associate

---

*Hunter Rawlings resigned in May 2011 upon his appointment as President, Association of American Universities.

vi

Foreword

REQUEST FROM CONGRESS

In 2005 a bipartisan group in Congress asked the National Academies to identify the key steps that the U.S. Congress should take to ensure a science and technology enterprise that would enable the United States to compete in the global economy of the 21st century. In response, the National Academies appointed a committee, under the leadership of Norman Augustine, that produced *Rising Above the Gathering Storm: Energizing and Employing America for a Brighter Economic Future*.[1] That report provided a powerful framework for discussing America's competitiveness as well as recommendations that formed the basis of the America COMPETES Act.[2]

Four years later, in 2009, Senators Lamar Alexander and Barbara Mikulski and Representatives Bart Gordon and Ralph Hall requested that the National Academies provide a follow-up report that examines more deeply the health and competitiveness of the nation's research universities. They noted that America's research universities "have been the critical assets that have laid the groundwork—through research and doctoral education—for the development of many of the competitive advantages that make possible the high American standard of living." But they also

---

[1] National Academy of Sciences, National Academy of Engineering, and Institute of Medicine, Rising Above the Gathering Storm: Energizing and Employing America for a Brighter Economic Future. Washington, DC: National Academies Press, 2007.

[2] America Creating Opportunities to Meaningfully Promote Excellence in Technology, Education, and Science Act, Public Law No. 110-69.

noted that, while our research universities are admired throughout the world and their contributions cannot be overstated, they are nonetheless "under stress, even as other countries are measurably improving the quality of their research institutions." Consequently, they requested that the Academies "assess the organizational, intellectual, and financial capacity of public and private American research universities relative to research universities internationally."[3]

CHARGE TO THE STUDY COMMITTEE

The Governing Board of the National Research Council accepted the request from Congress. The NRC then empanelled a study committee composed of individuals who are leaders in academia, industry, government, and national laboratories. In selecting the committee, the NRC sought not only balance across sectors, but also diversity among academic institutions, balance across fields, and wide geographic distribution, including individuals with significant international experience. The committee was charged with the following task:

> An ad hoc committee will author a consensus report with findings and recommendations that answer the question:
>
> What are the top ten actions that Congress, the federal government, state governments, research universities, and others could take to assure the ability of the American research university to maintain the excellence in research and doctoral education needed to help the United States compete, prosper, and achieve national goals for health, energy, the environment, and security in the global community of the 21st century.
>
> The study committee will, in carrying out its work, focus on:
>
> • Research and doctoral programs carried out by research universities and associated medical centers;
> • Basic and applied research in research universities, along with collaborative research programs with other components of the research enterprise (e.g., national and federal laboratories, federally funded research and development centers, and corporate research laboratories);
> • Doctoral education and, to the extent necessary, the pathways to graduate education and research careers; and
> • Fields of study and research that are critical to helping the United States compete, prosper, and achieve national goals for health, energy, the environment, and security, with a focus on science, engineering, and medicine.

---

[3] See Appendix A for Letter of Request.

In carrying out this charge, the study committee will, in addition to other tasks it identifies:

- Describe and assess the historical development, current status, trends, and societal impact of research universities and the "ecosystem" of this set of institutions in the United States, placing these institutions in the context of the nation's research, innovation, and industrial enterprises and the nation's system of higher education;
- Assess the organizational, financial, and intellectual capacity of public and private research universities in the United States, including reference to research universities internationally to the extent possible with existing data; and
- Envision the mission and organization of these diverse institutions 10–20 years into the future and the steps needed to get there.

THE REPORT

The study committee has taken stock of the health of our nation's research universities today and envisioned the role we would like them to play in our nation's life 10 to 20 years from now. They have found that without reservation, our research universities are, today, the best in the world, yet they face critical threats and challenges that may seriously erode their quality. In response to its charge, the committee produced this report—their vision for strengthening these institutions so that they may remain dynamic assets over the coming decades—as the launch of a decade-long effort involving many constituencies. In order for the program they outline to ensure we have strong research universities 20 years from now that remain critical national assets, the actions necessary to implement their recommendations and achieve our goals will necessarily evolve as their details are thought through, new challenges and opportunities arise, and as we surely emerge from the economic circumstances present at the time of their writing. Experience with earlier reports, such as *Rising Above the Gathering Storm*, suggests that the role of this report should be to lay out and justify the findings concerning the challenges and needs, provide general recommendations that may be adapted to changing circumstances, and then develop implementation plans for each constituency that will evolve and adapt in a changing world (e.g., the economy).

America's research universities have been "breaking through" to create a better life for Americans for more than a century. While Bell Labs and their counterparts have given way to Silicon Valley and their counterparts, American research universities continue to provide the heartbeat that keeps major innovation alive. The plan for action in this report, when followed for the remainder of this decade, will set the course for continued American leadership and good jobs for Americans. As this report is finalized, citizens from all over the world question America's capability to lead the world to a new century of growth. As Americans, we must accept this challenge, and these 10 recommendations hold a critical key to that success.

Charles M. Vest, President   Charles O. Holliday, Jr., Chair
National Academy of Engineering   Committee on Research Universities

Acknowledgments

This report has been reviewed in draft form by individuals chosen for their diverse perspectives and technical expertise, in accordance with procedures approved by the National Academies' Report Review Committee. The purpose of this independent review is to provide candid and critical comments that will assist the institution in making its published report as sound as possible and to ensure that the report meets institutional standards for objectivity, evidence, and responsiveness to the study charge. The review comments and draft manuscript remain confidential to protect the integrity of the process.

We wish to thank the following individuals for their review of this report: Patrick Aebischer, École Polytechnique Fédérale de Lausanne; Nancy Andrews, Duke University; Robert Atkinson, Information Technology and Innovation Foundation; William Banholzer, Dow Chemical Company; Steven Beckwith, University of California; Robert Berdahl, Association of American Universities; Richard Celeste, Colorado College; Jonathan Cole, Columbia University; Rita Colwell, University of Maryland; Anthony DeCrappeo, Council on Government Relations; David Goldston, Natural Resources Defense Council; Stephen Emerson, Haverford College; Leroy Fletcher, Texas A&M University; Paul Gray, Massachusetts Institute of Technology; Peter McPherson, Association of Public and Land-grant Universities; William Press, University of Texas; Alison Richard, Yale University; Michael Rothschild, Princeton University; Debra Stewart, Council of Graduate Schools; Ronald Sugar, Northrop Grumman Corporation; Jack Martin Wilson, University of Massachusetts; and Nancy Fugate Woods, University of Washington.

Although the reviewers listed above have provided many constructive comments and suggestions, they were not asked to endorse the conclusions or recommendations, nor did they see the final draft of the report before its release. The review of this report was overseen by Maxine Savitz, Honeywell Inc. (retired) and Stephen Fienberg, Carnegie Mellon University. Appointed by the National Academies, they were responsible for making certain that an independent examination of this report was carried out in accordance with institutional procedures and that all review comments were carefully considered. Responsibility for the final content of this report rests entirely with the authoring committee and the institution.

The study committee thanks the National Science Foundation, the U.S. Department of Energy, the Alfred P. Sloan Foundation, and the John D. and Catherine T. MacArthur Foundation for the financial support they provided for this study and the many experts who met with the committee to provide their insights on the policy, organizational, financial, and intellectual issues central to the committee's charge. Special thanks to Ariella Barrett, Research Librarian for her assistance verifying the citations. We also thank the staff of the National Research Council who helped organize our committee meetings and draft the report.

Contents

xv

Boxes, Figures, and Tables

Note: In three-digit box, figure, and table numbers, the middle number indicates the Recommendation that the box, table, or figure corresponds to.

BOXES

xvii

FIGURES

TABLES

Knowledge will forever govern ignorance: And a people who mean to be their own governours must arm themselves with the power which knowledge gives.

—President James Madison, 1822
Entrance to the James Madison Building of the
Library of Congress

Summary

America is driven by innovation—advances in ideas, products, and processes that create new industries and jobs, spur economic growth and support a high standard of living, and achieve national goals for defense, health, and energy. In the last half-century, innovation in turn has been increasingly driven by educated people and the knowledge they produce. Our nation's primary source of both new knowledge and graduates with advanced skills continues to be its research universities.

These institutions, with the strong and sustained support of government and working in partnership with American industry, are widely recognized as the best in the world, admired for both their research and their education. They are, however, confronted by many pressures: the economic challenges faced by the nation and the states, the emergence of global competitors, changing demographics, and rapidly evolving technologies. Even as other nations around the world have emulated the United States in building research universities to drive economic growth, America's commitment to sustaining the research partnership that built a great industrial nation has weakened under these pressures.

Expressing concern that the nation's universities are at risk, U.S. Senators Lamar Alexander and Barbara Mikulski and U.S. Representatives Bart Gordon and Ralph Hall in 2009 asked the National Academies to assess the competitive position of American research universities, both public and private, and to respond to the following question: "What are the top ten actions that Congress, state governments, research universities, and others can take to maintain the excellence in research and doctoral education needed to help the United States compete, prosper, and achieve national goals for health, energy, the environment, and security in the global community of the 21st century?"

In response, the National Research Council (NRC) convened a committee of individuals who are leaders in academia, industry, government, and national laboratories. In selecting the committee, the NRC sought not only balance across sectors, but also diversity among academic institutions, balance across fields, and wide geographic distribution, including individuals with significant international experience. This report is the committee's response to its charge.

We believe that America's research universities are, today, a key asset for our nation's future. They are so because of the considered and deliberate decisions made in the past by policy makers, even in difficult times. Our future now depends on the willingness of our current policy makers to follow their example and make the decisions that will allow us to continue to compete, prosper, and shape our destiny. *It is essential that we as a nation reaffirm, revitalize, and strengthen substantially the unique partnership that has long existed among the nation's research universities, the federal government, the states, and philanthropy by enhancing their roles and linkages and also providing incentives for stronger partnership with business and industry.* In doing so, we will encourage the ideas and innovations that will lead to more high-end jobs, increasing middle-class incomes, and the security, health, and prosperity we expect.

FINDINGS

In the course of our history, America has set and accomplished grand goals that have defined us as a nation. Our national assets strongly position the United States to accomplish our current goals and lead the world in the 21st century. However, the relative rankings of the United States in the global knowledge economy at a time when new knowledge and technological innovation are critical to economic growth and other national goals have shown that other countries increasingly are investing in their own competitiveness.

As America pursues economic growth and other national goals, its research universities have emerged as a major national asset perhaps even its most potent one. This did not happen by accident; it is the result of prescient and deliberate federal and state policies. These began with the Morrill Act of 1862 and subsequent land-grant acts that established a partnership between the federal government and the states in building universities that would address the challenges of creating a modern agricultural and industrial economy for the twentieth century. They were amplified as the partnership was powerfully rebuilt in the decades following World War II. The importance of government-sponsored university research intensified during the World War II partnership that led to breakthrough discoveries that helped win the war, including radar, the proximity fuse, penicillin, DDT, the computer, jet propulsion, and the atomic bomb.[1] Drawing on this experience, the government-university partnership was expanded in the 1950s and 1960s to contribute to national security, public health, and economic growth. Through this expanded partnership, basic research as the source of new ideas for the long term would be increasingly funded by the federal government and largely concentrated in the nation's research universities.

The results of this federal-state-university partnership have had great impact on our nation's economy, health, and other national achievements. Talented graduates of these institutions have created and populated many new businesses that go on to employ millions of Americans. As Jonathan Cole, former provost of Columbia University, relates, "The laser, magnetic-resonance imaging, FM radio, the algorithm for Google searches, global-positioning systems, DNA fingerprinting, fetal monitoring, bar codes, transistors, improved weather forecasting, mainframe computers, scientific cattle breeding, advanced methods of surveying public opinion, even Viagra had their origins in America's research universities. Those are only a few of the tens of thousands of advances, originating on those campuses that have transformed the world."[2]

In addition to their high productivity, the exceptional stature of American research universities globally can be measured in several additional ways. In global rankings, U.S. research universities typically account for 35 to 40 of the top 50 such institutions in the world. Since the 1930s, roughly 60 percent of Nobel Prizes have been awarded to scholars at American institutions. More international students enroll in U.S. research universities than their counterparts elsewhere.

Despite their current global leadership, American research universities are facing critical challenges. First, their financial health is endangered as each of their major sources of revenue has been undermined or contested. Federal funding for research has flattened or declined; in the face of economic pressures and changing policy priorities, states are either unwilling or unable to continue support for their public research universities at world-class levels; endowments have deteriorated significantly in the recent recession; and tuition has risen beyond the reach of many American families. At the same time, research universities also face

---

[1] Hugh Davis Graham and Nancy Diamond, The Rise of American Research Universities: Elites and Challengers in the Postwar Era. Baltimore, MD: The Johns Hopkins University Press, 1997, p. 28.

[2] Jonathan Cole, Can American research universities remain the best in the world? *The Chronicle of Higher Education*, January 3, 2010.

strong forces of change that present both challenges and opportunities: demographic shifts in the U.S. population, transformative technologies, changes in the organization and scale of research, a global intensification of research networks, and changing relationships between research universities and industry.

In addition, U.S. universities face growing competition from their counterparts abroad, and the nation's global leadership in higher education, unassailable for a generation, is now threatened. Our research universities have brought to this country the most outstanding students and scholars from around the world, and these individuals have contributed substantially to our research and innovative capacity. Now, other nations recognize the importance of world-class research universities and are rapidly strengthening their institutions to compete for the best international students and for faculty, resources, and reputation. These countries have developed national strategies for education and research and are also offering attractive opportunities to repatriate their citizens who are graduates of U.S. universities.

With these developments in mind, we have identified a set of specific challenges and opportunities that a reasoned set of policies must address in order to produce the greatest return to our society, our security, and our economy. The first group identifies issues in the partnership among the federal government, states, business, and universities:

- Federal funding for university research has been unstable and, in real terms, declining at a time when other countries have increased funding for research and development (R&D), both in nominal terms and as a percentage of gross domestic product.
- State funding for higher education, already eroding in real terms for more than two decades, has been cut further in the recent recession.
- Business and industry have largely dismantled the large corporate research laboratories that drove American industrial leadership in the twentieth century (e.g., Bell Labs), but have not yet fully partnered with our research universities to fill the gap at a time when we need to more effectively translate, disseminate, and transfer into society the new knowledge and ideas that emerge from university research.
- Research universities need to be responsive to stakeholders by improving management, productivity, and cost efficiency in both administration and academics.

The second group identifies issues that affect the operations of universities, the efficient administration of university research, the effectiveness of doctoral education, and the robustness of the pipeline of new talent:

- Insufficient opportunities for young faculty to launch academic careers and research programs;
- Underinvestment in campus infrastructure, particularly in cyber-infrastructure, that can lead to long-term increases in productivity, cost-effectiveness, and innovation in research, education, and administration;
- Research sponsors that do not pay the full cost of research they procure, meaning that universities have to cross-subsidize research from other sources;
- A burdensome accumulation of federal and state regulatory and reporting requirements that increases costs and sometimes challenges academic freedom and integrity;
- Opportunities to improve doctoral and postdoctoral preparation that increase both its productivity and its effectiveness in providing training for highly productive careers;
- Demographic change in the U.S. population that necessitates strategies for increasing the success of female and underrepresented minority students; and
- Competition for international students, researchers, and scholars.

The principles and recommendations that follow are designed to help federal and state policy makers, universities, and businesses overcome these hurdles and capitalize on these opportunities. Strong leadership—and partnership—will be needed by these parties if our research universities and our nation are to thrive.

PRINCIPLES

For the past half-century, the research and graduate programs of America's research universities have been essential contributors to the nation's prosperity, health, and security. Today, our nation faces new challenges, a time of rapid and profound economic, social, and political transformation driven by the growth in knowledge and innovation. Educated people, the knowledge they produce, and the innovation and entrepreneurial skills they possess, particularly in the fields of science and engineering, have become the keys to America's future.

We have taken stock of the organizational, financial, and intellectual health of our nation's research universities today and have envisioned the role we would like them to play in our nation's life 10 to 20 years from now. We can say without reservation that our research universities are, today, the best in the world and an important resource for our nation, yet at the same time, they are in grave danger of not only losing their place of global leadership but of serious erosion in quality due to critical trends in public support.

Our vision for strengthening these institutions so that they may remain dynamic assets over the coming decades involves both increasing their productivity and ensuring their strong support for education and research. Therefore, it is essential that the unique partnership that has long existed among the nation's research universities, the federal government, the states, and business and industry be reaffirmed and strengthened. This will require

• A balanced set of commitments by each of the partners—federal government, state governments, research universities, and business and industry—to provide leadership for the nation in a knowledge-intensive world and to develop and implement enlightened policies, efficient operating practices, and necessary investments.

• Use of matching requirements among these commitments that provide strong incentives for participation at comparable levels by each partner.

• Sufficient flexibility to accommodate differences among research universities and the diversity of their various stakeholders. While merit, impact, and need should continue to be the primary criteria for awarding research grants and contracts by federal agencies, investment in infrastructure should consider additional criteria such as regional and/or cross-institutional partnerships, program focus, and opportunities for building significant research capacity.

• A commitment to a decade-long effort that seeks to both address challenges and take advantage of opportunities as they emerge.

• A recognition of the importance of supporting the comprehensive nature of the research university, spanning the full spectrum of academic and professional disciplines, including the physical, life, social, and behavioral sciences; engineering; the arts and humanities; and the professions, that enable it to provide the broad research and education programs required by a knowledge- and innovation-driven global economy.

Within this partnership, our research universities—with a historical commitment to excellence, academic freedom, and service to society—must pledge themselves to a new level of partnership with government and business; recommit to being the places where the best minds in the world want to work, think, educate, and create new ideas; and commit to delivering better outcomes for each dollar spent.

RECOMMENDATIONS

The United States can best leverage research universities for the breakthroughs it needs by ensuring they are properly resourced, increasingly productive, agile and innovative, and working creatively in partnership with business. With that in mind, we recommend that the federal government, the states, research universities, and business and industry take the following actions that reinforce their partnership:

Recommendation 1

Within the broader framework of United States innovation and research and development (R&D) strategies, the federal government should adopt stable and effective policies, practices, and funding for university-performed R&D and graduate education so that the nation will have a stream of new knowledge and educated people to power our future, helping us meet national goals and ensure prosperity and security.

Actors and Actions—Implementing Recommendation 1:

- *Federal government*: The federal government should review and modify those research policies and practices governing university research and graduate education that have become burdensome and inefficient, such as research cost reimbursement, unnecessary regulation, and awkward variation and coordination among federal agencies. (See Recommendations 6 and 7.)

- *Federal government—Congress, Administration, federal science and technology (S&T) agencies*: Over the next decade as the economy improves, Congress and the administration should invest in basic research and graduate education at a level sufficient to produce the new knowledge and educated citizens necessary to achieve national goals. As a core component of a national plan to raise total national R&D to 3 percent of gross domestic product (GDP), Congress and the Administration should provide full funding of the amount authorized by the America COMPETES Act that would double the level of basic research conducted by the National Science Foundation (NSF), National Institute of Standards and Technology (NIST), and Department of Energy (DOE) Office of Science as well as sustain our nation's investment in other key areas of basic research, including biomedical research. Within this investment, as recommend by *Rising Above the Gathering Storm*,[3] a portion of the increase should be directed to high-risk, innovative, and unconventional research.

- *Federal government—White House Office of Science and Technology Policy (OSTP), President's Council of Advisors on Science and*

---

[3] National Academy of Sciences, National Academy of Engineering, and Institute of Medicine, Rising Above the Gathering Storm: Energizing and Employing America for a Bright Economic Future, Washington, DC: National Academies Press, 2007.

Technology (PCAST), U.S. Office of Management and Budget (OMB), National Economic Council (NEC), and Council of Economic Advisors (CEA): On an annual basis in the President's annual budget request, OMB should develop and present, in coordination with OSTP, a federal science and technology budget that addresses priorities for sustaining a world-class U.S. science and technology enterprise. On a quadrennial basis, OSTP, in conjunction with PCAST, and OMB, in conjunction with the NEC and CEA, should review federal science and technology spending and outcomes, internationally benchmarked, to ensure that federal S&T spending is adequate in size to support our economy and appropriately targeted to meet national goals. We recommend that this process consider U.S. global leadership, a focus on developing new knowledge, balance in the science and technology portfolio, reliable and predictable streams of funding, and a commitment to merit review.

Budget Implications

This recommendation calls for stable and effective federal research policies and practices, the budget implications of which are outlined under several recommendations below. The recommendation also aims to ensure robust financial support for critical federal basic research programs. It supports funding increases that Congress has *already authorized* through the America COMPETES Act for the doubling of funding for the NSF, NIST, and DOE Office of Science. These increases target stronger investment in physical sciences and engineering research, but do not imply any disinvestment in critical fields such as the life sciences and social, behavioral, and economic sciences. Indeed, we recommend Congressional action to at least *maintain* current levels of funding for basic research across other federal agencies, including the National Institutes of Health (NIH), as adjusted for inflation. Research universities, along with other research performers (national laboratories, nonprofit research and development organizations, and industry), will only benefit from these actions through their success in competing for federal grants and contracts from these agencies.

Expected Outcomes

Supportive federal research policies would ensure stable funding and cost-efficient regulation sufficient to enable corresponding university investment in research facilities and graduate programs. By completing the funding of the America COMPETES Act, the nation would achieve a balanced research portfolio capable of driving innovation necessary for economic prosperity. As research and education are deliberately intertwined in our American research universities, such funding will also ensure that we continue to produce the scientists, engineers, physicians, teachers, scholars, and other knowledge professionals essential to the nation's security, health, and prosperity.

Recommendation 2

Provide greater autonomy for public research universities so that these institutions may leverage local and regional strengths to compete strategically and respond with agility to new opportunities. At the same time, restore state appropriations for higher education, including graduate education and research, to levels that allow public research universities to operate at world-class levels.

Actors and Actions—Implementing Recommendation 2:

- *State governments*: States should move rapidly to provide their public research universities with sufficient autonomy and agility to navigate an extended period with limited state support. (See also regulatory environment, below.)
- *State governments*: For states to compete for the prosperity and welfare of their citizens in a knowledge- and innovation-driven global economy, the advanced education, research, and innovation programs provided by their research universities are absolutely essential. Hence, as state budgets recover from the current recession, states should strive to restore and maintain per-student funding for higher education, including public research universities, to the mean level for the 15-year period 1987-2002, as adjusted for inflation.[4]
- *Federal government*: To provide further incentives for state actions to protect the quality of public research universities as both a state and a national asset, federal programs designed to stimulate innovation and workforce development at the state level, including those recommended in this report, should be accompanied by strong incentives to stimulate and sustain state support for their public universities.

---

[4] A 15-year period was used so as to ensure the funding recommendation was not unduly influenced by year-to-year fluctuations in state appropriations. The year 2002 was used as the endpoint of the period, as that year represents the beginning of a period of significant decline in appropriations.

Budget Implications

This recommendation addresses the alarming erosion in state support of higher education over the past decade that has put the quality and capacity of public research universities at great risk. While the committee urges the states to strive to restore over time appropriation cuts to public research universities estimated to average 25 percent (and ranging as high as 50 percent for some universities),[5] it acknowledges that current state budget challenges and shifting state priorities may make this very difficult in the near term. Hence, the committee views as equally important a strong recommendation that the states provide their public research universities with sufficient autonomy and ability to navigate what could be an extended period with inadequate state funding. The committee strongly believes that such recommendations are in the long-term interests of both the states and the nation.

Expected Outcomes

State appropriations per enrolled student have declined by 25 percent or more over the past two decades, resulting in the need for universities to increase tuition or reduce activities, or quality. As states strive to compete in a knowledge- and innovation-driven global economy, restoring state appropriations to levels sufficient to maintain advanced education, research, and innovation programs provided by research universities is absolutely essential for the prosperity and welfare of their citizens. Increasing the autonomy and agility of public research universities should increase their efficiency and productivity as well as their ability to respond to changing state and regional needs during an extended period when states may not be able to restore adequate support.

---

[5] The National Science Board reports, "Over the decade [2002 to 2010], per-student state support to major research universities dropped by an average of 20 percent in inflation-adjusted dollars. In 10 states, the decline ranged from 30 percent to 48 percent." National Science Board, Science and Engineering Indicators 2012, p. 8-68. Available at: http://www.nsf.gov/statistics/seind12/pdf/c08.pdf (accessed March 8, 2012). The states have enacted further and deeper cuts in 2011 and 2012, which suggests an overall decline for 2002-2012 of at least 25 percent. For example, the State Higher Education Executive Officers Association (SHEEO) recently reported, "FY 2012 state appropriations [for higher education] (including a small residual of ARRA funding) were $72.5 billion, a decrease of 7.6 percent from $78.5 billion in FY 2011." See SHEEO, "Commentary on FY 2012 state appropriations for higher education," press release, January 23, 2012. Available at: http://grapevine.illinoisstate.edu/tables/FY12/SHEEO%20Commentary%20(2).pdf (accessed March 8, 2012).

Recommendation 3

Strengthen the business role in the research partnership, facilitating the transfer of knowledge, ideas, and technology to society and accelerate "time to innovation" in order to achieve our national goals.

Actors and Actions—Implementing Recommendation 3:

- *Federal government*: Continue to fund and expand research support mechanisms that promote collaboration and innovation.
- *Federal government*: Within the context of also making the R&D tax credit permanent, implement new tax policies that incentivize business to develop partnerships with universities (and others as warranted) for research that results in new U.S.-located economic activities.
- *Business, universities*: The relationship between business and higher education should evolve into more of a peer-to-peer nature, stressing collaboration in areas of joint interest rather than the traditional customer-supplier relationship in which business procures graduates and intellectual property from universities.
- *Business, universities*: Business and universities should work closely together to develop new graduate degree programs that address strategic workforce gaps for science-based employers.
- *National laboratories, business, universities*: Collaboration among research by the nation's national laboratories, business, and universities should also be encouraged, since the latter's capacity for large-scale, sustained research projects both supports and depends critically on both the participation of university faculty and graduate students and the marketplace.
- *Universities*: Improve management of intellectual property to improve technology transfer.

Budget Implications

Tax policies that create incentives for new university-industry research and development partnerships will have a cost to the federal budget as a "tax expenditure." Although we are not in a position to estimate what that cost would be, it would be a relatively minor component of the cost of current proposals to make permanent the R&D tax credit.

Expected Outcomes

Effective use of research support mechanisms that promote collaboration will lead to the creation and efficient use of knowledge to achieve national goals.

The outcomes from the new tax policies would be new research partnerships; new knowledge and ideas; new products, processes, and industries located in the United States; economic growth; and new jobs. The outcomes from these efforts would be the creation of new partnerships, new knowledge and ideas, achieving national goals in key policy areas, and the economic growth and jobs that result from new activity.

Improvements in university management of intellectual property will result in more effective dissemination of research results, generating economic activity and jobs.

Recommendation 4

Increase university cost-effectiveness and productivity in order to provide a greater return on investment for taxpayers, philanthropists, corporations, foundations, and other research sponsors.

Actors and Actions—Implementing Recommendation 4:

- *Universities*: The nation's research universities should set and achieve bold goals in cost-containment, efficiency, and productivity in business operations and academic programs. Universities should strive to constrain the cost escalation of all ongoing activities—academic and auxiliary—to the inflation rate or lower through improved efficiency and productivity. Beyond the implementation of efficient business practices, universities should review existing academic programs from the perspectives of centrality, quality, and cost-effectiveness, adopting modern instructional methods such as cyberlearning, and encouraging greater collaboration among research investigators and institutions, particularly in the acquisition and utilization of expensive research equipment and facilities.

- *University associations*: University associations should develop and implement more powerful and strategic tools for financial management and cost accounting that better enable universities to determine the most effective methods for containing costs and increasing productivity and efficiency. As part of this effort, they should develop metrics that allow universities to communicate their cost-effectiveness to the general public.

- *Universities, working together with key stakeholders*: Universities and key stakeholders should intensify efforts to educate key audiences about the unique character of U.S. research universities and their importance to state, regional, and national goals, including economic prosperity, public health, and national security.

Budget Implications

There may be an initial cost to institutions as they examine their operations in order to identify actions that will increase efficiency and as they invest in new infrastructure. In the long term, however, research universities will reap the rewards of these investments through greater productivity. Many institutions have already demonstrated that significant cost efficiencies are attainable. If research universities can take action, states and the nation will realize greater returns on their investments, and the savings associated with cost containment and greater productivity can then be deployed to other priorities such as constraining tuition increases (a major national concern), increasing student financial aid, or launching new programs.

Expected Outcomes

By increasing cost-effectiveness and productivity, institutions will realize significant cost savings in their operations that may be used to improve performance by shifting resources strategically and/or to reduce growth in their need for resources (e.g., tuition). There are many ways to do this, but one of the easiest is to implement a "priority fund" in which the base funding of ongoing activities is reduced by 1 percent or so each year (with the "savings" reallocated to new university priorities).

Recommendation 5

Create a "Strategic Investment Program" that funds initiatives at research universities critical to advancing education and research in areas of key national priority.

Actors and Actions—Implementing Recommendation 5:

- *Federal government*: The federal government should create a new "Strategic Investment Program" supporting initiatives that advance education and research at the nation's research universities. The program is designed to be a "living" program that responds to changing needs and opportunities. As such, it will be composed of term-limited initiatives requiring matching grants in critical areas that will change over time. The committee recommends the program begin with two 10-year initiatives: (1) an endowed faculty chairs program to facilitate the careers of young investigators and (2) a research infrastructure program initially focused on advancement of campus cyberinfrastructure, but perhaps evolving later to address as well emerging needs for physical research infrastructure as they arise. The federal investments in human capital and research infrastructure are intended for both public and private research universities. They require matching funds that different types of institutions may obtain from different sources. For example, public research universities may secure their matching funds from states sources, while private research universities may obtain their matches from private sources. However, the source that a particular institution taps for matching funds is not prescribed, so public and private institutions may draw from state support, philanthropy, business, or other sources for matching funds. While merit, impact, and need should continue to be important criteria for the awarding of grants, consideration should also be given to regional and/ or cross-institutional partnerships, program focus, and opportunities for building significant research capacity, subject, of course, to the matching requirements for the federal grants.

• *Universities in partnership with state governments, business, philanthropy, and others*: Universities should compete for funding under these initiatives, bringing in partners—states, business, philanthropy, others—that will support projects by providing required matching funds.

Budget Implications

In addition to increases in federal funding for basic research (in Recommendation 1), the committee recommends federal support for these first two initiatives in the program that will cost $7 billion per year over the next decade. These funds will leverage an additional $9 billion per year through matching grants from other partners.

Expected Outcomes

This program develops and leverages the human-, physical-, and cyberinfrastructures necessary for cutting-edge research and advanced education. Of particular importance is the investment in rapidly evolving cyberinfrastructure that will increase productivity and collaboration in research, but may also provide opportunities to increase productivity in administration and education. Also of critical importance is the endowment of chairs, particularly for promising young faculty, during a time of serious financial stress and limited faculty retirements. This will ensure that we are building our research faculty for the future, as we can reap the rewards of their work over the long term.

Recommendation 6

The federal government and other research sponsors should strive to cover the full costs of research projects and other activities they procure from research universities in a consistent and transparent manner.

Actors and Actions—Implementing Recommendation 6:

• *Federal government and research sponsors*: The federal government and other research sponsors should strive to support the full cost, direct and indirect, of research and other activities they procure from research universities so that it is no longer necessary to subsidize these sponsored grants by allocating resources (e.g., undergraduate tuition and patient fees for clinical care) away from other important university missions. Both sponsored research policies and cost recovery negotiations should be developed and applied in a consistent fashion across all federal agencies and academic institutions, public and private.

Budget Implications

Federal coverage of a higher portion of indirect costs would, at the margins, shift part of federal research funding from direct to indirect costs, so there will be no net change in cost to the federal government.

Expected Outcomes

This change will allow our research universities to hold steady or reduce the amount of their funding from other sources, such as tuition revenue or patient clinical fees that they have had to provide for research procured by the federal government, amounts that have increased over the past two decades. Consequently, they will be able to use the flexibility this provides to allocate their resources from other sources more strategically for their intended purpose.

Recommendation 7

Reduce or eliminate regulations that increase administrative costs, impede research productivity, and deflect creative energy without substantially improving the research environment.

Actors and Actions—Implementing Recommendation 7:

• *Federal government (OMB, Congress, agencies), state governments*: Federal and state policy makers and regulators should review the costs and benefits of federal and state regulations, eliminating those that are redundant, ineffective, inappropriately applied to the higher education sector, or impose costs that outweigh the benefits to society.

• *Federal government*: The federal government should also harmonize regulations and reporting requirements across federal agencies so universities can maintain one system for all federal requirements rather than several, thereby reducing costs.

Budget Implications

While the staff time-to-review regulatory and reporting requirements has a small, short-term cost, the savings to universities and federal and state governments over the long term will be substantial. Quantifying the burdens is difficult, so it is not feasible to estimate the savings in advance of a review, but we believe they could run into the billions of dollars over the next decade.

Expected Outcomes

Reducing or eliminating regulations can reduce administrative costs, enhance productivity, and increase the agility of institutions. We agree with the conclusion of the Association of American Universities, Association of Public and Land-grant Universities, and Council on Governmental Relations that "minimizing administrative and compliance costs ultimately will also provide a cost benefit to the federal government and to university administrators, faculty, and students by freeing up resources and time to directly support educational and research efforts."[6] With greater resources and freedom, they will be better positioned to respond to the needs of their constituents in an increasingly competitive environment.

Recommendation 8

Improve the capacity of graduate programs to attract talented students by addressing issues such as attrition rates, time to degree, fund-

---

[6] Association of American Universities, Association of Public and Land-grant Universities, and Committee on Government Relations, Regulatory and Financial Reform of Federal Research Policy: Recommendations to the NRC Committee on Research Universities, January 21, 2011. Available at : http://www.aau.edu/policy/reports_presentations.aspx.

ing, and alignment with both student career opportunities and national interests.

Actors and Actions—Implementing Recommendation 8:

- *Research universities*: Research universities should restructure doctoral education to enhance pathways for talented undergraduates, improve completion rates, shorten time-to-degree, and strengthen the preparation of graduates for careers both in and beyond the academy.
- *Research universities, federal agencies*: Research universities and federal agencies should ensure, as they implement the above measures, that they improve education across the full spectrum of research university graduate programs, because of the increasing breadth of academic and professional disciplines necessary to address the challenges facing our changing world, including the physical, life, social, and behavioral sciences; engineering; the arts and humanities; and the professions.
- *Federal government*: The federal government should significantly increase its support for graduate education through balanced programs of fellowships, traineeships, and research assistantships provided by all science agencies dependent upon individuals with advanced training.
- *Employers*: Business, government agencies, and nonprofits that hire master's- and doctorate-level graduates should more deeply engage programs in research universities to provide internships, student projects, advice on curriculum design, and real-time information on employment opportunities.

Budget Implications

Increasing the number of federal fellowships and traineeships to support 5,000 new graduate students per year in science and engineering would amount to $325 million in year one, climbing to a steady state expenditure of $1.625 billion per year. This funding is not designed to increase the overall numbers of doctoral students per se, but to provide incentives for students to pursue areas of national need and to shift support from the research assistantship to mechanisms that strengthen doctoral training. At the same time that the committee recommends increased federal funding for graduate education, the implementation of other aspects of our recommendation will also save money for the federal government, universities, and students. Reducing attrition and time-to-degree in doctoral programs, for example, will increase the cost-effectiveness of federal and other investments in this area.

Expected Outcomes

Improving pathways will ensure that we draw strongly from among the "best and brightest" for our nation's future doctorates in science and engineering fields that are critical to our nation's future.

Improving completion rates and shortening time-to-degree to an optimal length is the right thing to do for students and also increases cost-effectiveness, ensuring good stewardship of resources from the federal government and other sources.

Strengthening preparation of doctorates for a broad range of careers, not just those in academia, assists the students in their careers, and also assists employers who need their staff to be productive in the short term. This benefits new doctorates, employers, and society.

Recommendation 9

Secure for the United States the full benefits of education for all Americans, including women and underrepresented minorities, in science, mathematics, engineering, and technology.

Actors and Actions—Implementing Recommendation 9:

- *Research universities*: Research universities should engage in efforts to improve education for all students at all levels in the United States by engaging in outreach to K–12 school districts and undertaking efforts to improve access and completion in their own institutions.
- *Research universities*: Research universities should assist efforts to improve teacher education and preparation for K–12 STEM education and improve undergraduate education, including persistence and completion in STEM.
- *Federal government, states, local school districts, industry, philanthropy, universities*: All stakeholders should take action—urgent, sustained, comprehensive, intensive, and informed—to successfully increase the participation and success of women and underrepresented minorities across all academic and professional disciplines and, especially, in science, mathematics, and engineering education and careers.

Budget Implications

Increasing federal support for programs that enable the participation and success of women and underrepresented minorities in STEM disciplines has already been stated as a priority by both the America COMPETES Act and the Office of Science and Technology Policy. The committee supports the investments recommended for these purposes by these efforts.

Expected Outcomes

Our people are our greatest asset. Improving the educational success of our citizens at all levels improves our democracy, culture and society, social mobility, and both individual and national economic success. As career opportunities in science, technology, engineering, and math continue to expand at a rapid pace, recruiting more underrepresented minorities and women into STEM careers and ensuring that they remain in the pipeline is essential and strategic not only for meeting the workforce needs of an increasingly technological nation but also for obtaining the intellectual vitality and innovation necessary for economic prosperity, national security, and social well-being that such diversity brings.

Recommendation 10

Ensure that the United States will continue to benefit strongly from the participation of international students and scholars in our research enterprise.

Actors and Actions—Implementing Recommendation 10:

- *Federal government*: Federal agencies should ensure that visa processing for international students and scholars who wish to study or conduct research in the United States is as efficient and effective as possible, consistent also with homeland security considerations.
- *Federal government*: As we benefit from the contributions of highly skilled, foreign-born researchers, the federal government should also streamline the processes for non-U.S. doctoral researchers to obtain permanent residency or U.S. citizenship in order to ensure that a high proportion remain in the United States. The United States should consider taking the strong step of granting residency (a Green Card) to each non-U.S. citizen who earns a doctorate in an area of national need from an accredited research university. The Department of Homeland Security should set the criteria for and make selections of areas of national need and of the set of accredited institutions in cooperation with the National Science Foundation and the National Institutes of Health.
- *Federal government*: Engage in the proactive recruitment of international students and scholars.

Budget Implications

There is no additional cost.

Expected Outcomes

The United States has benefited significantly over the last half-century and more from highly talented individuals who have come to the United States from abroad to study or conduct research. Today, there is increasing competition for these individuals as students or researchers both in general and from their home countries. It is in the interest of the United States to attract and keep individuals who will create new knowledge and/or convert it to new products, industries, and jobs in the United States.

CONCLUSION

During past eras of challenge and change, our national leaders have acted decisively to create innovative partnerships to enable our universities to enhance American security and prosperity.

While engaged in the Civil War, Congress passed the Morrill Land-Grant Act of 1862 to forge a partnership between the federal government, the states, higher education, and industry aimed at creating universities capable of extending educational opportunities to the working class while conducting the applied research to enable American agriculture and industry to become world leaders. Among the results were the green revolution in agriculture that fed the world, an American manufacturing industry that became the economic engine of the 20th century and the arsenal of democracy in two world wars, and an educated middle class that would transform the United States into the strongest nation on Earth.

In the 20th century, emerging from the Great Depression and World War II, Congress acted once again to strengthen this partnership by investing heavily in basic research and graduate education to build the world's finest research universities, capable of providing the steady stream of well-educated graduates and scientific and technological innovations central to our robust economy, vibrant culture, vital health enterprise, and national security. This expanded research partnership enabled America to win the Cold War and put a man on the Moon. It also developed new technologies such as computers, the Internet, global positioning systems, and new medical procedures and pharmaceuticals that contribute immensely to national prosperity, security, and public health.

Today, our nation faces new challenges, a time of rapid and profound economic, social, and political transformation driven by an exponential growth in knowledge and innovation. A decade into the 21st century, a resurgent America must stimulate its economy, address new threats, and position itself in a competitive world transformed by technology, global competitiveness, and geopolitical change. In this milieu, educated people, the knowledge they produce, and the innovation and entrepreneurial skills they possess, particularly in the fields of science and engineering, are keys to America's future.

It is essential as a nation to reaffirm and revitalize the unique partnership that has long existed among the nation's research universities, federal government, states, and business and industry. The actions recommended will require significant policy changes, productivity enhancement, and investments on the part of each member of the research partnership. Yet they also comprise a fair and balanced program that will generate significant returns to a stronger America.

1

Prologue

Innovation is the strong driver of economic growth, new industries and jobs, and a high standard of living, both in the United States and globally. In the last half-century, innovation in turn has been increasingly driven by educated people and the knowledge they produce, particularly though scientific and technological research and development. In the United States, the primary source of the new knowledge and talented individuals who apply it to achieve our security, health, prosperity, and other national goals continues to be the basic research and graduate education programs of our nation's research universities.

America's research universities, with the strong and sustained support of government and working in partnership with American industry and philanthropy, are widely recognized as the best in the world, admired for both their research and their education. They are, however, confronted by many forces: the economic challenges faced by the nation and the states, the emergence of global competitors, changing demographics, and rapidly evolving technologies. Even as other nations around the world have emulated the United States in building research universities, America's commitment to sustaining the research partnership that has helped power our economy has weakened.

Federal policies no longer place a priority on university research and graduate education; because of economic challenges and the priorities of aging populations, states no longer are either capable of supporting or willing to support their public research universities at world-class levels; business and industry have largely dismantled the large corporate research laboratories that drove American industrial leadership in the twen-

23

tieth century (e.g., Bell Labs), but have not yet fully partnered with our research universities to fill the gap; and research universities themselves have failed to achieve the cost efficiency and productivity enhancement in teaching and research required of an increasingly competitive world.

Yet a time of crisis can also stimulate a call to action. We have reached a fork in the road at which critical decisions about the future of American higher education must be made. The actions we take in the next few years will determine whether our children and grandchildren will have well-paying jobs and whether our nation will continue to have a vibrant economy, and a healthy and secure populace. It is essential that, at this fork, we as a nation take the path that reaffirms, revitalizes, and strengthens substantially the unique partnership that has long existed among the nation's research universities, the federal government, the states, and business and industry.

At this time in history, the United States faces a range of important challenges: economic recovery and growth, budget deficits, unemployment, security challenges, and spiraling health care costs. These issues must be addressed. Yet the United States can also utilize and leverage a range of extraordinary assets that will allow us to create our own destiny in the 21st century. Among those assets are our nation's research universities, which can help us address our short-term challenges even as they create new opportunities. The United States can best leverage research universities for the breakthroughs it needs for the high-end jobs, increasing middle-class incomes, and the security, health, and prosperity we expect, by ensuring these institutions are properly resourced; increasingly productive, agile, and innovative; and working creatively in partnership with business.

2

National Goals and Assets

NATIONAL GOALS

In the course of our history, our nation has set grand goals that have defined us as a nation. And then we accomplished them. We created a republic, defeated totalitarianism, and extended civil rights to our citizens. We joined our coasts with a transcontinental railroad, linked our cities through the interstate highway system, and networked ourselves and the globe through the Internet. We electrified the nation. We sent men to the Moon. We created a large, strong, and dynamic economy, the largest in the world since the 1870s and today comprising one-quarter of nominal global gross domestic product (GDP).

In this century, education, research, new ideas, and technological innovation will help us sustain our quality of life and ensure our health, security, and prosperity.

- Advances in medicine and health care:
   − Biomedical research, such as that funded by the National Institutes of Health, seeks "fundamental knowledge about the nature and behavior of living systems." The application of that knowledge enhances health, lengthens life, and reduces the burdens of illness and disability.[1]
   − Behavioral and social research help us understand and address mental illness, addiction, and health disparities; provide insights that allow us to increase prevention and wellness, manage disease, and support

---

[1] See http://www.nih.gov/about/mission.htm (accessed March 12, 2012).

an aging population; suggest approaches to improve the development and use of health information technology; and formulate policies that improve the use of resources in health care.

- A sustainable, healthier environment:
  - Basic research in the environmental sciences helps us better understand our natural environment, how and why it is changing, and the policy options for maintaining and restoring environmental quality.
  - Social science research helps us understand how population change and economic development affect the environment, how societies adapt to environmental change, how people understand environmental risks, and ways to encourage the invention, adoption, and use of technologies that improve environmental conditions.
  - Advances in technology improve water and air quality, reduce pollution, facilitate environmental cleanup, and improve agricultural productivity and sustainability.
- Energy security:
  - Basic and applied energy research leads to new or improved technologies that improve the efficiency of existing technologies or provide new alternatives that diversify or enhance our energy sources.
  - Social and behavioral research helps encourage and measure the adoption of new technologies, match technological design to societal needs, and facilitate more efficient energy consumption.
- Improved standards of living:
  - Research in the physical and life sciences creates knowledge and ideas that can be developed into new products, and into processes that create companies, jobs, and economic growth and new solutions for health, agriculture, transportation, communication, and information technologies and infrastructure.
  - Social and behavioral research provides insight into how research impacts innovation, economic growth, and other aspects of societal well-being so that our policies help to facilitate these changes. The tools of social and behavioral science are instrumental in the design, marketing, and distribution of new products and services.
- Education for our children and adults:
  - Research in cognitive sciences has provided new knowledge and insights into the way students learn, creating the potential for powerful changes in curricula, teaching, and learning in all fields, but especially in science, technology, engineering, and mathematics.
- Enhanced security:
  - Scientific and engineering research lead to the development of technologies that improve public safety and emergency and public health preparedness, counter terrorism, and ensure homeland security, national defense, and cybersecurity.

   – Research in the social sciences and humanities has allowed us to better understand other cultures we may be allied or in conflict with so we can adapt strategies to improve diplomatic and military outcomes. Research in the cognitive sciences and on computerized language techniques has improved intelligence analysis and improved threat detection.

• Civic life:
   – Research in engineering and the information sciences has led to the development of computing technologies that permit the analysis of large and complex bodies of data and elegant communication of findings from such analyses.

   – The behavioral and social sciences have provided tools—social surveys, censuses, and administrative record systems and the methods for analyzing them—that inform governments, businesses, and the general public about the state of our nation and about political, social, and economic processes.

As the National Governors Association notes, "colleges and universities play a critical role in state economies through the production of workers in critical occupations, the conduct of research, and the dissemination and commercialization of new knowledge." [2] These institutions have a global impact as well as their research which translates into new knowledge and innovative technologies plays a strong role in addressing global grand challenges that affect all of humankind (see Box 2-1). University basic research and education are investments for the long term that ensure we will have new ideas not just for today but also for driving change that will improve the lives of our children and grandchildren.

ASSETS FOR INNOVATION

   Our assets strongly position the United States to accomplish its goals and lead the world in the 21st century. These assets include the following:

• A large country geographically, with substantial natural resources and a large, barrier-free internal market.
• A political culture characterized by freedom, democracy, and the rule of law.
• An economic culture that rewards entrepreneurship, openness to change, and a willingness to take and reward risk.

---

[2] National Governors Association, Higher Education's Contribution to Economic Growth Strategies. Available at: http://www.nga.org/cms/home/nga-center-for-best-practices/center-issues/page-ehsw-issues/col2-content/main-content-list/higher-educations-contribution-t.html (accessed September 16, 2011).

BOX 2-1
Grand Challenges of Engineering

From urban centers to remote corners of Earth, the depths of the ocean to space, humanity has always sought to transcend barriers, overcome challenges, and create opportunities that improve life in our part of the universe. In the last century alone, many great engineering achievements became so commonplace that we now take them mostly for granted. Technology allows an abundant supply of food and safe drinking water for much of the world. We rely on electricity for many of our daily activities. We can travel the globe with relative ease, and bring goods and services wherever they are needed. Growing computer and communications technologies are opening up vast stores of knowledge and entertainment. As remarkable as these engineering achievements are, certainly just as many more great challenges and opportunities remain to be realized. While some seem clear, many others are indistinct and many more surely lie beyond most of our imaginations. Today, we begin engineering a path to the future.

Here are the Grand Challenges for engineering as determined by a committee of the National Academy of Engineering:

- Make solar energy economical
- Provide energy from fusion
- Develop carbon sequestration methods
- Manage the nitrogen cycle
- Provide access to clean water
- Restore and improve urban infrastructure
- Advance health informatics
- Engineer better medicines
- Reverse-engineer the brain
- Prevent nuclear terror
- Secure cyberspace
- Enhance virtual reality
- Advance personalized learning
- Engineer the tools of scientific discovery

Source: National Academy of Engineering, Grand Challenges of Engineering, http://www.engineeringchallenges.org/ (accessed September 16, 2011).

- A strongly growing and increasingly diverse population, enriched by its capacity to attract talented immigrants from around the world.
- A historic commitment to education that, until recently, pioneered and led the world in the expansion of high school and college education.[3]
- An ecosystem of public and private research universities that in-

---

[3] Claudia Goldin and Lawrence F. Katz, The Race Between Education and Technology. Cambridge, MA: Harvard University Press, 2008.

cludes, according to one ranking, 35 of the top 50 such institutions in the world.[4]

- Tremendous wealth, with substantial public and private capital to fund education, infrastructure, research, and corporate growth.

By mixing stability, freedom, knowledge, and individual empowerment, our culture creates a fertile milieu for opportunity, innovation, and change. Consequently, our assets have allowed us to make the United States a nation of unparalleled economic, cultural, and military strength. Yet the late-twentieth-century creation of a global knowledge economy has made the environment for innovation and competitiveness more complex and the need for action to sustain and strengthen our assets central to any strategy for meeting our national goals.

We cannot take our continued strength for granted. While economists have attributed much of our economic growth in the last half-century to technological innovation,[5] the relative ranking of the United States in the global knowledge economy has shown that other countries are investing in their own competitiveness. Recently, for example, indexes of innovation and/or competitiveness have placed the United States variously at 4th, 8th, or 11th globally, depending on the indicators and methodology used.[6]

The National Academies' *Rising Above the Gathering Storm*, which provided a detailed analysis of our nation's competitiveness, expressed pride in the vitality of the American economy, "derived in large part from the productivity of well-trained people and the steady stream of scientific and technological innovations they produce." However, they also noted,

---

[4] Shanghai Jiao Tong University, Academic Rankings of World Universities—2010. Available at: http://www.arwu.org/ARWU2010.jsp (accessed February 9, 2011).

[5] Robert M. Solow, Technical change and the aggregate production function," *The Review of Economics and Statistics*, Vol. 39, No. 3 (Aug. 1957), pp. 312-320, identified technological change as a key driver of economic growth in the twentieth century. Since its publication, economists have continued to explore through complex formulations just how much our economic growth is due to technological change, and how much is due to human capital, managerial improvement, process innovation, and other factors. A recent examination of the economic returns more specifically to research can be found in National Research Council, Measuring the Impacts of Federal Investments in Research: A Workshop Summary, Washington, DC: National Academies Press, 2011.

[6] Information Technology and Innovation Foundation and European-American Business Council, The Atlantic Century II, July 2011. Available at: http://www.itif.org/files/2011-atlantic-century.pdf (accessed September 16, 2011). Boston Consulting Group/National Association of Manufacturers, International Innovation Index, March 2009. Available at: http://www.bcg.com/media/pressreleasedetails.aspx?id=tcm:12-8040 (accessed May 13, 2011). INSEAD, Global Innovation Index Report, 2009-2010. Available at: http://www.global innovationindex.org/gii/main/analysis/showindexranking.cfm?vno=a (accessed May 13, 2011).

BOX 2-2
The Context for Innovation and Competitiveness Policy

"The United States takes deserved pride in the vitality of its economy, which forms the foundations of our high quality of life, our national security, and our hope that our children and grandchildren will inherit ever greater opportunities. That vitality is derived in large part from the productivity of well-trained people and the steady stream of scientific and technical innovations they produce. Without high-quality, knowledge-intensive jobs and the innovative enterprises that lead to discovery and new technology, our economy will suffer and our people will face a lower standard of living. Economic studies conducted even before the information-technology revolution have shown that as much as 85% of measured growth in U.S. income per capita was due to technological change.

"Today, Americans are feeling the gradual and subtle effects of globalization that challenge the economic and strategic leadership that the United States has enjoyed since World War II. A substantial portion of our workforce finds itself in direct competition for jobs with lower wage workers around the globe, and leading-edge scientific and engineering work is being accomplished in many parts of the world. Thanks to globalization, driven by modern communications and other advances, workers in virtually every sector must now face competitors who live just a mouse-click away in Ireland, Finland, China, India, or dozens of other nations whose economies are growing. This has been aptly referred to as 'the Death of Distance.'

"Having reviewed trends in the United States and abroad, the committee is deeply concerned that the scientific and technological building blocks critical to our economic leadership are eroding at a time when many other nations are gathering strength....Although the U.S. economy is doing well today, current trends indicate...that the United States may not fare as well in the future without government intervention. This nation must prepare with great urgency to preserve

---

"A substantial portion of our workforce finds itself in direct competition for jobs with lower wage workers around the globe, and leading-edge scientific and engineering work is being accomplished in many parts of the world. Thanks to globalization, driven by modern communications and other advances, workers in virtually every sector must now face competitors who live just a mouse-click away in Ireland, Finland, China, India, or dozens of other nations whose economies are growing. This has been aptly referred to as 'the Death of Distance.'"

The authors of the report were "deeply concerned that the scientific and technological building blocks critical to our economic leadership are

its strategic and economic security. Because other nations have, and probably will continue to have, the competitive advantage of a low-wage structure, the United States must compete by optimizing its knowledge-based resources, particularly in science and technology, and by sustaining the most fertile environment for new and revitalized industries and the well-paying jobs they bring."

—Excerpted from National Academy of Sciences, National Academy of Engineering, and Institute of Medicine, Rising Above the Gathering Storm: Energizing and Employing Americans for a Brighter Economic Future, (Washington, DC: National Academies Press, 2007), pp. 1-4.

"Because we have been so blessed in this country, we tend to assume that we are the best in the world. Yet we should take note of the areas in which we are not, by most metrics, ranked number one. For example, we are sixth in global innovation-based competitiveness and fortieth in the rate of change in that measure over the last decade. We are eleventh among OECD countries in the fraction of our young adults who have graduated from high school (a number that is truly appalling) and sixteenth in college completion rate. We are twenty-second in our provision of broadband Internet access to our citizens; twenty-fourth in life expectancy at birth; and twenty-seventh among developed nations in the fraction of our college students receiving degrees in science or engineering. Finally, according to the World Economic Forum . . . we are forty-eighth in the quality of our K–12 math and science education. These figures put American exceptionalism in context: we are number one, except when we are not."

—Excerpted from Charles M. Vest,
Remarks in "Making America More Competitive, Innovative, and Healthy,"
Bulletin of the American Academy of Arts and Sciences, Summer, 2011, p. 32.

eroding at a time when many other nations are gathering strength"[7] (see Box 2-2). Consequently, they provided recommendations for improving K–12 science and mathematics education, science and engineering human capital, research, and the innovation environment. These critical recommendations are the starting point for ensuring a competitive U.S. innovation capacity.

In the past quarter-century, several deeply significant developments

---

[7] National Academy of Sciences, National Academy of Engineering, and Institute of Medicine, Rising Above the Gathering Storm: Energizing and Employing America for a Brighter Economic Future. Washington, DC: National Academies Press, 2007, pp. 1-4.

have changed the global economy and the kinds of actions that nations must take to remain competitive:

- Coinciding with the end of the Cold War, the economic policies of the world's two largest countries—China and India—shifted in two important ways: (1) They moved from planned to more capitalistic economic systems, and (2) they developed strong export sectors that produced low-cost goods or provided low-costs services (e.g., call centers) through the use of abundant low-wage labor.[8]
- Global trade intensified and supply chains have extended further and further. Because of revolutions in shipping (e.g., containerization) and telecommunications (i.e., the Internet), global sourcing moved production of many goods to low-wage economies.[9]
- Countries that benefited from lower-cost production of goods for export—first, Japan, then Taiwan and South Korea, now China and India—took the profits and reinvested them in the innovation capacity—including educational and research infrastructure—that will allow them to advance further.[10]
- More advanced countries have also noted the importance of and have invested in education and research, particularly in science and technology. So, while the United States has increased the percentage of its 24-year-olds who have earned a first university degree in the natural sciences or engineering, other countries such as Finland, France, and the United Kingdom, have increased it further and now outpace us on this key indicator.[11] Similarly, while the United States has continued to fund research and development at a high level, other countries have increased their spending at a still faster rate.[12]

These are powerful trends that led Thomas Friedman to argue that "the world is flat."[13] The United States must continue to capitalize on its assets in this flatter world, but to do so requires a concerted and strategic effort.

In this competitive world, the ingredients for national success are

---

[8] L. Alan Winters and Shahid Yusuf, eds., Dancing with Giants: China, India, and the Global Economy. Washington, DC: The World Bank, 2007.

[9] Thomas Friedman, The World Is Flat: A Brief History of the Twenty-First Century, Release 2.0. New York: Farrar, Straus, and Giroux, 2006.

[10] National Research Council, The Dragon and the Elephant: Understanding the Development of Innovation Capacity in China and India. Washington, DC: National Academies Press, 2010.

[11] National Science Board, Science and Engineering Indicators 2004. Arlington, VA: National Science Foundation, 2004, Figure 2-34, p. 2-36.

[12] National Science Board, Science and Engineering Indicators 2010. Arlington, VA: National Science Foundation, 2010, Figures 4-13 and 4-16, pp. 4-35 and 4-36.

[13] Thomas Friedman, The World Is Flat. Op. cit.

many.[14] They include the assets outlined at the beginning of this chapter. Models for understanding the role of scientific research and technological innovation more specifically and indexes for ranking countries on their innovation and competitiveness capacity include a lengthy range of diverse indicators. One index, developed by the Information Technology and Innovation Foundation (ITIF) in coordination with the European-American Business Council (EABC), placed the United States fourth globally in 2011. This index was built on 16 indicators measuring human capital, innovation capacity, entrepreneurship, information technology infrastructure, economic policy factors, and economic performance. (See Table 2-1 for ITIF–EABC rankings of the United States on each of these indicators in 2011.)[15] A "scoreboard" on science, technology, and industry, developed by the Organisation for Economic Co-operation and Development (OECD), examines country performance on 57 indicators, including competing in the world economy, connecting to global research, and investing in the knowledge economy.[16] *Rising Above the Gathering Storm, Revisited: Rapidly Approaching Category 5* examined multiple "ingredients for innovation" across knowledge capital, human capital, and the innovation environment.[17]

The importance of research universities to knowledge generation and innovation is evident in all of these indicators. Five of the ITIF–EABC indicators—corporate research and development (R&D), government R&D, higher education attainment, science and technology researchers, and science and technology publications—are inputs to or outputs from our nation's research universities. The OECD looks intensively at R&D funding and performing trends across sectors and fields, international cooperation in research, trends in researchers, human resources in science and technology, new university graduates, new doctoral degrees,

---

[14] The relatively new field of the "science of science and innovation policy" seeks to increase our understanding of knowledge generation and innovation; to improve models, metrics, indicators, and data for measuring them; and to enhance the scientifically rigorous and quantitative basis for science policy. See NSF, Science and Science and Innovation Policy Program. Available at: http://www.nsf.gov/funding/pgm_summ.jsp?pims_id=501084 (accessed May 13, 2011), and Executive Office of the President, Office of Science and Technology Policy, Science of Science Policy, available at: http://scienceofsciencepolicy.net/ (accessed May 13, 2011).

[15] Information Technology and Innovation Foundation and European-American Business Council, The Atlantic Century II, July 2011.

[16] See http://www.oecd-ilibrary.org/content/book/sti_scoreboard-2009-en (accessed May 10, 2011).

[17] Members of the "Rising Above the Gathering Storm" Committee, Rising Above the Gathering Storm Revisited: Rapidly Approaching Category 5, Prepared for the Presidents of the National Academy of Sciences, National Academy of Engineering, and Institute of Medicine, Washington, DC: National Academies Press, 2010.

TABLE 2-1 U.S. Ranking Relative to Other Countries on Innovation and Competitiveness, 2011

Indicator	U.S. Rank 2011
Overall Rank	4
Higher Education Attainment: Percentage of adults aged 25-34 with a tertiary degree	10
Science and Technology Researchers: Science and technology researchers per 1,000 population	6
Corporate Investment in R&D: Investments in research and development by business as a percentage of GDP	5
Government Investment in R&D: Investments in R&D by government as a percentage of GDP	8
Share and Quality of World's Scientific and Technical Publications: S&T publications per million people and the relative prominence of those publications	14
Venture Capital: Venture capital investment as a percentage of GDP	11
New Firms: New corporations as a percent of total corporations	11
E-Government: A measure of the utilization of digital technology in national government	2
Broadband Telecommunications: Broadband quality and subscription rates per capita	11
Corporate Investment in Information Technology: Business investments in IT as a share of GDP	5
Effective Corporate Tax Rates: Average 5-year effective marginal corporate tax rate	35
Ease of Doing Business: A measurement of the regulatory and business climate	4
Trade Balance: Trade balance as a percentage of GDP	37
Foreign Direct Investment Inflows: Inflows from foreign direct investment as a share of GDP	34
GDP per Working-Age Adult: GDP (PPP) per adult age 25-64	1
Productivity: GDP (PPP) per hour worked	3

Source: ITIF–EABC, Atlantic Century II.

international mobility of doctoral students, and foreign students in the United States.

Gathering Storm, Revisited argues, "Given the trend of industry to invest less in fundamental research, focusing on more predictable development projects, it is increasingly left to government to fund the former type of activity. This is consistent with the notion that governments should assume responsibility for supporting activities that produce benefits to society as a whole but not necessarily to the individual performer or underwriter. In such a scenario the nation's research universities will have to assume even greater responsibility for performing much of the nation's research—with that research largely being funded by the federal government."[18]

---

[18] Members of the "Rising Above the Gathering Storm" Committee, Rising Above the Gathering Storm, Revisited: Rapidly Approaching Category 5, p. 45.

3

America's Research Universities

America's research universities, through education and basic research, have emerged as a major asset—some would say the most potent asset— for the United States as the nation seeks economic growth and national goals. *This did not happen by accident; it is the result of prescient and deliberate federal and state policies that have powerfully shaped these institutions.*

CREATING THE AMERICAN RESEARCH UNIVERSITY

Before World War II, the federal government and research universities played only a small role in scientific research and its dissemination, with a couple of notable exceptions in agricultural research and extension and early efforts in public health. Scientific research and technological change were carried out by individual researchers and inventors and by industry, which either capitalized on the innovations of others or developed their own industrial laboratories to incorporate science and engineering directly into product development.

The structure and power of the nation's science and engineering enterprise changed dramatically during World War II. Critical to the war effort, a federal-university partnership created by President Franklin Roosevelt and led by Vannevar Bush led to significant uses of scientific and technological breakthroughs in the war—including radar, the proximity fuse, penicillin, DDT, the computer, jet propulsion, and the atomic bomb—and in industry.[1] As Vannevar Bush wrote in the 1945 report *Science: The Endless Frontier*:

> We all know how much the new drug, penicillin, has meant to our grievously wounded men on the grim battlefronts of this war—the countless lives it has saved—the incalculable suffering which its use has prevented. Science and the great practical genius of this nation made this achievement possible.
>
> Some of us know the vital role which radar has played in bringing the United Nations to victory over Nazi Germany and in driving the Japanese steadily back from their island bastions. Again it was painstaking scientific research over many years that made radar possible.
>
> What we often forget are the millions of pay envelopes on a peacetime Saturday night which are filled because new products and new industries have provided jobs for countless Americans. Science made that possible, too.[2]

With the value of the partnership clearly demonstrated during wartime, this set up a model for the postwar future.

The model was harnessed to both civilian and military goals in the post–World War II era. Bush proposed, in *Science: The Endless Frontier,* a new partnership to achieve economic growth, national security, and the public health. Through this partnership, basic research would be increasingly funded by the federal government and largely concentrated in the nation's research universities.

This partnership gradually emerged over the next 15 years, encompassing a range of federal agencies and an increasing number of public and private research universities. The federal government science establishment expanded through the creation of the National Science Foundation (NSF), the expansion of the National Institutes of Health, the establishment of the National Aeronautics and Space Administration and the "Space Race," the research and development programs of the Departments of Defense, Energy, and Commerce (National Institute for Standards and Technology and the National Oceanic and Atmospheric Administration). At the same time, university research expanded. For example, from 1958 to 1968, academic research and development (R&D)

---

[1] Hugh Davis Graham and Nancy Diamond, The Rise of American Research Universities: Elites and Challengers in the Postwar Era. Baltimore: The Johns Hopkins University Press, 1997, p. 28.

[2] Vannevar Bush, Science: The Endless Frontier. Washington, DC: U.S. Government Printing Office, 1945. Available at: http://www.nsf.gov/about/history/nsf50/vbush1945.jsp (accessed September 16, 2011).

grew by 417 percent; academic research expenditures, by 587 percent; federally funded academic R&D, by 618 percent; and federally funded basic research, by 702 percent. At the same time, the G.I. Bill led to the vast expansion of the university enterprise in a way that reinforced the growth of research. Consequently, as Clark Kerr asserts, "At the end of World War II, perhaps six American universities could be called research universities, in the sense that research was the dominant faculty activity. . . . By the early 1960s, there were about 20 research universities and they received half of all federal research and development funds going to higher education. In the year 2000, there were at least 100, and many more were aspiring to this status."[3]

AN ECOSYSTEM OF DIVERSE INSTITUTIONS

This federal-university partnership has led to the creation of a large, diverse ecosystem of public and private research universities in which each institution plays critical local, regional, and national roles. An expansive view of the ecosystem would identify perhaps as many as 200 or more institutions that either award research doctorates or have more than $35 million in annual R&D expenditures. One observer has argued that about half of these, or 125 institutions, generate most of the new knowledge from research. This more limited set of institutions include about 60 institutions that are large, comprehensive research universities and rank among the top 100 universities globally. There are another 60 or so that educate undergraduate and graduate students and conduct research, but have a more limited set of fields in which they seek to excel in either doctoral education or research.[4] The ecosystem also includes our national laboratories that provide a unique capacity for large-scale, sustained research projects that would be inappropriate for universities, such as the deep space missions of the Jet Propulsion Laboratory or the Advanced Light Source at Lawrence Berkeley National Laboratory. Yet it is important to note that most of these large laboratory projects involved both university faculty and graduate students as key players.

For our purposes, research universities are those that share certain values and characteristics and participate in an "ecosystem" of research universities in which institutions interact—through cooperation and competition (see Box 3-1). Many of these values and characteristics distinguish

---

[3] Clark Kerr, The Gold and the Blue: A Personal Memoir of the University of California, 1949-1967, Volume Two: Political Turmoil, Berkeley: University of California Press, 2002, p. 92. Cited in Irwin Feller, Presentation to AAAS Science and Technology Policy Forum, April 2011.

[4] Jonathan Cole, The Great American University: Its Rise to Preeminence, Its Indispensable National Role, Why it Must be Protected, New York: Public Affairs, 2009.

BOX 3-1
Values and Characteristics of American Research Universities

The values that these institutions share include:

1. Intellectual freedom: The research university is a place of free inquiry that and a place of original ideas, a value that distinguishes U.S. research universities from many around the world.
2. Initiative and creativity: The U.S. Research University is a place that provides support for student initiative and creativity. This distinguishes us from research universities in Asia (e.g., Singapore and China) where student creativity is not supported.
3. Excellence: There is a competitive drive for talent in students and faculty and quality in research.
4. Openness: The openness of the US academy in the last century to foreign-born students and faculty, both political refugees from Europe and Asia and more purely scientifically curious.

The characteristics they share include:

5. Large and comprehensive: With some notable exceptions, they tend to be large institutions with multiple divisions comprising the "multiversity" described by Clark Kerr.
6. Undergraduate experience: The U.S. Research University includes an undergraduate residential experience that distinguishes these institutions from counterparts in Europe (e.g., France, Germany, and the Netherlands). This experience provides an opportunity to learn outside the classroom as well as within. The undergraduate experience is also enriched by the opportunity to participate in the research activities of faculty.
7. Graduate education: These institutions emphasize high caliber advanced training for graduate students, with a relatively high ratio of graduate students to undergraduates and the integration of graduate education and research.
8. Faculty: These institutions have faculty intensely who are engaged in research and scholarship and compete for external research funding. Research performance plays a critical role in the decision for tenure.
9. Research: Characterized by high levels of research, generally linked to scholarship, economic productivity, and world leadership.
10. Leadership: Enlightened and bold leadership.

Sources: Cole, The Great American University. Graham and Diamond, The Rise of American Research Universities.

American research universities from their counterparts around the world and the ecosystem they participate in may also be distinguished from its counterparts. The traditional European model of higher education emphasizes centralized planning, state control, state funding, little competition, and a focus on research and advanced training. In the American ecosystem, by contrast, there is significant diversity among research universities in size, geography, and missions. The ecosystem is characterized by decentralization, pluralism (public and private institutions), diverse funding sources (endowment, federal, state, tuition), high levels of competition, and a hybrid model that includes undergraduate education, graduate study, and research "in the same place, done by the same people, frequently at the same time."[5] These distinctions have made our ecosystem extremely productive. Indeed, the success of the U.S. system has prompted others to move toward our system, for example, the ongoing debates about the higher education sector in the United Kingdom.

The U.S. ecosystem and its productivity, argues Jonathan Cole, is importantly defined by "unprecedented, vast" federal funding for science and technology research. Hugh Graham and Nancy Diamond note that higher education grew substantially in the post–World War II era because of growing economic prosperity, the baby boom, and revolution in federal science policy. The last of these more specifically drove the expansion of the nation's research universities. And, as a consequence, "American universities, not widely respected in the international community of scholars and scientists prior to World War II, subsequently won preeminence among the world's leading institutions."[6]

The U.S. ecosystem and its productivity, argue Graham and Diamond, also are importantly defined by a large, competitive, national market for faculty in which state funding has also played a critical role. This market emerged among a small set of prominent institutions between 1900 and 1925. In this system, faculty careers were defined by upward mobility through lateral movement that made the curriculum vitae all important, a primary attachment to profession rather than institution, and research productivity. In this environment, public research universities could only provide salaries competitive with those of private research universities through economies of scale and state appropriations.[7]

QUALITY AND IMPACT

Measuring the direct contribution of universities, through this federal-state-university partnership, on the economy and society is a complex task,[8] yet a series of indicators reveal a pattern of quality and impact.

---

[5] Graham and Diamond, Rise of American Research Universities, p. 1.

[6] Cole, Great American University; Graham and Diamond, Rise of American Research Universities, pp. 1 and 11.

[7] Graham and Diamond, Rise of American Research Universities, pp. 20-22.

[8] National Research Council, Measuring the Impact of Federal Investments in Research: Summary of a Workshop. Washington, DC: National Academies Press, 2011.

2001
Worldwide: 2 million students
U.S.: 547,000 students

2008
Worldwide: 3 million students
U.S.: 624,000 students

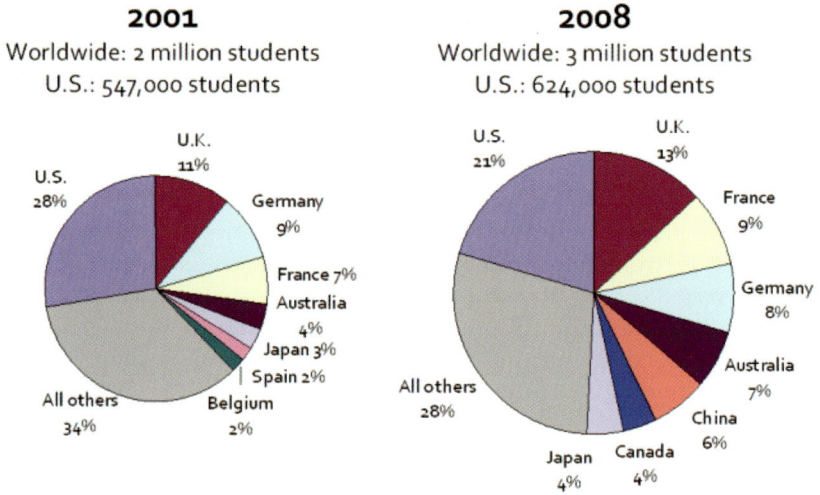

FIGURE 3-1 Foreign students in tertiary education by country of enrollment, 2001 and 2008.
Source: IIE Atlas of Student Mobility.

First, in indicators of relative success and quality as measured against their peers globally, American research universities and the work they do are ranked individually and collectively as the best in the world:[9]

- *Nobel Prizes*: Before World War I, Nobel Prizes were largely awarded to Europeans at European institutions such as the University of Berlin, University of Göttingen, L'Ecole Polytechnique, Cambridge University, and Oxford University. Indeed, until Adolph Hitler came to power, German universities were considered the best in the world. Afterwards, there was a great intellectual migration out of Germany, mainly to the United States. Consequently, as Cole relates, "Today, there is not one German university in the world's top 50." Meanwhile, since the 1930s, roughly 60 percent of Nobel Prizes have been awarded to scholars at American institutions.[10]

- *International students*: American higher education represents one of the few sectors of the U.S. economy with a favorable balance of trade. We attract talented young people from around the world who seek opportunities at American universities as students, scholars, and

---

[9] Graham and Diamond, Rise of American Research Universities p. 10; Cole, Great American University, pp. 4-5.
[10] Cole, Great American University, p. 4.

scientists. As shown in Figure 3-1, the United States has the largest market share of foreign students in tertiary education. That share has been shrinking in recent years, but may be on the rise again with increases in Chinese undergraduates at American institutions. As seen in Figure 3-2, a very high percentage of these intellectual migrants stay here and work in science, technology, engineering, and mathematics occupations.

• *Global rankings*: There are numerous global rankings of research universities and substantial debates about the indicators useful in compiling them. While we do not endorse any particular ranking or methodology, we do note that in almost every case they indicate the general dominance of U.S. institutions. For example, as shown in Box 3-2, the most recent Academic Ranking of World Universities (ARWU) produced

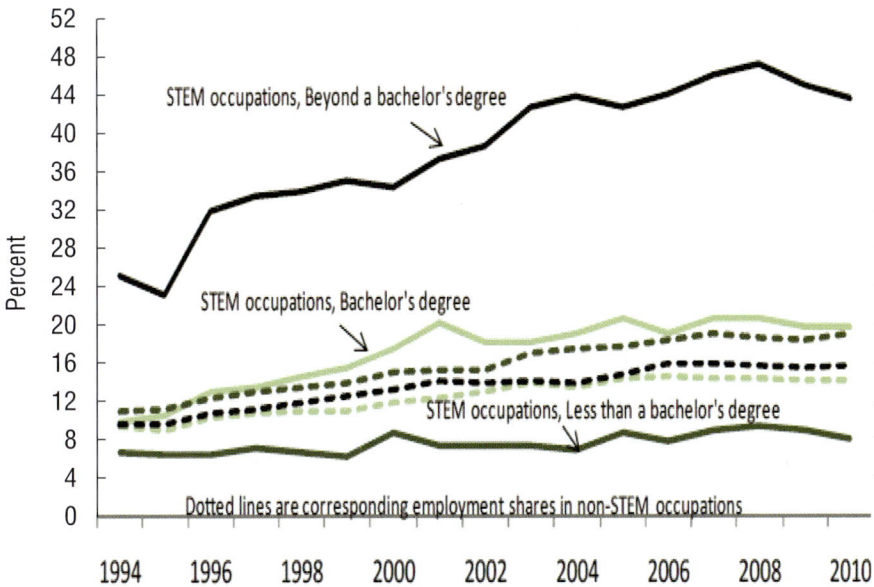

FIGURE 3-2 Foreign-born share of STEM workers, by educational attainment, 1994-2010.

Source: U.S. Department of Commerce, Economic and Statistics Administration, "Education Supports Racial and Ethnic Equality in STEM," ESA Issue Brief, #05-11, September 2011. http://www.esa.doc.gov/sites/default/files/reports/documents/educationsupportsracialandethnicequalityinstem_0.pdf (accessed September 16, 2011).

BOX 3-2
Top 50 Research Universities,
Academic Ranking of World Universities, 2010

1. Harvard University
2. University of California, Berkeley
3. Stanford University
4. Massachusetts Institute of Technology (MIT)
5. University of Cambridge
6. California Institute of Technology
7. Princeton University
8. Columbia University
9. University of Chicago
10. University of Oxford
11. Yale University
12. Cornell University
13. University of California, Los Angeles
14. University of California, San Diego
15. University of Pennsylvania
16. University of Washington
17. University of Wisconsin - Madison
18. The Johns Hopkins University
19. University of California, San Francisco
20. The University of Tokyo
21. University College London
22. University of Michigan - Ann Arbor
23. Swiss Federal Institute of Technology Zurich
24. Kyoto University
25. University of Illinois at Urbana-Champaign
26. The Imperial College of Science, Technology and Medicine
27. University of Toronto
28. University of Minnesota, Twin Cities
29. Northwestern University
30. Washington University in St. Louis
31. New York University
32. University of California, Santa Barbara
33. University of Colorado at Boulder
34. Rockefeller University
35. Duke University
36. University of British Columbia
37. University of Maryland, College Park
38. The University of Texas at Austin
39. Pierre and Marie Curie University - Paris 6
40. University of Copenhagen
41. University of North Carolina at Chapel Hill
42. Karolinska Institute
43. Pennsylvania State University - University Park
44. The University of Manchester
45. University of Paris Sud (Paris 11)
46. University of California, Davis
47. University of California, Irvine
48. University of Southern California
49. The University of Texas Southwestern Medical Center at Dallas
50. Utrecht University

Source: Academic Rankings of World Universities, 2010. Shanghai Jiao Tong University. http://www.arwu.org/ARWU2010.jsp (accessed February 9, 2011).

TABLE 3-1 Indicators and Weights for ARWU

Criteria	Indicator	Code	Weight
Quality of Education	Alumni of an institution winning Nobel Prizes and Fields Medals	Alumni	10%
	Staff of an institution winning Nobel Prizes and Fields Medals	Award	20%
Quality of Faculty	Highly cited researchers in 21 broad subject categories	HiCi	20%
	Papers published in Nature and Science*	N&S	20%
Research Output	Papers indexed in Science Citation Index-expanded and Social Science Citation Index	PUB	20%
Per Capita Performance	Per capita academic performance of an institution	PCP	10%
Total			100%

* For institutions specialized in humanities and social sciences such as London School of Economics, N&S is not considered, and the weight of N&S is relocated to other indicators. Source: http://www.arwu.org/ARWUMethodology2010.jsp (accessed February 9, 2011).

at Shanghai Jiao University (2010), placed 8 U.S. institutions in the top 10, 17 in the top 20, 35 in the top 50, and 54 in the top 100.[11]

• *Productivity*: Jonathan Cole argues that "we are the greatest because we are able to produce a very high proportion of the most important fundamental knowledge and practical research discoveries in the world."[12] This can be glimpsed, for example, in the indicators used in the ARWU, as shown in Table 3-1, that emphasize publications and citations and, in particular, the number of highly cited faculty in an institution. It can also be seen in, as shown in Box 3-3, the Organisation for Economic Co-operation and Development's Science, Technology, and Industry Scoreboard 2011, which demonstrates that, "as measured by normalised citations to academic publications across all disciplines, 40 of the world top 50 universities are located in the United States, with some U.S. universities excelling in a wide range of disciplines."[13]

Our preeminence can be seen not just in these indicators, but in the

---

[11] Shanghai Jiao Tong University, Academic Rankings of World Universities–2010. Available at: http://www.arwu.org/ARWU2010.jsp (accessed February 9, 2011).

[12] Cole, Great American University, p. 5.

[13] Organisation for Economic Co-operation and Development (OECD), Science, Technology, and Industry Scoreboard 2011: Highlights, p. 8. Available at: http://www.oecd.org/dataoecd/63/32/48712591.pdf (accessed April 20, 2012).

BOX 3-3
OECD Analysis of Geographical Distribution of Highest
Impact Institutions, Overall and By Field, 2009

"While research efforts are increasing across the globe, top research remains highly concentrated. A new indicator of research impact—measured by normalized citations to academic publications across all disciplines—shows that 40 of the world top 50 universities are located in the United States, with some US universities excelling in a wide range of disciplines. Stanford University features among the top 50 for all 16 subject areas, and 17 other US universities feature in the top 50 in at least 10 scientific fields.

"A more diverse picture emerges on a subject-by-subject basis. The United States accounts for less than 25 of the top 50 universities in social sciences, a field in which the United Kingdom plays a key role. The universities producing the top-rated publications in the areas of earth sciences, environmental science and pharmaceutics are more evenly spread across economies. Universities in Asia are starting to emerge as leading research institutions: China has six in the top 50 in pharmacology, toxicology and pharmaceutics. The Hong Kong University of Science and Technology is among the top universities in computer science, engineering and chemistry."

Excerpted from: Organisation for Economic Cooperation and Development, OECD Science, Technology, and Industry Scoreboard 2011. Highlights, p.8. Available at: http://www.oecd.org/dataoecd/63/32/48712591.pdf (accessed April 20, 2012).

---

actions of others. Leaders in nations around the world are reshaping their universities to compete with ours by emulating them and our system. For example, in the Bologna Process, the Council of Europe in conjunction with the European Commission is reforming European higher education, including doctoral education, across 47 countries. The goal of the process is to improve Europe as a knowledge society. The strategies of the process include greater harmonization of degrees across nations; a greater convergence with the U.S. model to promote quality, easier interaction with

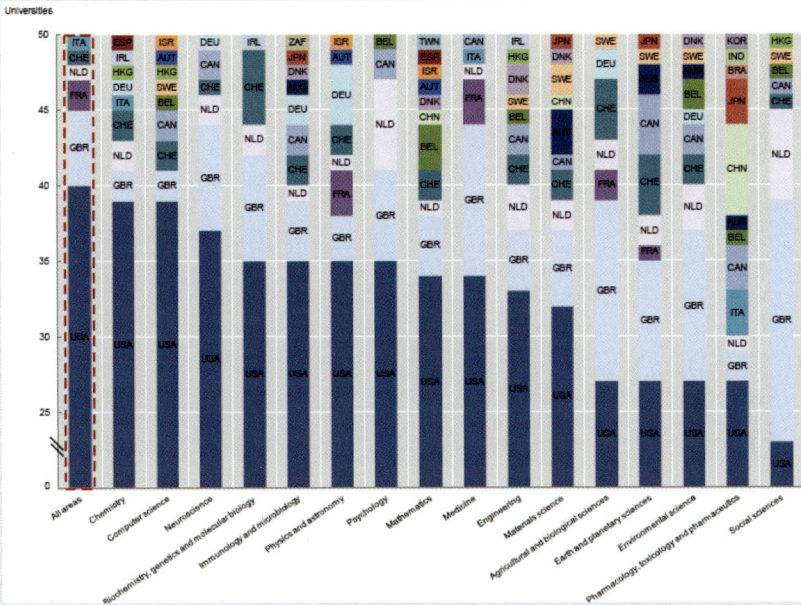

**University hotspots—geographical distribution of highest impact institutions, 2009
Location of top-50 universities by main subject areas**

Source: OECD and SCImago Research Group (CSIC) (forthcoming), Report on Scientific Production, based on Scopus Custom Data, Elsevier, June 2011.

the United States, and attractiveness to non-European students; and an increase in the overall competitiveness of European higher education.[14]

Second, reports of specific institutions have demonstrated their significant economic impact locally, regionally, and nationally, as talented graduates of these institutions have created and populated many new businesses that go on to employ millions of Americans. For example, Jonathan Cole notes:

> Stanford University reports, for example, that faculty members, students, and alumni have founded more than 2,400 companies—and a

---

[14] See http://www.ehea.info/ (accessed September 16, 2011).

subset, including Cisco Systems, Google, and Hewlett-Packard, generated $255-billion of total revenue among the "Silicon Valley 150" in 2008.

and

> The Massachusetts Institute of Technology (MIT) has reported that 4,000 MIT-related companies employ 1.1 million people and have annual world sales of $232-billion—a little less than the gross domestic product of South Africa and of Thailand, which would make MIT companies among the 40 largest economies in the world.[15]

Meanwhile, to provide the example of a public institution that has been significantly supported by the federal government and its state, the University of Alabama (UAB) Birmingham reports:

- $4.6 billion in total economic impact is generated by UAB in the state of Alabama.
- $1 invested by the state in UAB generates $16.23 in the total state economy.
- 61,205 jobs are supported in the state of Alabama.
- $302.2 million is generated in state and local tax revenue.

The UAB report asserts further that "the economic and employment impact of UAB's expansion in 2020 (mid-range scenario) is projected to grow to $6.6 billion, generate 72,449 jobs and create $431.4 million state and local tax revenue."[16] These impacts are generated by just three diverse institutions. Expand this to 120 or more institutions and the impact grows enormously.

Third, examples of specific products and companies demonstrate the economic and social impact and penetration of the results of university education and research. For example, Jonathan Cole summarized many of the examples in his book as follows:

> The laser, magnetic-resonance imaging, FM radio, the algorithm for Google searches, global-positioning systems, DNA fingerprinting, fetal monitoring, bar codes, transistors, improved weather forecasting, mainframe computers, scientific cattle breeding, advanced methods of surveying public opinion, even Viagra had their origins in America's research universities. Those are only a few of the tens of thousands of advances, originating on those campuses that have transformed the world.

---

[15] Jonathan Cole, Can American research universities remain the best in the world? *The Chronicle of Higher Education*, January 3, 2010.

[16] Tripp Umbach, The Economic Impact of UAB: Current and Projected Economic, Employment, and Government Revenue Impacts. Final Executive Report, November 9, 2010.

BOX 3-4
National Science Foundation, Selected Examples of
"Sensational" Products That Have Resulted from
or Drawn on NSF-Funded Basic Research

- Bar code scanners
- Computer-assisted design
- Anti-freeze proteins used in ice cream, cosmetics, fish farming, and tissue transplants
- Genetic plant research that has led to the development of new crops
- Improved biofuels
- The application of modified Buckeyballs in medicine and in building materials
- Low-cost, low-energy use methods for obtaining clean drinking water
- Improved understanding of business cycles and economic policies
- Forensic DNA analysis
- The development of revolutionary weather-sensing networks
- MRI technology
- Reaction injection molding that has led to lighter and more fuel-efficient automobiles
- solid-state physics and ceramics/glass engineering essential to the optical fibers
- The PageRank method that led to Google
- NSFNET, the telecommunications that developed into the Internet

Source: National Science Foundation, NSF Sensational 60. http://www.nsf.gov/about/history/sensational60.pdf. (accessed February 3, 2011).

"Such discoveries, he writes, "have provided industry with the material needed for the growth of new, high-technology businesses—and universities have trained most of the highly skilled work force that populates our major industrial laboratories."[17]

To add to Cole's list, the National Science Foundation and the Science Coalition have also catalogued how federal funding for research, and in particular, for research performed in universities, has led to important products, companies, and jobs. Box 3-4 provides a partial list of NSF's Sensational 60 products that resulted from or drew on research the foundation funded.[18] The Science Coalition report, meanwhile, provides details on the origin, size, and revenue of 100 successful companies, just a small sample of the many that have grown out of federally funded uni-

---

[17] Cole, *The Chronicle of Higher Education*.

[18] National Science Foundation, NSF Sensational 60. Available at : http://www.nsf.gov/about/history/sensational60.pdf (accessed February 3, 2011).

versity research. Some of these companies are well known, like Google and SAS. Google, of course, grew out of research on a better search engine at Stanford University funded by the National Science Foundation. Others, like Sharklet Technologies of Alachua, Florida, or A123 Systems of Watertown, Massachusetts, are not yet household names but contribute importantly to their local economies. A123, which grew out of materials research at MIT funded by the U.S. Department of Energy, now employs 1,740 people and had annual revenue in 2008 of $54 million. What conveys the power of university research, perhaps even more than the data on the 100 companies that can be reviewed in the coalition report, are the quotes in Box 3-5 from company founders that demonstrate, through their own words, how important it can be for jobs, economic growth, and the outcomes for the health, security, or quality of life for Americans that their products bring.

Research in the social, behavioral, and economic (SBE) sciences also contribute to critical national goals. As a recent report from the National Science and Technology Council contends, "The quest for deeper understanding of humans is key to managing society's most critical challenges." It continues by noting:

These challenges include:

- Developing more effective education programs
- Developing better health care programs
- Understanding violence, suicide, abuse, neglect, addiction, and mental illness
- Mitigating fanaticism, extremism, and terrorism
- Protecting confidentiality and privacy
- Fostering societal resilience in the face of both natural and human-made disasters
- Fostering a culture of creativity and innovation and maintaining America's competitiveness in an era of rapid globalization
- Addressing the long-term sustainability of civilization within Earth's ecosystems.

These challenges all share a human element, which makes them resistant to untested interventions or technological solutions, and makes evidence-based policy making difficult. After a half-century of progress, however, the SBE sciences can offer more rigorous, evidence-based strategies to address this human element.[19]

---

[19] National Science and Technology Council, Subcommittee on Social, Behavioral, and Economic Sciences, Social, Behavioral, and Economic Research in the Federal Context, January 2009. Available at: http://www.nsf.gov/sbe/prospectus_v10_3_17_09.pdf (accessed March 8, 2009).

BOX 3-5
Selected Statements of Individuals Who
Founded or Lead Companies That Grew Out of
Federally Funded University Research

The core technology of TomoTherapy was developed by National Cancer Institute funding. Each year, the technology is responsible for the treatment of tens of thousands of difficult to treat patients. In addition, it generates many times its original funding level in salaries and taxes returned to both the U.S. and Wisconsin governments.

—Rock Mackie, Professor, University of Wisconsin-Madison, and Co-Founder and Chairman of the Board, TomoTherapy Incorporated.

Basic research provides the critical 'seed corn' for our nation's technological innovations. Certainly, that was true in the case of A123 which grew out of DOE-funded basic research into new battery concepts at MIT and us today developing batteries and battery systems to enable the electrification of transportation and improved efficiency in the 'smart' electric grid.

—Yel-Ming Chiang, Professor, MIT, and Co-Founder A123 Systems.

Our lab at Arizona State University received substantial support from both the Office of Naval Research and the National Science Foundation to develop scanning probe microscopy for biological applications right from the first discovery of the technique (1985-6). This background led directly to the intellectual property that Molecular Imaging licensed from ASU when it was founded in 1993. Today, Agilent AFM in Chandler is a significant employer of scientists and engineers, manufacturing and further developing the instruments pioneered by Molecular Imaging.

—Dr. Stuart Lindsay, Director Arizona State University's The Biodesign Institute, Single Molecule Biophysics; and Founder Molecular Imaging.

SAS was originally created to analyze crop data through a grant from the Department of Agriculture. Forty years later, SAS is used in every industry around the world. There are plenty of success stories still to be told. Federally supported university research is vitally important to keeping America at the forefront of technology innovation.

—Dr. Jim Goodnight, Chief Executive Officer, SAS.

Source: The Science Coalition, Sparking Economic Growth: How federally funded university research creates innovation, new companies, and jobs, April 2010. See www.sciencecoalition. org (accessed September 16, 2010).

BOX 3-6
Multidisciplinary Social Science Research
Program for National Energy Policy

A recent report of the President's Council of Advisors on Science and Technology (PCAST) addressed ways to accelerate the pace of change in energy technologies through and integrated Federal energy policy. Among its recommendations, PCAST included action that social science researchers could take to improve the adoption of energy technology:

A Multidisciplinary Social Science Research Program

DOE's energy mission is to support basic and "use-inspired" research, but in fact it devotes little time or investment to understanding how energy technologies ultimately succeed in the marketplace. DOE needs to "close the innovation cycle" through support of a significant new multidisciplinary program into the processes of energy innovation. Understanding how the department's technologies proceed as they pass from invention to innovation to adoption to diffusion and how the innovation system as a whole is functioning is critical to understanding the overall success of DOE's mission, as well as the performance of government in energy innovation and technology deployment.

RECOMMENDATION 4-4: DOE, along with NSF, should initiate a multidisciplinary social science research program to examine the U.S. energy technology innovation ecosystem, including its actors, functions, processes, and outcomes. This research should be fully integrated into DOE's energy research and applied programs.

This research program should fund experts from the physical sciences, engineering, economics, sociology, public policy, political science, international relations, business, and other disciplines. Examples of questions that might be rigorously studied are:

University research in the SBE sciences, therefore, also play a strong role in national efforts to meet our goals both generally and in specific areas. Box 3-6, for example, describes how SBE research contributes to federal energy policy and the acceleration of energy innovation.

- How and why are advanced energy technologies accepted or rejected by consumers?
- What are the barriers to adoption?
- Will the public accept a specific technology and why?
- What market conditions are needed for a technology to compete?
- What is the role of public policy to efficiently and effectively push and pull advanced technologies into the marketplace?
- How are technologies transferred and diffused internationally?

Other types of multidisciplinary research that are needed include strategic energy analyses and full life cycle assessments of new energy technologies. The potential benefits of such a research program are significant. Estimates are as high $1.2 trillion in energy savings through 2020 from wide scale implementation of energy efficiency technologies in the U.S. With or without new technologies, more behavioral research is also needed concerning the patterns, incentives, and decisions that determine individuals' energy usage. Well-designed social science experiments can yield important insights about how people react to various policies and technologies. Continuity is important. In many cases, large-scale datasets exist or can be easily collected concerning such questions, but are not easy to study because of proprietary or regulatory obstructions. DOE should work with OMB, energy providers, and researchers to facilitate the compilation of energy usage data under both routine and experimental conditions. Other disciplines, such as history and international case studies, can also deliver important lessons.

—Excerpted from President's Council of Advisors on Science and Technology, Report to the President on Accelerating the Pace of Change in Energy Technologies Through an Integrated Federal Energy Policy, November 2010. Available at: http://www.whitehouse.gov/sites/default/files/microsites/ostp/pcast-energy-tech-report.pdf (accessed March 8, 2012).

4
Threats and Weaknesses

While American research universities are a strong set of assets for America, these institutions must have adequate resources, sound organizational structures, and a vibrant intellectual community in order to continue to fulfill their obligations in the twenty-first century. They require a renewal of the national partnership that was forged in the last half of the twentieth century.

CHALLENGES AND OPPORTUNITIES FOR OUR RESEARCH UNIVERSITIES

American research universities are facing critical concerns.[1] Public universities have experienced a long-term erosion of state support in the face of increasing demands for expenditures in other areas. As state budgets have tightened during the recent economic crisis, public research universities have been further challenged by steep reductions in state appropriations for higher education. (See figures under Recommendation 2 in Chapter 5.) Meanwhile, private and public universities saw their endowments seriously erode in the recession, with 1-year returns in 2009 of −18.7 percent. There has been some recovery in 2010, but operating budgets may not recover for some time as institutions continue to address both current needs and those postponed during the downturn

---

[1] For additional background, see, for example, James J. Duderstadt and Farris W. Womack, The Future of the Public University in America: Beyond the Crossroads. Baltimore, MD: The Johns Hopkins University Press, 2003.

(see Table 4-1). Meanwhile, demand for student aid continues to increase while federal funding for basic and applied research at public and private universities has, in real terms, declined in the face of competing priorities for funding. (See figures under Recommendation 1 in Chapter 5.)

With these developments in mind, the committee has identified a set of specific challenges and opportunities that a reasoned set of policies must address in order to produce the greatest return to our society, our security, and our economy. The first group identifies issues in the partnership among the federal government, states, business, and universities:

- Federal funding for university research has been unstable and, in real terms, declining at a time when other countries have increased funding for research and development (R&D), both in nominal terms and as a percentage of gross domestic product.
- State funding for higher education, already eroding in real terms for more than two decades, has been cut further in the recent recession.
- Business and industry have largely dismantled the large corporate research laboratories that drove American industrial leadership in the twentieth century (e.g., Bell Labs), but have not yet fully partnered with our research universities to fill the gap at a time when we need to more effectively translate, disseminate, and transfer into society the new knowledge and ideas that emerge from university research.
- Research universities need to be responsive to stakeholders by improving management, productivity, and cost efficiency in both administration and academics.

The second group identifies issues that affect the operations of universities, the efficient administration of university research, the effectiveness of doctoral education, and the robustness of the pipeline of new talent:

- Insufficient opportunities for young faculty to launch academic careers and research programs;
- Underinvestment in campus infrastructure, particularly in cyberinfrastructure, that can lead to long-term increases in productivity, cost-effectiveness, and innovation in research, education, and administration;
- Research sponsors that do not pay the full cost of research they procure, meaning that universities have to cross-subsidize research from other sources;
- A burdensome accumulation of federal and state regulatory and reporting requirements that increases costs and sometimes challenges academic freedom and integrity;
- Opportunities to improve doctoral and postdoctoral preparation

TABLE 4-1 Average One-, Three-, Five-, and Ten-Year Net Returns on University Endowments, By Endowment Size, Fiscal Years 2009 and 2010

Numbers in Percent	Total Institutions		Over $1 Billion		$501 Million – $1 Billion		$101 Million–$500 Million		$51 Million–$100 Million		$25 Million – $50 Million		Under $25 Million	
	842	**850**	52	**60**	60	**66**	219	**226**	164	**169**	137	**145**	210	**184**
Fiscal Years	2009	**2010**	2009	**2010**	2009	**2010**	2009	**2010**	2009	**2010**	2009	**2010**	2009	**2010**
FY2010 annual total net return	–18.7	**11.9**	–20.5	**12.2**	–19.8	**11.9**	–19.7	**11.9**	–18.6	**11.8**	–18.5	**12.0**	–16.8	**11.6**
3-year net return	–2.5	**–4.2**	–0.8	**–3.5**	–2.0	**–3.9**	–2.5	**–4.4**	–2.7	**–4.3**	–3.2	**–4.2**	–2.3	**–3.9**
5-year net return	2.7	**3.0**	5.1	**4.7**	3.5	**3.6**	2.6	**3.0**	2.7	**2.7**	2.1	**2.6**	2.1	**2.2**
10-year net return	4.0	**3.4**	6.1	**5.0**	4.3	**3.6**	3.7	**3.3**	3.7	**3.3**	3.4	**2.9**	3.9	**2.8**

SOURCE: National Association of College and University Business Officers, "Educational Endowments Earned Investment Returns Averaging 11.9 percent in FY2010," http://www.nacubo.org/Documents/research/2010NCSE_Full_Data_Press_Release_Final.pdf (accessed September 17, 2011). Reprinted with permission from the 2010 NACUBO Commonfund Study of Endowments, National Association of College and University Business Officers (NACUBO), Copyright 2011.

that increase both its productivity and its effectiveness in providing training for highly productive careers;
- Demographic change in the U.S. population that necessitates
strategies for increasing the success of female and underrepresented minority students; and
- Competition for international students, researchers, and scholars.

We will need strong leadership from the federal government, our state
capitals, business, and our higher education institutions to overcome
these hurdles, address our challenges, and capitalize on our opportunities and the partnerships that will allow our research universities and,
through them, our nation, to thrive.

PUBLIC RESEARCH UNIVERSITIES: A SPECIAL CASE

America's public research universities, in scale and breadth, are the
backbone of advanced education and research in the United States today.
They conduct most of the nation's academic research (62 percent) while
producing the majority of its scientists, engineers, doctors, teachers, and
other learned professionals (70 percent). They are committed to public
engagement in every area where knowledge and expertise can make a difference: basic and applied research, agricultural and industrial extension,
economic development, health care, national security, and cultural enrichment.[2] In fact, it was the public research university, through its land-
grant tradition, its strong engagement with society, and its commitment
to educational opportunity in the broadest sense, that was instrumental
in creating the middle class, transforming American agriculture and industry into the economic engine of the world during the 20th century, and
defending democracy during two world wars.

Yet today, despite their importance to their states, the nation, and the
world, America's public research universities are at great risk. There is
ample evidence from the past three decades of declining support that the
states are simply not able—or willing—to provide the resources to sustain
growth in public higher education, at least at the rate experienced in the
decades following World War II. Despite the growth in enrollments and
the increasing demand for university services such as health care and
economic development, most states will find it difficult to sustain even
the present capacity and quality of their institutions. In the wake of the
recent global financial crisis, many states have already enacted drastic

---

[2] Paul N. Courant, James J. Duderstadt, and Edie N. Goldenberg, Needed: A national
strategy to preserve public research universities, The Chronicle of Higher Education, January 3, 2010.

cuts in state appropriations ranging from 20 percent to 50 percent. Leading public research universities such as the University of California, the University of Colorado (Boulder), and Pennsylvania State University have been pushed to the brink by deep and permanent reductions in their state appropriations. In this budget-constrained climate, state support of higher education and research is no longer viewed as an investment in the future but rather as an expenditure competing with the other priorities of aging populations, for example, health care, retirement security, safety from crime, and tax relief.[3]

In fact, many states are encouraging their public universities to reduce the burden of higher education on limited state tax revenues by diversifying their funding sources, for example, becoming more dependent upon tuition, particularly that paid by out-of-state students, intensifying efforts to attract gifts and research contracts, and generating income from intellectual property transferred from campus laboratories into the marketplace. Yet such efforts to "privatize" the support of public universities through higher tuition or increasing out-of-state enrollments also subject public universities to strong public outrage and political intrusion. Furthermore, since state support is key to the important public university mission of providing educational opportunities to students regardless of economic means, shifting to high-tuition funding, even accompanied by increased financial aid, usually leads to a sharp decline in the socioeconomic diversity of students.[4]

While several public research universities might be able to survive as "privately funded but publicly committed" institutions (the Universities of Virginia and Michigan provide interesting case studies), most will be unable to accomplish such a transition from public to private support with their quality and capacity intact. Their key public missions to their states—including broad educational opportunities and economic development—will go unfulfilled. Furthermore, their capacity to conduct research and graduate education at the world-class levels required by our nation will rapidly erode without adequate state support.

Today, many nations have recognized the positive impact that their public research universities can have in a world increasingly dependent upon advanced education and research. They are investing heavily to upgrade the quality of their institutions to world-class levels. America already has such leading public research universities. They are one of our

---

[3] Duderstadt and Womack, The Future of the Public University in America, p. 127.

[4] Danette Gerald and Kati Haycock, Engines of Inequality: Diminishing Equity in the Nation's Premier Public Universities. Washington, DC: The Education Trust, 2006. Available at: http://www.edtrust.org/sites/edtrust.org/files/publications/files/EnginesofInequality. pdf (accessed April 20, 2012).

nation's greatest assets. However, preserving their quality and capacity will require not only sustained investments but also significant paradigm shifts in university financing, management, and governance. It also will likely demand that many of our public research universities broaden their public purpose and stakeholders far beyond state boundaries. Preserving the quality and capacity of the extraordinary resource represented by our public research universities must remain a national priority, even if the support required to sustain these institutions at world-class levels is no longer viewed as a priority by our states.

GLOBAL THREATS

Meanwhile, the global leadership of the United States in higher education, unassailable for a generation, is now also threatened. Our research universities have attracted the most outstanding students and scholars from abroad who have contributed substantially to our research and our innovative capacity, but, as they return home, to universities of their own countries as well. Indeed, other nations have recognized the importance of world-class research universities and of university-driven research and advanced education to economic prosperity and social well-being. They are strategically and rapidly strengthening their research universities to compete for international students and faculty, resources, and reputation and, in some instances, have closely tied university research to business. These countries have developed national strategies for education and research with the aim of both offering attractive opportunities to repatriate their citizens who are graduates of U.S. universities and attaining world-class levels, where they will strongly compete with the United States (see Box 4-1).

As Jonathan Cole has written, "China aspires to the excellence that wins Nobel Prizes just as they aspired to gold medals at the 2008 Olympic Games in Beijing."[5] In order to increase its competitiveness, China, in particular, has implemented plans to increase scientific and technological innovation and to develop, attract, and retain highly skilled individuals in six broad sectors of the economy.[6] Evidence of the results of these aspirations is already apparent in data. Figures 4-1 through 4-5 show

---

[5] Jonathan Cole, The Great American University: Its Rise to Preeminence, Its Indispensable National Role, Why it Must be Protected, New York: Public Affairs, 2009, p. 3.

[6] Dieter Ernst, China's Innovation Policy is a Wake-Up Call for America, East-West Center, Analysis from the East-West Center, No. 100, May 2011. Available at: http://www.eastwestcenter.org/fileadmin/stored/pdfs/api100.pdf (accessed September 17, 2011).

Wang Huiyao, China's National Talent Plan: Key Measures and Objectives. Brookings Institution. Available at: http://www.brookings.edu/~/media/Files/rc/papers/2010/1123_china_talent_wang/1123_china_talent_wang.pdf (accessed September 17, 2011).

increases in postsecondary educational attainment in the natural sciences and engineering, doctoral degrees in the natural sciences and engineering, science and engineering article output, and research and development expenditures, each figure showing relative advances of countries and regions compared to the United States.

Meanwhile, the rise of Indian universities has been so remarkable that science-focused high school students in India are now increasingly less likely to seek education in the United States. Thus, the United States is not benefitting from the intellectual capital of those students who might have come here, nor are the students themselves benefitting from ours, except via publication. And while electronic Web-based intellectual interaction is increasing, unless universities themselves become internationalized or virtual, there is no substitute for direct intellectual engagement. The remarkable investments by Singapore in the National University of Singapore, Nanyang Technological University, and Singapore Management University push the agenda one step further, demonstrating that the United States may actually lose significant numbers of the best members of our academy, and perhaps students as well, if we are seriously under-supporting our research universities and faculty and students choose not to come to our institutions but rather to others where investment continues to grow. This loss in brain circulation and the benefits from it for all is of great concern.

The U.S. form of doctoral education is now being adopted by many countries, and the global growth in doctoral education via the American model contests the preeminence of U.S. doctoral education. To elaborate on just one data point, the number of doctorates across all fields in China has increased from a few hundred in 1990 to 49,698 in 2008 and, in so doing, surpassed the number awarded by U.S. institutions that conferred 48,763 doctorates that same year. There is a distribution in the quality of these Ph.D. programs, to be sure, but some of the institutions that graduate doctorates in science and engineering are highly ranked. Tables 4-2a and 4-2b speak to this point: While U.S. research universities dominate global rankings of such institutions, it is clear that other countries are making strides in particular fields. Chinese programs are highly ranked, particularly in engineering and technology (in both the Academic Ranking of World Universities [ARWU] and the QS World University Rankings) and also in the life sciences and medicine and the natural sciences (in the QS World University Rankings). Several universities have climbed into the top 25 globally. Peking University is ranked 21st in the life sciences and in the natural sciences in the QS World University Rankings and Tsinghua University is 11th in engineering and technology. In the ARWU, Hong Kong University of Science and Technology is 39th in en-

---

BOX 4-1
Strategies of Countries to Strengthen Research Universities

Europe: The Bologna Process

"At its inception, the Bologna Process was meant to strengthen the competitiveness and attractiveness of the European higher education and to foster student mobility and employability through the introduction of a system based on undergraduate and postgraduate studies with easily readable programmes and degrees. Quality assurance has played an important role from the outset, too. However, the various ministerial meetings since 1999 have broadened this agenda and have given greater precision to the tools that have been developed. The undergraduate/postgraduate degree structure has been modified into a three-cycle system, which now includes the concept of qualifications frameworks, with an emphasis on learning outcomes. The concept of social dimension of higher education has been introduced and recognition of qualifications is now clearly perceived as central to the European higher education policies."

—European Higher Education Area.
Available at: http://www.ehea.info/ (accessed September 17, 2011).

China: National Mid- and Long-Term Talent Development Plan

"China's National Talent Development Plan was jointly issued by the Central Committee of the Chinese Communist Party (CCP) and the State Council on June 6, 2010. It is remarkably unusual that these two leadership bodies would jointly endorse a plan on such a high note. The announcement of this plan was also very unusual in that President Hu Jintao and all of the other eight Politburo Standing Committee Members attended its formal release ceremony, where President Hu, Premier Wen Jiabao and Vice President Xi Jinping all delivered important speeches. . . . During the meeting, President Hu stated that 'talent is the most important resource and it is a key issue that concerns the development of the Party and country' . . . . Among the plan's goals is the transformation of China from a manufacturing hub to a world leader in innovation, a grand objective that, according to the targets laid out in the plan, will be met in part by an increase in the pool of highly skilled workers from the current total of 114 million to 180 million by 2020, with government-allocated spending on human resources increasing from 10.75 percent of the country's gross domestic product (GDP) now to 15 percent by 2020."

—Wang Huiyao, China's National Talent Plan: Key Measures and
Objectives, Brookings Institution. Available at: http://www.brookings.edu/~/media/
Files/rc/papers/2010/1123_china_talent_wang/1123_china_talent_wang.pdf
(accessed September 17, 2011).

Singapore: Government Investment in Principal Universities

"The IAAP [Ministry of Education's International Academic Advisory Panel] commends the excellent progress made by the existing autonomous universities (AUs)—the National University of Singapore (NUS), Nanyang Technological University (NTU) and the Singapore Management University (SMU)—in continuously innovating in their education and research programmes to produce high-quality graduates and research outcomes. The IAAP supports the healthy balance of competition and collaboration among the various educational institutions, even as each institution seeks to distinguish itself in its offerings and competes for students and faculty.

"The IAAP applauds Singapore's continued commitment to invest in research, innovation, and enterprise. Research funding from agencies, such as MOE, the National Research Foundation (NRF) and the Agency for Science, Technology and Research (A*STAR), have helped universities to grow their research enterprises. The IAAP endorses Singapore's steps towards establishing a more sustainable model of university funding, with appropriate support coming from multiple sources, including Government grants, student fees, research grants and income from endowment funds."

"The IAAP notes that since its last meeting in 2008, NUS, NTU and SMU have made remarkable progress in becoming world-class research-intensive universities, without neglecting their key mission of providing a strong foundation in undergraduate education through a student centric approach. Individually, each AU has succeeded in bringing talent into the system—be it students or faculty, both local and international. As a system, it has generated intellectual and social capital which has contributed to the vibrancy of Singapore and drawn top talent to the country. In pursuing their development strategies, each AU would need to distinguish itself from the others and continually assess its progress against various metrics, including benchmarking its progress against peer institutions."

—Singapore Government, Ministry of Education, International Academic Advisory Panel, press release, November 12, 2010. Available at: http://www. moe.gov.sg/media/press/2010/11/advisory-panel-endorses-continuing- investments-in-higher-education.php (accessed February 22, 2012).

Saudi Arabia: Creation of King Abdullah University of Science and Technology

"It is my desire that this new University become one of the world's great institutions of research; that it educate and train future generations of scientists, engineers and technologists; and that it foster, on the basis of merit and excellence, collaboration and cooperation with other great research universities and the private sector. The University shall have all the resources that it needs to pursue these goals."

—King Abdullah Bin Abdulaziz Al Saud, Message on the Creation of King Abdullah University of Science and Technology. Available at: http://www.kaust. edu.sa/about/kingsmessage.html (accessed September 17, 2011).

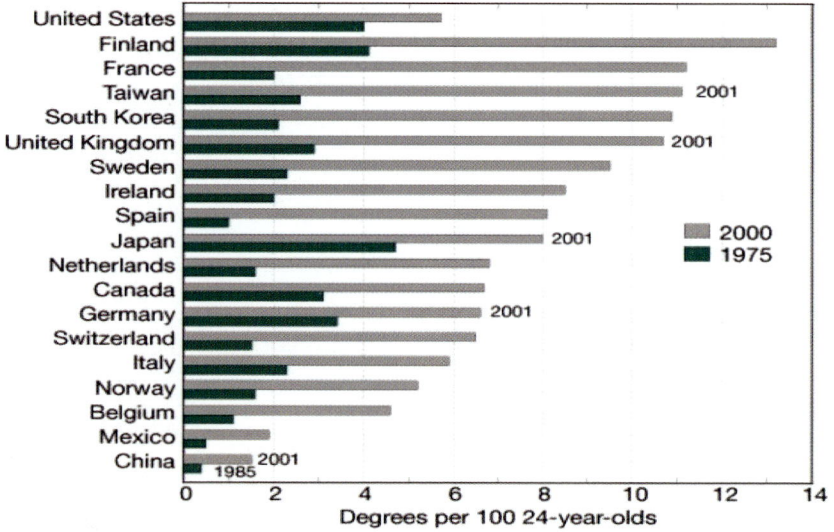

FIGURE 4-1 Ratio of first university NS&E degrees to 24-year-old population, by selected country/economy, 1975 and 2000 or most recent year.
Source: National Science Board, Science and Engineering Indicators 2004. (NSB 04-01) Arlington, VA: National Science Foundation, 2004, Figure 2-34, page 2-36.

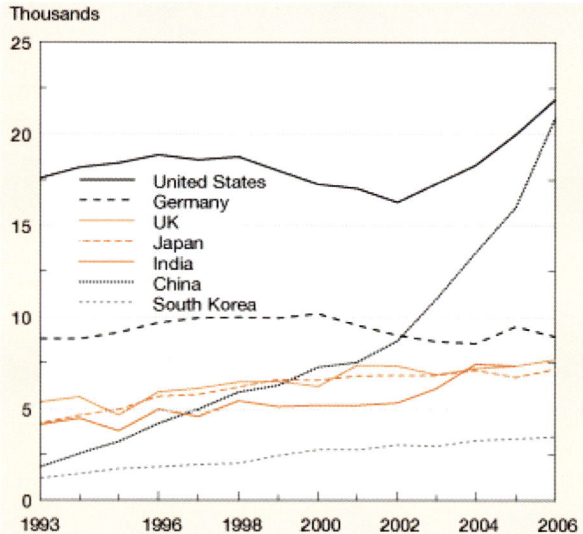

FIGURE 4-2 Natural science and engineering doctorate awards, selected countries, 1993-2006 (thousands).
Source: National Science Board, Science and Engineering Indicators 2010. (NSB 10-01) Arlington, VA: National Science Foundation, 2010, Figure 2-27, page 2-35.

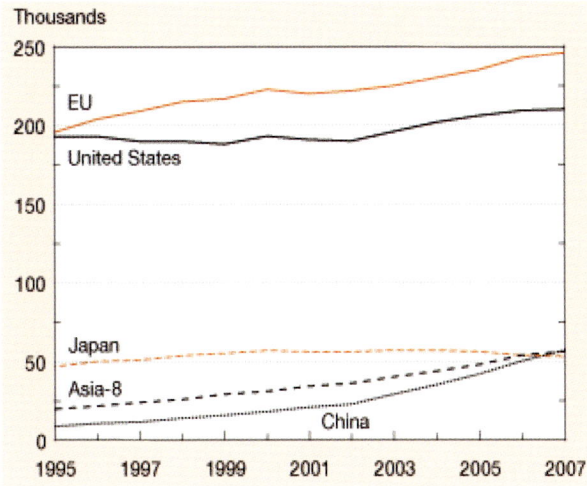

FIGURE 4-3 S&E article output, by major S&E publishing region or country/ economy, 1999-2007.
Source: National Science Board, Science and Engineering Indicators 2010. (NSB 10-01) Arlington, VA: National Science Foundation, 2010, Figure 5-20, page 5-32.

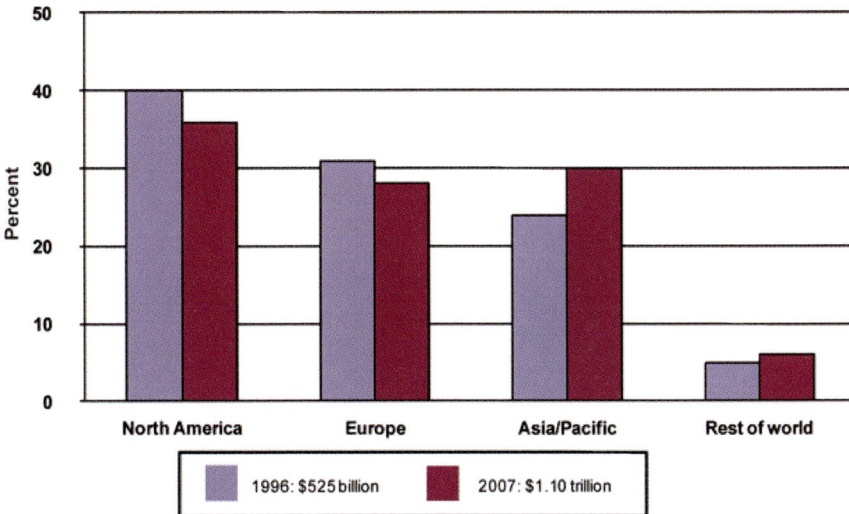

FIGURE 4-4 Location of estimated worldwide R&D expenditures, 1996 and 2007. Source: National Science Board, Globalization of Science and Engineering: A Companion to Science and Engineering Indicators 2010. (NSB 10-03) Arlington, VA: National Science Foundation, 2010, Figure 1, page 1.

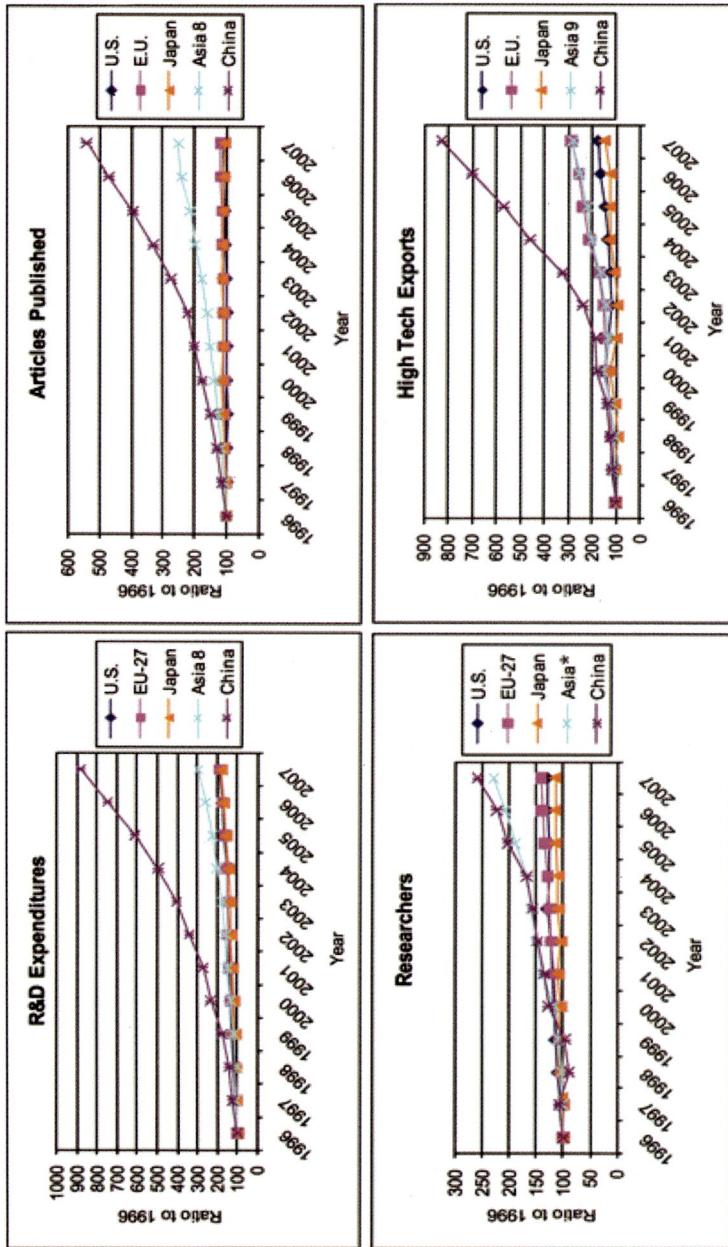

FIGURE 4-5 Normalized growth in S&T globalization, data indexed as a ratio to 1996 = 100.
Source: National Science Board, Globalization of Science and Engineering: A Companion to Science and Engineering Indicators 2010. (NSB 10-03) Arlington, VA: National Science Foundation, 2010, Figure 3, page 4.

TABLE 4-2a Chinese University Programs in QS World University Rankings, by Field

Life Science and Medicine	Natural Sciences	Engineering and Technology
21 Peking University 37 University of Hong Kong (HKU) 55 Tsinghua University 62 Hong Kong University of S&T 67 Chinese University of Hong Kong 69 Fudan University	21 Peking University 27 Tsinghua University 56 University of Hong Kong (HKU) 77 University of Science and Technology of China 91 Chinese University of Hong Kong 92 Fudan University 94 Hong Kong University of S&T	11 Tsinghua University 26 Hong Kong University of S&T 33 Peking University 43 Shanghai Jiao Tong University 52 University of Hong Kong (HKU) 70 Hong Kong Polytechnic University 71 University of Science and Technology of China 79 Zhejiang University 85 Chinese University of Hong Kong

Source: Presentation of Bill Berry, National Research Council, Policy and Global Affairs Committee, November 2010.

TABLE 4-2b Chinese University Programs in Shanghai Jiao Tong Academic Ranking of World Universities, by Field, 2010

Life Science and Agricultural Sciences	Natural Sciences and Mathematics	Engineering and Technology
None	None	39 Hong Kong University of S&T 43 City University of Hong Kong 45 Tsinghua University 52-75 Shanghai Jiao Tong University 52-75 Chinese University of Hong Kong 52-75 Hong Kong Polytechnic University Peking University 52-75 University of Science and Technology of China 52-75 Zhejiang University 76-100 Harbin Institute of Technology

Source: http://www.arwu.org/index.jsp (accessed September 17, 2011).

gineering and technology, with City University of Hong Kong, 43rd, and Tsinghua University, 45th.

In science and engineering, the United States still leads other nations in the number of Ph.D.'s conferred each year, but at the present rate of growth, the number of doctorates in China will soon rival the United States in Ph.D. production (see Figure 4-2). Other countries, such as India, Japan, South Korea, and some European counties have also increased the number of Ph.D.'s they produce in these fields. The ramifications of this for U.S. institutions are that the best and brightest students may no longer come to the United States for study and may not stay here as much as in the past. U.S. institutions will need to draw more heavily on students coming through the U.S. educational system, with special attention to minority groups that are making up a larger proportion of the population.

To be sure, both the United States and others will benefit from increasing global investments in higher education and research as ideas and talent circulate globally. Indeed, the United States needs to consider actions that allow us to continue to benefit and appropriate from global sources of ideas and talent, such as changes in immigration law suggested in Recommendation 10. Meanwhile, just as the global rise in higher education and research is multidimensional, so the response to these global changes for the United States and its institutions should be considered, nuanced, and varied. One key response must continue to be the increasing globalization of networks among researchers, which enhances research and its outcomes for everyone. Institutions should continue to explore the establishment of overseas campuses and research centers either as stand-alone entities or in partnership with local institutions. Yet a third response must also be to ensure that our national investments in research and doctoral education are responsive to both national needs and the realities of an increasingly competitive world. Our research universities are the best in the world. But a leadership position is easy to lose and difficult to regain.[7]

---

[7] For more discussion on issues in the globalization of higher education and research universities, see the series of reports that have emerged from the Glion Colloquium at http://www.glion.org/ (accessed December 19, 2011).

5

Action

REPOSITIONING OUR RESEARCH UNIVERSITIES IN A CHANGED WORLD

The emergence of our nation's research universities and the establishment of a strong federal-university partnership driving research and doctoral education has been a success story for the American people, contributing to our economic prosperity and national goals. Through education and research, American research universities have produced the talent and knowledge that generates innovation critical to economic growth and a high American standard of living.

The Great Recession and the "flattening of the world," though, have made it clear that there is an *urgent need* to develop a compelling and effective national strategy for sustaining our world-class research universities that reinforces the partnership of research universities with federal and state governments and expands it to include a larger role for business. It is time to act. In the midst of the Civil War, one of our nation's deepest crises, Congress passed, and President Abraham Lincoln signed, the Morrill Act, thereby laying the foundation for the land-grant universities that generated a productive agricultural and industrial society. So too, the nation now needs to act in the context of present circumstances to assure the vitality of its research universities in a global knowledge economy. For our research universities to continue to fulfill their obligations to the nation, they must have sufficient resources and a robust infrastructure, sound organizational and administrative structures, a vibrant intellectual community, and the ability to translate research discoveries into societal benefits. Without these, states and regions that are currently sustained by their research universities may lose their competitive edge, and our nation may fall short in both meeting its national goals and continuing its strong global leadership.

PRINCIPLES

For the past half-century, the research and graduate programs of America's research universities have been essential contributors to the nation's prosperity, health, and security. Today, our nation faces new challenges, a time of rapid and profound economic, social, and political transformation driven by the growth in knowledge and innovation. Educated people, the knowledge they produce, and the innovation and entrepreneurial skills they possess, particularly in the fields of science and engineering, have become the keys to America's future. We have taken stock of the organizational, financial, and intellectual health of our nation's research universities today and have envisioned the role we would like them to play in our nation's life 10 to 20 years from now. We can say without reservation that our research universities are, today, the best in the world and an important resource for our nation, yet, at the same time, in grave danger of not only losing their place of global leadership but of serious erosion in quality due to critical trends in public support.

Our vision for strengthening these institutions so that they may remain dynamic assets over the coming decades involves both increasing their productivity and ensuring their strong support for education and research. Therefore, it is essential that the unique partnership that has long existed among the nation's research universities, the federal government, the states, and business and industry be reaffirmed and strengthened. This will require

• A balanced set of commitments by each of the partners—federal government, state governments, research universities, and business and industry—to provide leadership for the nation in a knowledge-intensive world and to develop and implement enlightened policies, efficient operating practices, and necessary investments.

• Use of matching requirements among these commitments that provide strong incentives for participation at comparable levels by each partner.

• Sufficient flexibility to accommodate differences among research universities and the diversity of their various stakeholders. While merit, impact, and need should continue to be the primary criteria for awarding research grants and contracts by federal agencies, investment in infrastructure should consider additional criteria such as regional and cross-institutional partnerships, program focus, and opportunities for building significant research capacity.

- • A commitment to a decade-long effort that seeks to both address challenges and take advantage of opportunities as they emerge.
- • A recognition of the importance of supporting the comprehensive nature of the research university, spanning the full spectrum of academic and professional disciplines, including the physical, life, and social and behavioral sciences; engineering; the arts and humanities; and the professions, that enable it to provide the broad research and education programs required by a knowledge- and innovation-driven global economy.

Within this partnership, our research universities with a historical commitment to excellence, academic freedom, and service to society must pledge themselves to a new level of partnership with government and business, recommit to being the places where the best minds in the world want to work, think, educate, and create new ideas, and commit to delivering better outcomes for each dollar spent. As articulated in the Millennium Declaration of 2001 on the future of research universities:

> For a thousand years the university has benefited our civilization as a learning community where both the young and the experienced could acquire not only knowledge and skills, but the values and discipline of the educated mind. It has defended and propagated our cultural and intellectual heritage, while challenging our norms and beliefs. It has produced the leaders of our governments, commerce, and professions. It has both created and applied new knowledge to serve our society. And it has done so while preserving those values and principles so essential to academic learning: the freedom of inquiry, an openness to new ideas, a commitment to rigorous study, and a love of learning. There seems little doubt that these roles will continue to be needed by our civilization. There is little doubt as well that the university, in some form, will be needed to provide them. The university of the 21st century may be as different from today's institutions as the research university is from the colonial college. But its form and its continued evolution will be a consequence of transformations necessary to provide its ancient values and contributions to a changing world.[1]

RECOMMENDATIONS

With these principles in mind, the committee provides 10 recommendations that the federal government, the states, research universities,

---

[1] Declaration summarized in James J. Duderstadt, A University for the 21st Century. Ann Arbor, MI: The University of Michigan Press, 2003, p. 324. Original text of the declaration is available at: http://www.glion.org/pub_1999_millennium.aspx (accessed March 23, 2012).

and business and industry can act on to maintain the level of world-class excellence in research and graduate education necessary for the United States to compete, prosper, and achieve national goals for health, energy, the environment, and security in the global community of the twenty-first century. The first four recommendations reaffirm the commitments of each major partner, and the following six enable these commitments. It is important that these recommendations must be implemented together, as they reinforce each other in critical ways.

Universities are today among the most complex institutions in modern society. As James Duderstadt has noted, research universities are comprised of many activities, some nonprofit, some publicly regulated, and some operating in intensely competitive marketplaces. They teach students, conduct research for various clients, provide health care, engage in economic development, stimulate social change, and provide mass entertainment (e.g., athletics). In systems terminology, the modern university is a "loosely coupled, adaptive system," with a growing complexity, as its various components respond to changes in its environment.[2]

As the major focus of the charge to the committee was graduate education and research, we preface our recommendations by reinforcing the importance of undergraduate education, both in the research universities that we are examining and in other important institutions, from liberal arts colleges to state universities that also provide undergraduate education. The strength of undergraduate teaching and learning to our nation's workforce and prosperity and to preparing students who go on to graduate study cannot be overstated.

Similarly, the unusually broad intellectual needs of the nation and the increasing interdependence of the academic disciplines provide compelling reasons why such federal support should encompass all areas of scholarship, including the natural sciences, the social sciences, the humanities, the arts, and professional disciplines such as engineering, education, law, and medicine. Our report and its recommendations are designed to encourage support across all of these areas.[3]

Recommendation 1

Within the broader framework of United States innovation and research and development (R&D) strategies, the federal government should adopt stable and effective policies, practices, and funding for university-performed R&D and graduate education so that the nation will have a

---

[2] James J. Duderstadt, A University for the 21st Century, p. 50.

[3] We look forward to a Congressionally requested report on the role of the humanities and social sciences in our nation, due in 2012 from the American Academy of Arts and Sciences.

*stream of new knowledge and educated people to power our future, help-
ing us meet national goals and ensure prosperity and security.*

Actors and Actions—Implementing Recommendation 1:

- *Federal government*: The federal government should review and
modify those research policies and practices governing university research and graduate education that have become burdensome and inefficient, such as research cost reimbursement, unnecessary regulation,
and awkward variation and coordination among federal agencies. (See
Recommendations 6 and 7.)

- *Federal government—Congress, Administration, federal science
and technology (S&T) agencies*: Over the next decade as the economy
improves, Congress and the administration should invest in basic research and graduate education at a level sufficient to produce the new
knowledge and educated citizens necessary to achieve national goals. As
a core component of a national plan to raise total national R&D to 3 percent of gross domestic product (GDP), Congress and the Administration
should provide full funding of the amount authorized by the America
COMPETES Act that would double the level of basic research conducted
by the National Science Foundation (NSF), National Institute of Standards and Technology (NIST), and Department of Energy (DOE) Office
of Science as well as sustain our nation's investment in other key areas of
basic research, including biomedical research. Within this investment, as
recommend by *Rising Above the Gathering Storm*,[4] a portion of the increase
should be directed to high-risk, innovative, and unconventional research.

- *Federal government—White House Office of Science and Technology Policy (OSTP), President's Council of Advisors on Science and
Technology (PCAST), U.S. Office of Management and Budget (OMB),
National Economic Council (NEC), and Council of Economic Advisors
(CEA)*: On an annual basis in the President's annual budget request,
OMB should develop and present, in coordination with OSTP, a federal
science and technology budget that addresses priorities for sustaining a
world-class U.S. science and technology enterprise. On a quadrennial basis, OSTP, in conjunction with PCAST, and OMB, in conjunction with the
NEC and CEA, should review federal science and technology spending
and outcomes, internationally benchmarked, to ensure that federal S&T
spending is adequate in size to support our economy and appropriately
targeted to meet national goals. We recommend that this process consider

---

[4] National Academy of Sciences, National Academy of Engineering, and Institute of Medicine, Rising Above the Gathering Storm: Energizing and Employing America for a Brighter
Economic Future, Washington, DC: National Academies Press, 2007.

U.S. global leadership, a focus on developing new knowledge, balance in the science and technology portfolio, reliable and predictable streams of funding, and a commitment to merit review.

Budget Implications

This recommendation calls for stable and effective federal research policies and practices, the budget implications of which are outlined under several recommendations below. The recommendation also aims to ensure robust financial support for critical federal basic research programs. It supports funding increases that Congress has *already authorized* through the America COMPETES Act for the doubling of funding for the NSF, NIST, and DOE Office of Science. These increases target stronger investment in physical sciences and engineering research, but do not imply any disinvestment in critical fields such as the life sciences and social, behavioral, and economic sciences. Indeed, we recommend Congressional action to at least *maintain* current levels of funding for basic research across other federal agencies, including the National Institutes of Health (NIH), as adjusted for inflation. Research universities, along with other research performers (national laboratories, nonprofit research and development organizations, and industry), will only benefit from these actions through their success in competing for federal grants and contracts from these agencies.

Expected Outcomes

Supportive federal research policies would ensure stable funding and cost-efficient regulation sufficient to enable corresponding university investment in research facilities and graduate programs. By completing the funding of the America COMPETES Act, the nation would achieve a balanced research portfolio capable of driving innovation necessary for economic prosperity. As research and education are deliberately intertwined in our American research universities, such funding will also ensure that we continue to produce the scientists, engineers, physicians, teachers, scholars, and other knowledge professionals essential to the nation's security, health, and prosperity.

Discussion

Context

Nations around the world have recognized the importance of investment in research and doctoral education, both of which build their nation's research universities, contribute to economic growth, and improve global competitiveness. In most instances, they have developed comprehensive national strategies designed to strengthen their research base and their institutions to compete for students and faculty, resources, and reputation (see Box 4-1).

The United States has begun to lag on a key, internationally recognized indicator of national investment in the development of new knowledge: national (public and private) R&D expenditures as a percentage of GDP. As shown in Figure 5-1.1, public and private R&D expenditures in the United States have hovered between 2.5 and 2.8 percent of GDP over the last three decades. It stood at 2.79 percent in 2008. By comparison, as shown in Figures 5-1.1 and 5-1.2, Japan has increased its national R&D funding from about 2.8 percent of GDP in 1996 to 3.4 percent in 2007, while South Korea has increased its spending even further, reaching 3.5 percent of GDP in that year. While R&D in Germany as a percent of GDP is slightly lower than that of the United States, its nondefense R&D as a percentage of GDP is higher than that of the United States and the gap between the two countries is growing. The annual rate of growth in national R&D expenditures was 5-6 percent for the United States and the European Union (EU-27), while rates of growth for many Asian countries were far higher. China's annual growth in national R&D expenditures was 20 percent for the period 1996 to 2007.[5]

Targets

Embedded in a broader federal innovation strategy that addresses national research and development priorities, the nation must develop a framework of national funding goals and supportive policies that sustain the nation's research universities at world-class levels. The current Administration developed and issued the National Innovation Strategy in September 2009 and presented an updated version drafted by the National Economic Council, the Council of Economic Advisors, and the Office of Science and Technology Policy in February 2011. This strategy provides a broad policy context and includes a short section focused on strengthening and broadening "American leadership in fundamental research." This provides an excellent foundation from which to craft a more detailed strategy for sustaining the nation's R&D enterprise, fundamental research, and U.S. research universities. For example, it sets a national goal "for America to invest more than three percent of our GDP in public and private research and development" noting that "this investment rate

---

[5] National Science Board, Science and Engineering Indicators, 2010, (NSB 10-01), Arlington, VA: National Science Foundation, 2010, Figures 4-13 and 4-16, pages 4-35 and 4-36.

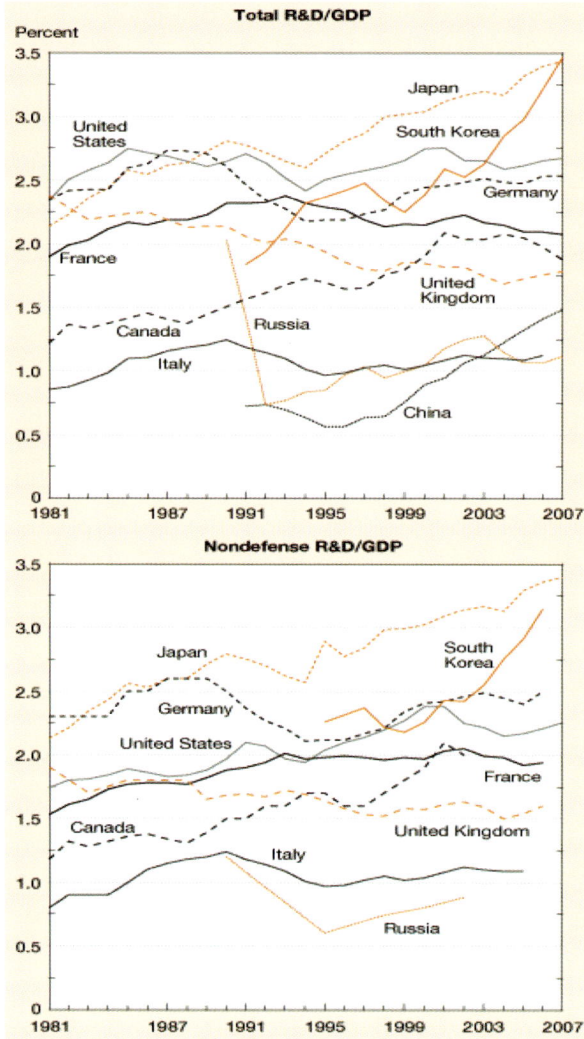

FIGURE 5-1.1 Gross expenditures on R&D as share of gross domestic product, for selected countries: 1981-2007.
Source: National Science Board, Science and Engineering Indicators 2010. (NSB 10-01) Arlington, VA: National Science Foundation, 2010, Figure 4-16, page 4-36.

Constant 2000 PPP dollars (billions)

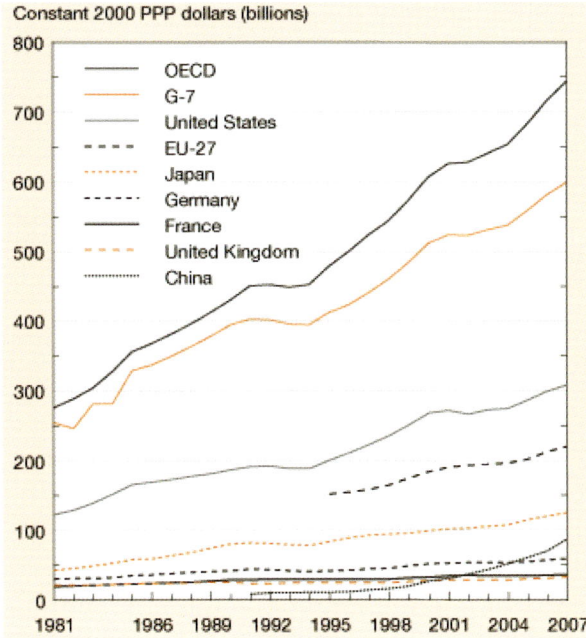

FIGURE 5-1.2 Gross domestic expenditures on R&D by United States, EU-27, OECD, and selected other countries: 1981-2007.
Source: National Science Board, Science and Engineering Indicators 2010. (NSB 10-01) Arlington, VA: National Science Foundation, 2010, Figure 4-13, page 4-35.

will surpass the level achieved at the height of the space race, and can be achieved through policies that support basic and applied research, create new incentives for private innovation, promote breakthroughs in national priority areas, and improve [science, technology, engineering, and mathematics] STEM education."[6] Table 5-1.1 displays 2008 U.S. R&D in current dollars and as a percentage of GDP and shows total national R&D spending in that year at 2.79 percent. An increase to 3 percent of GDP would potentially lift all components of R&D, including federally funded, university-performed research.

Indeed, the committee recommends federal R&D appropriations levels that would sustain and enhance university-based research. We strongly support the goals articulated by *Rising Above the Gathering Storm* and au-

_____

[6] The White House, A Strategy for American Innovation: Securing Our Economic Growth and Prosperity, February 2011.

TABLE 5-1.1 U.S. R&D, 2008 Expenditures

	Current Funding ($ billions)	Current Percent of GDP
Gross Domestic Product	14,264.6	100.00
National R&D (all sources, all performers)	397.3	2.79
Federally funded R&D	103.7	0.73
National basic research (all sources)	69.10	0.48
Federally funded basic research	39.4	0.28
University-performed R&D	51.9	0.36
Federally funded, university-performed R&D	31.3	0.22
University-performed basic research	39.4	0.28
Federally funded, university-performed basic research	24.5	0.17

Sources: NSF/NCSES, Academic R&D Expenditures, Fiscal Year 2009, Tables 1, 2, and 3. Available at: http://www.nsf.gov/statistics/nsf11313/content.cfm?pub_id=4065&id=2 (accessed September 4, 2011). NSF/NCSES, national patterns of R&D Resources, Tables 6 and 13. Available at: http://www.nsf.gov/statistics/natlpatterns/ (accessed September 4, 2011).

thorized in the America COMPETES Act of 2010 that would increase the support of basic research key to sustaining the nation's innovation necessary for prosperity and national security by doubling the budgets of the NSF, DOE Office of Science, and NIST. We also strongly urge that federal appropriations for basic research in support of other key national goals such as health (NIH), defense (Department of Defense [DOD]), space (National Aeronautics and Space Administration), and agriculture (U.S. Department of Agriculture) be sustained at least at the rate of inflation. Figure 5-1.3 shows that federally funded, university-performed R&D as a percentage of GDP increased from 1998 to 2005, while the NIH budget doubled, from about 0.17 percent to about 0.24 percent, and has since decreased to 0.22 percent. This mirrors the flattening of federally funded university R&D and the decline of federally funded research generally (in constant dollars) seen in Figures 5-1.4 and 5-1.5. Providing the appropriations we recommend can help reverse these declines and ensure that we are strongly investing for the future.

Principles

The following are important principles for federal R&D funding, many articulated in previous National Academies reports:

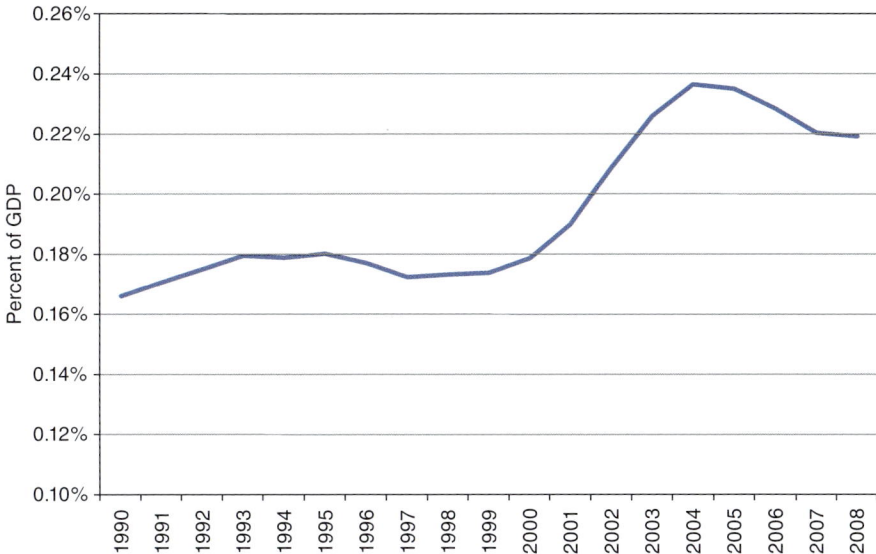

FIGURE 5-1.3 Federally funded, university-performed research and development as a percentage of GDP, 1990-2008.
Source: NSF/NCSES, Academic R&D Expenditures, Fiscal Year 2009, Table 1. Available at: http://www.nsf.gov/statistics/nsf11313/content.cfm?pub_id=4065&id=2 (accessed September 4, 2011). NSF/NCSES, National Patterns of R&D Resources, Table 13. Available at: http://www.nsf.gov/statistics/natlpatterns/ (accessed September 4, 2011).

- *Focus on global leadership*: At the end of the Cold War, the U.S. Congress asked the National Academies to identify priority areas for future federal investment and to provide a foundation upon which federal science and technology (FS&T) budgetary policy can be built and analyzed. In *Science, Technology, and the Federal Government: National Goals for a New Era* (1993), the National Academies recommended two goals to guide federal investment in science and technology:

    o First, the United States should be among the world leaders in all major areas of science. Achieving this goal would allow this nation to quickly apply and extend advances in science wherever they occur.

    o Second, the United States should maintain clear leadership in some areas of science. The decision to select a field for leadership would

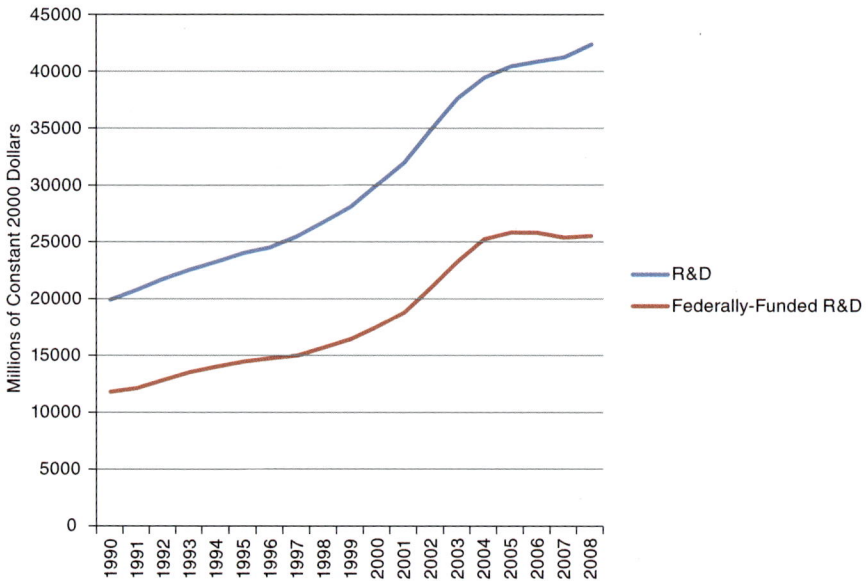

FIGURE 5-1.4 University-performed research and development and federally funded, university-performed research and development, 1990-2008 (in millions of constant 2000 dollars).

Sources: NSF/NCSES, Academic R&D Expenditures, Fiscal Year 2009, Table 1. Available at: http://www.nsf.gov/statistics/nsf11313/content.cfm?pub_id=4065&id=2 (accessed September 4, 2011).

Data adjusted for inflation using implicit price deflator in NSF/NCSES, national patterns of R&D Resources, Table 13. Available at: http://www.nsf.gov/statistics/natlpatterns/ (accessed September 4, 2011).

be based on national objectives and other criteria external to the field of research.[7]

These remain critical national goals for federal R&D investment.

• **_Focus on new knowledge_**: The National Academies' _Allocating Federal Funds for Science and Technology_ (1995) urged the Executive Office of the President and the U.S. Congress to develop a more coherent budget process for determining federal investment in programs that create new knowledge and technologies (i.e., the federal science and technology budget). It recommended that the President present annually a Federal

---

[7] National Academy of Sciences, National Academy of Engineering, Institute of Medicine, Science, Technology, and the Federal Government: National Goals for a New Era. Washington, DC: National Academy Press, 1993.

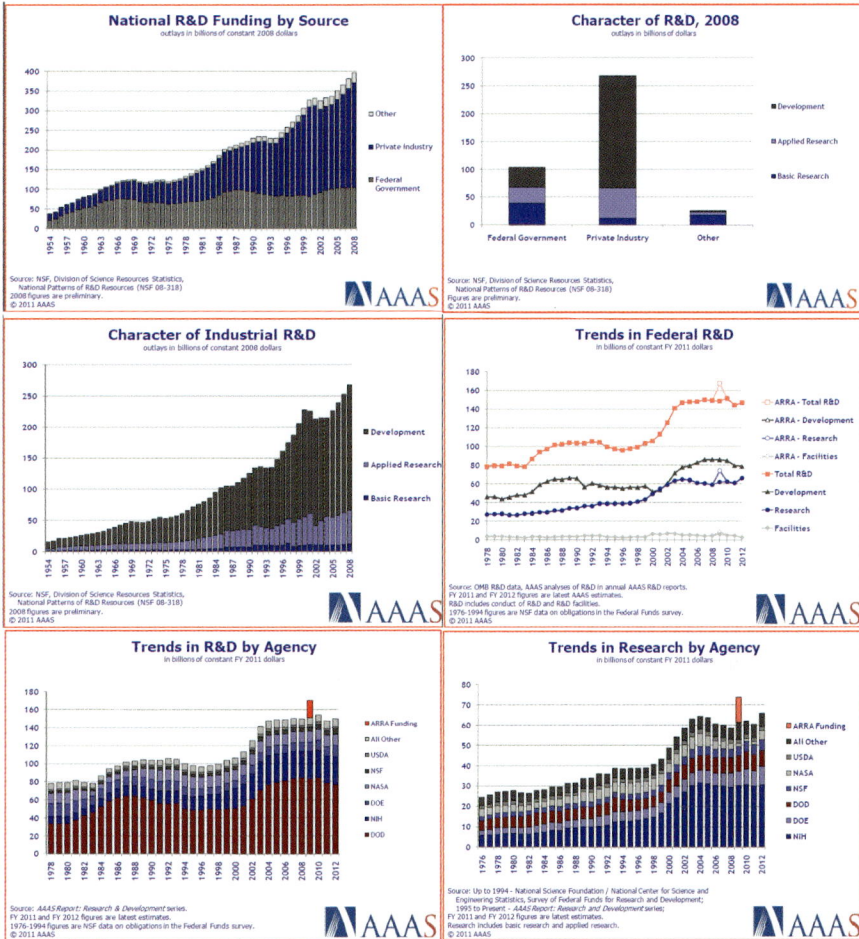

FIGURE 5-1.5 Trends in and characteristics of national, industrial, and federal R&D, 1954-present.

Note: Fiscal 2012 is Administration Budget Proposal, not yet enacted at time of original figure composition.

Source for AAAS Figures: Patrick Clemins, Research and Development in the Federal Budget Presentation, AAAS S&T Policy Forum, May 5, 2011. Available at: http://www.aaas.org/spp/rd/forum2011/presentations/PatrickClemins_AAASForum2011.pdf (accessed September 4, 2011).

Science and Technology budget proposal that addresses priorities for sustaining a world-class U.S. science and technology enterprise.[8] Within broader R&D appropriations, FS&T more narrowly focuses on the production of new knowledge and is roughly analogous to basic and applied research. This FS&T presentation was adopted in the late 1990s by the U.S. Office of Management and Budget and was continued into the early 2000s.[9] The presentation has since been dropped from the President's annual federal budget proposal. We recommend that it be restored.

•   *Balance in the science and technology portfolio*: *Rising Above the Gathering Storm* recommended to "increase the federal investment in long-term basic research by 10% each year over the next 7 years through reallocation of existing funds or, if necessary, through the investment of new funds." The report also recommended "special attention should go to the physical sciences, engineering, mathematics, and information sciences and to Department of Defense (DOD) basic-research funding. This special attention does not mean that there should be a disinvestment in such important fields as the life sciences or the social sciences. A balanced research portfolio in all fields of science and engineering research is critical to U.S. prosperity."[10]

•   *Focus on accelerating scientific and technological advances*: *Rising Above the Gathering Storm* also argued that "increasingly, the most significant new scientific and engineering advances are formed to cut across several disciplines" and that federal research agencies should "allocate at least 8% of the budgets of federal research agencies to discretionary funding…focused on catalyzing high-risk, high-payoff research of the type that often suffers in today's increasingly risk-averse environment."[11]

•   *Reliable and predictable streams of funding*: The nation will increase the performance of its research enterprise by providing steady, predictable streams of funding for research over time. The last decade has seen damaging fluctuations in research appropriations. Instead, the federal government should provide steady, sustainable, predictable support for university research over the longer term. This would enable universities to plan their own investments in research, and it would make federal research expenditures more effective and efficient.

•   *Commitment to merit review*: The nation's investments in university research should continue to emphasize the characteristics that have

---

[8] National Research Council, Allocating Federal Funds for Science and Technology. Washington, DC: National Academy Press, 1995, p. v.

[9] National Academy of Sciences, National Academy of Engineering, Institute of Medicine, Observations on the President's Fiscal Year 2003 Federal Science and Technology Budget. Washington, DC: National Academies Press, 2002.

[10] National Academy of Sciences et al., Rising Above the Gathering Storm.

[11] Ibid.

made it the most effective research investment in the world a research agenda driven by science and scientific opportunity and a commitment to peer-reviewed and competitively awarded research grants. In particular, the committee strongly encourages both federal sponsors and universities to avoid the use of earmarks or other political mechanisms for determining grant awards that both increase costs and erode research quality.

- **Importance of evaluation**: *Rising Above the Gathering Storm* also recommended that federal investments "should be evaluated regularly to realign the research portfolio to satisfy emerging needs and promises—unsuccessful projects and venues of research should be replaced with research projects and venues that have greater potential."[12]

Recommendation 2

Provide greater autonomy for public research universities so that these institutions may leverage local and regional strengths to compete strategically and respond with agility to new opportunities. At the same time, restore state appropriations for higher education, including graduate education and research, to levels that allow public research universities to operate at world-class levels.

Actors and Actions—Implementing Recommendation 2:

- **State governments**: States should move rapidly to provide their public research universities with sufficient autonomy and agility to navigate an extended period with limited state support. (See also regulatory environment, below.)
- **State governments**: For states to compete for the prosperity and welfare of their citizens in a knowledge- and innovation-driven global economy, the advanced education, research, and innovation programs provided by their research universities are absolutely essential. Hence, as state budgets recover from the current recession, states should strive to restore and maintain per-student funding for higher education, including public research universities, to the mean level for the 15-year period 1987-2002, as adjusted for inflation.[13]
- **Federal government**: To provide further incentives for state actions to protect the quality of public research universities as both a state

---

[12] Ibid.

[13] A 15-year period was used so as to ensure the funding recommendation was not unduly influenced by year-to-year fluctuations in state appropriations. The year 2002 was used as the endpoint of the period, as that year represents the beginning of a period of significant decline in appropriations.

and a national asset, federal programs designed to stimulate innovation and workforce development at the state level, including those recommended in this report, should be accompanied by strong incentives to stimulate and sustain state support for their public universities.

Budget Implications

This recommendation addresses the alarming erosion in state support of higher education over the past decade that has put the quality and capacity of public research universities at great risk. While the committee urges the states to strive to restore over time appropriation cuts to public research universities estimated to average 25 percent (and ranging as high as 50 percent for some universities),[14] it acknowledges that current state budget challenges and shifting state priorities may make this very difficult in the near term. Hence, the committee views as equally important a strong recommendation that the states provide their public research universities with sufficient autonomy and ability to navigate what could be an extended period with inadequate state funding. The committee strongly believes that such recommendations are in the long-term interests of both the states and the nation.

Expected Outcomes

State appropriations per enrolled student have declined by 25 percent or more over the past two decades, resulting in the need for universities to increase tuition or reduce activities, or quality. As states strive to compete in a knowledge- and innovation-driven global economy, restoring state appropriations to levels sufficient to maintain advanced education, research, and innovation programs provided by research universities is absolutely essential for the prosperity and welfare of their citizens. Increasing the autonomy and agility of public research universities should increase their efficiency and productivity as well as their ability to re-

---

[14] The National Science Board reports, "Over the decade [2002 to 2010], per-student state support to major research universities dropped by an average of 20 percent in inflation-adjusted dollars. In 10 states, the decline ranged from 30 percent to 48 percent." National Science Board, Science and Engineering Indicators 2012, p. 8-68. Available at: http://www. nsf.gov/statistics/seind12/pdf/c08.pdf (accessed March 8, 2012). The states have enacted further and deeper cuts in 2011 and 2012, which suggests an overall decline for 2002-2012 of at least 25 percent. For example, the State Higher Education Executive Officers Association recently reported, "FY 2012 state appropriations [for higher education] (including a small residual of ARRA funding) were $72.5 billion, a decrease of 7.6 percent from $78.5 billion in FY 2011." See SHEEO, "Commentary on FY 2012 state appropriations for higher education," press release, January 23, 2012. Available at: http://grapevine.illinoisstate.edu/tables/FY12/SHEEO%20Commentary%20(2).pdf (accessed March 8, 2012).

spond to changing state and regional needs during an extended period when states may not be able to restore adequate support.

Discussion

Support for public research universities is a *national* challenge of immense importance, since these institutions produce the *majority* of advanced-degree recipients and basic research for the United States. Any loss of world-class quality for America's public research institutions seriously damages national prosperity, security, and quality of life. In fact, for many state research universities, the national importance of these institutions is underscored by the fact that their federal support, through student financial aid and research grants, now exceeds state appropriations. But states still have a critically important role to play—one that supports these institutions and meets the local and regional needs of states and their residents.

The nation's public research universities face great risk as the states that support them not only face serious financial challenges due to the recent recession, they also often no longer give priority to the support of graduate education and research. With increasing national and even international mobility of campus-generated knowledge and doctorates, states may support undergraduate education and the goal of broadening access at world-class levels, but they are less inclined to invest in research and graduate education at their public research universities given the uncertainty in their ability to capture the returns on their investments. However, state leaders should realize that a restoration of an adequate level of support for public postsecondary education generally—and their research universities more specifically—remains very much in their long-term interest. These institutions provide both the talent and ideas necessary for regional economic growth and for other local needs, including health, public safety, transportation planning, cultural enrichment, new elementary and secondary teachers, and more. The importance of highly educated citizens and universities with the ability to discover new knowledge, develop innovative applications of research, and transfer them into the marketplace is critical to the prosperity and welfare of the states just as it is to the nation. Yet the benefits of graduate education and university research are public goods whose high mobility extends far beyond state boundaries. Hence, with budget constraints and the shifting priorities of aging populations, many states have concluded that they can no longer justify giving high priority to sustaining their public research universities at world-class levels. Yet such actions represent not only a marked decline in regional advantage at the state level but also seriously harm the national interest. To be sure, not all states have the capacity to build and

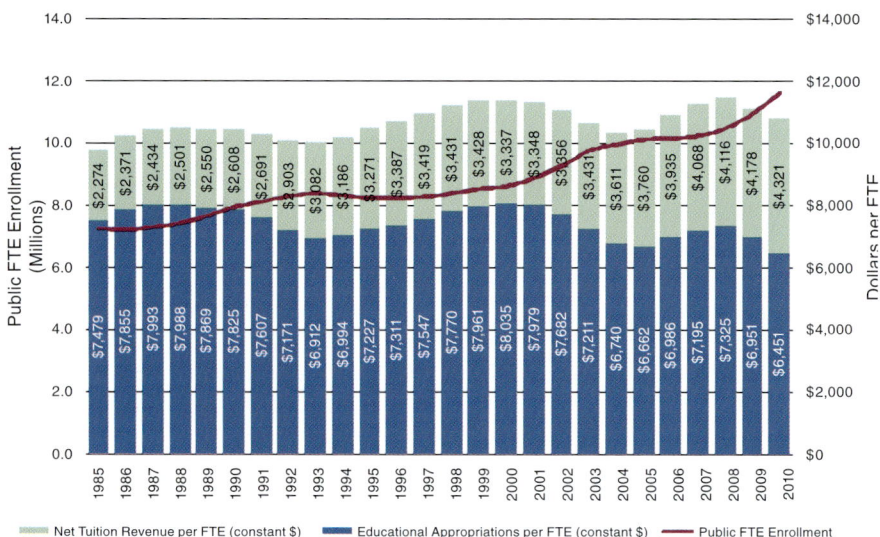

FIGURE 5-2.1 Public FTE enrollment and state educational appropriations per FTE student, U.S., fiscal 1985-2010 (constant dollars).
Note: Net tuition revenue used for capital debt service is included in the above figures.
Source: State Higher Education Officers (SHEEO), State Higher Education Finance 2010, Figure 3, page 20. Available at: http://www.sheeo.org/finance/shef_fy10.pdf.

maintain large, comprehensive research universities at world-class levels, but all states have the capacity to focus resources to build high-quality graduate and research programs in select areas of high local priority.

Indeed, the states vary significantly in both the levels of, and trends in, support they provide for public higher education.[15] However, for the nation as a whole, state postsecondary educational appropriations per full-time equivalent (FTE) student decreased 3.1 percent in constant dollars from FY 2005 to FY 2010. A 7.2 percent decrease in the past year due to the impact of the recession on the states wiped out interim gains from 2005 to 2008. In fact, as shown in Figures 5-2.1 and 5-2.2, state educational appropriations per FTE student in constant dollars have ebbed and flowed over time, but there has been a long-term downward trend since the late 1980s, and they were at their lowest levels in constant dollars in FY 2010

---

[15] State educational appropriations per FTE at public higher education institutions in FY 2010 varied from a low of $3,781 in Colorado to $13,090 in Wyoming. The 5-year change in educational appropriations per FTE varied from –27.4 percent in Rhode Island to +26.6 percent in North Dakota. State Higher Education Executive Officers (SHEEO), State Higher Education Finance, FY 2010, pp. 10, 29, available at: http://www.sheeo.org/finance/shef_fy10.pdf.

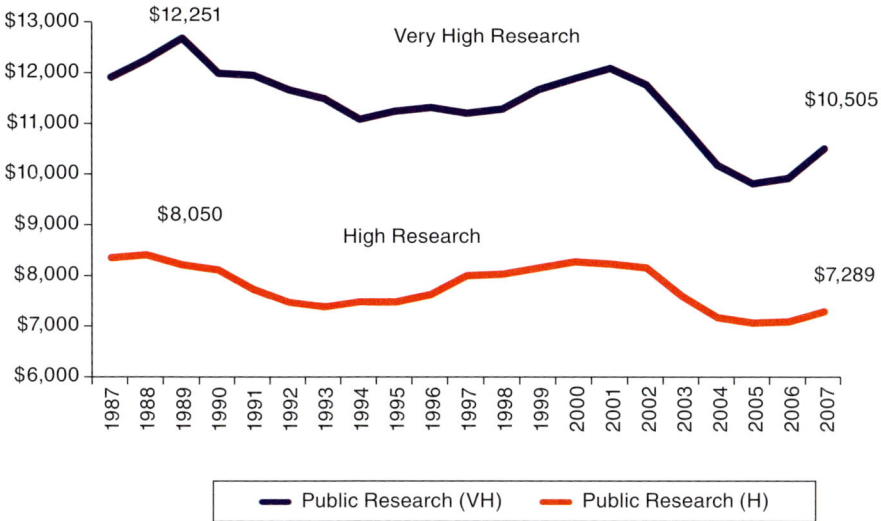

FIGURE 5-2.2 Real state and local appropriations per student (FTE) in public research universities, by very high research and high research institutions, fiscal 1987-2007 (2007 constant dollars).

Source: Peter M. McPherson, President, Association of Public and Land-grant Universities, Presentation to the NRC Committee on Research Universities, November 2010.

than at any time in the past 25 years.[16] This trend has resulted not just from the recession. State Higher Education Executive Officers (SHEEO) reports, "The proportion of state and local tax revenue allocated to higher education declined from 6.9 percent in 1998 to 6.6 percent in 2008."[17]

There are important consequences for public research universities and their students that flow from these cuts in state appropriations. As shown in Figure 5-2.3, per FTE student expenditures at public institutions are lower than those at private institutions and have been growing more slowly. As shown in Figure 5-2.4, the median salaries of assistant, associate, and full professors at public institutions have decreased over time relative to their peers at private institutions. Consequently, the private institutions have the upper hand in hiring and have the additional ability to lure away "star" professors from public research universities. As shown in Figure 5-2.5, the ratio of students to full-time faculty has been lower in private institutions, and the gap between public and private institutions

---

[16] Ibid., pp. 7, 20, 29.
[17] Ibid., p. 10.

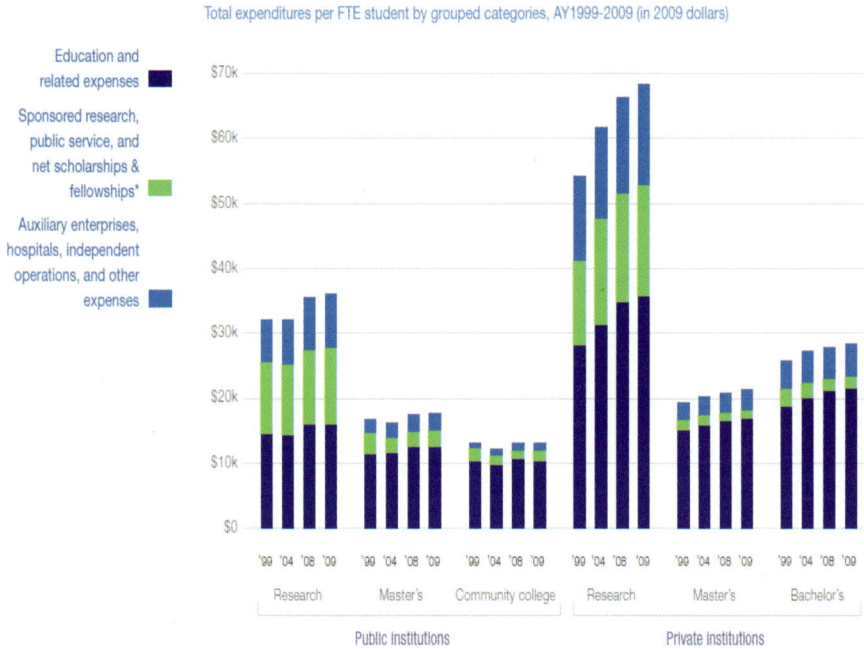

FIGURE 5-2.3 Total expenditures per FTE student at private and public nonprofit institutions, by institution category and type of expenses, 1999, 2004, 2008, and 2009 (2009 constant dollars).
Source: Donna M. Desrochers and Jane V. Wellman, Trends in College Spending, 1999-2009, Where does the money come from? Where does it go? What does it buy? A report of the Delta Cost Project. Available at: http://www.deltacostproject.org/resources/pdf/Trends2011_Final_090711.pdf (accessed September 16, 2011).

for this indicator is growing. This presumably affects the educational experience of students.

While the current budget difficulties faced by the states call for choices to be made, high-quality public research universities remain essential to providing America's citizens with the advanced education and research necessary to compete in a knowledge- and innovation-driven global economy. As budgets revive, states should give high priority to restoring and maintaining funding sufficient to keep their research universities at world-class levels. The actions that each state may take will vary according to their particular needs and circumstances; yet the national aggregate of state postsecondary education appropriations per FTE student must be restored to at least the inflation-adjusted levels that existed in 1988 as

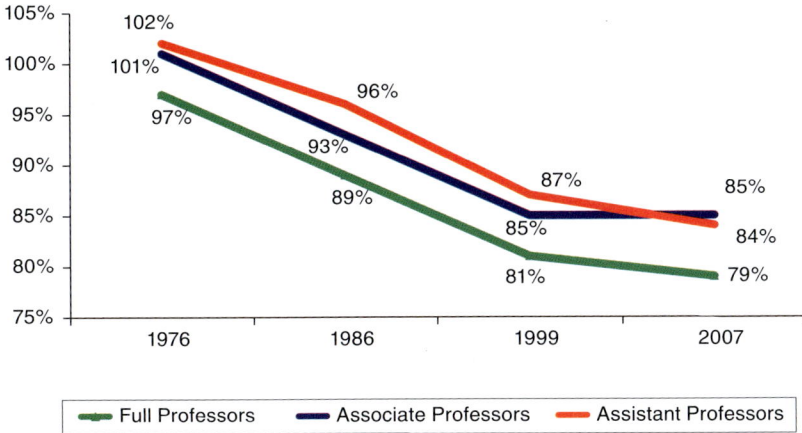

FIGURE 5-2.4 Ratio of salaries of full, associate, and assistant professors at private institutions to those at public institutions, 1976, 1986, 1999, and 2007.
Source: Peter M. McPherson, President, Association of Public and Land-grant Universities, Presentation to NRC Committee on Research Universities, November 2010.

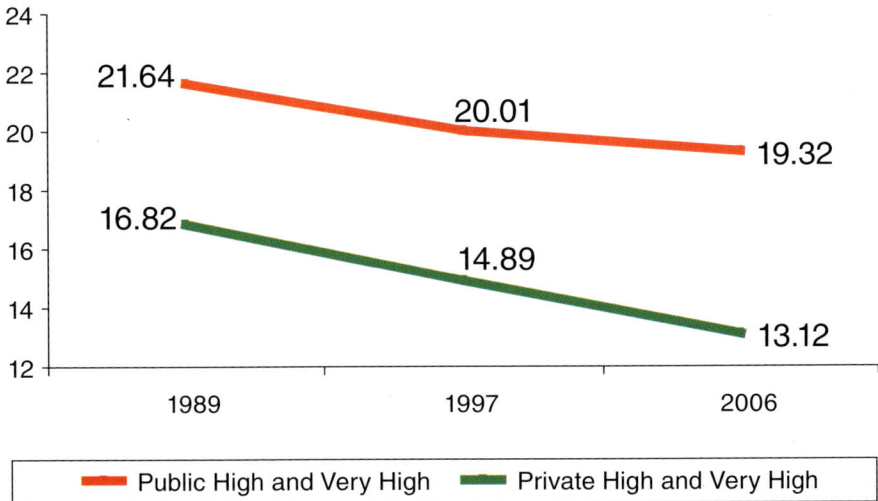

FIGURE 5-2.5 Ratio of students to full-time faculty, for public and private research universities, 1989, 1997, and 2006.
Source: Peter M. McPherson, President, Association of Public and Land-grant Universities, Presentation to Committee on Research Universities, November 2010.

rapidly as possible. To be sure, there are other competing claims on state funding, but the recommended average increase per state is reasonable, attainable, and a wise investment in the future.

Increased state funding, moreover, should be targeted to their best use in the local and regional economic environment. For example, increased state funding could be used to

- Fund expansion of undergraduate and graduate education at public research universities, including disciplines linked to the competitiveness of the state for retaining traditional business and attracting new business.
- Provide funding for research work undertaken by public research universities, including but not limited to research supportive of state and regional business activity.

There will be other reasonable targets that reflect local needs and conditions.

Critically important, the committee agrees with the Association of American Universities (AAU) that federal funding should be used to leverage, not substitute for, state funding. "The allocation of federal funds in support of public research universities cannot be a substitute for state funds; maintenance of efforts by states should be committed and audited. Where possible, federal funds could be employed as an incentive for state funding, for example with support for scientific infrastructure such as new research facilities, facility modernization and research instrumentation."[18] Indeed, federal and state governments could enter into complementary matching opportunities to advance fields that are critical to societal needs and incentivize collaboration to a greater degree on large national and state projects.

In addition to restoring appropriations, states should provide public research universities with the autonomy and agility to restructure their operations to enable them to survive current public underfunding and to position them to capitalize on future opportunities as the economy improves. Greater autonomy and agility can be accomplished in several ways, including

- Restructuring university governance so that boards better represent the broader "public" beyond just the states that now provide such small portions of overall university budgets.

---

[18] Association of American Universities, Recommendations to the National Research Council Committee on Research Universities, February 2, 2011.

- Allowing public research universities to set tuition and fees for their campuses.
- Allowing public research universities to do their own procurement independent of the state government.
- Allowing public research universities to obtain the bonds they need without state approval in order to move more quickly in the construction of dormitories, research facilities, and other buildings necessary to maintain high-quality education, research, and service. (In addition, moving construction projects ahead quickly creates jobs that are badly needed in this time of high unemployment.)
- Providing incentives for public universities to form regional compacts with other universities for the purpose of ensuring that programs that might not be of scale in a single university continue to be collaboratively offered or otherwise made available within the region in a cost-effective manner.
- Reducing state regulations that have attempted to take the place of university administrators and of university governing bodies that are already in place to effectively oversee the strategy and performance of the university as a whole, consistent with the particular mission and distinctive characteristics of the institution.
- Conducting complete reviews of state compliance requirements and regulations that affect research with a focus on identifying their costs, making judgments about their efficacy, and producing recommendations about modifying or eliminating compliance requirements and regulations as appropriate.

This list is illustrative. There are certainly more, perhaps even better, steps that may be taken. As states undertake steps in this area, they should examine experiments already under way, such as the Restructured Higher Education Financial and Administrative Operations Act (Restructuring Act) that provides a framework for transforming public higher education in Virginia. As the University of Virginia reports, "The Restructuring Act grants Virginia's public institutions of higher education including the University of Virginia greater financial and administrative autonomy allowing them to more effectively and efficiently manage day-to-day operations. In exchange for increased autonomy, each institution must commit to meet specific statewide goals. The Act provides for three levels of autonomy; the University, along with Virginia Tech, the College of William & Mary, and Virginia Commonwealth University, is currently operating at the highest degree of autonomy."[19]

---

[19] See http://www.virginia.edu/restructuring/ (accessed December 13, 2011).

Recommendation 3

Strengthen the business role in the research partnership, facilitating the transfer of knowledge, ideas, and technology to society and accelerate "time to innovation" in order to achieve our national goals.

Actors and Actions—Implementing Recommendation 3:

- *Federal government*: Continue to fund and expand research support mechanisms that promote collaboration and innovation.
- *Federal government*: Within the context of also making the R&D tax credit permanent, implement new tax policies that incentivize business to develop partnerships with universities (and others as warranted) for research that results in new U.S.-located economic activities.
- *Business, universities*: The relationship between business and higher education should evolve into more of a peer-to-peer nature, stressing collaboration in areas of joint interest rather than the traditional customer-supplier relationship in which business procures graduates and intellectual property from universities.
- *Business, universities*: Business and universities should work closely together to develop new graduate degree programs that address strategic workforce gaps for science-based employers.
- *National laboratories, business, universities*: Collaboration among research by the nation's national laboratories, business, and universities should also be encouraged, since the latter's capacity for large-scale, sustained research projects both supports and depends critically on both the participation of university faculty and graduate students and the marketplace.
- *Universities*: Improve management of intellectual property to improve technology transfer.

Budget Implications

Tax policies that create incentives for new university-industry research and development partnerships will have a cost to the federal budget as a "tax expenditure." Although we are not in a position to estimate what that cost would be, it would be a relatively minor component of the cost of current proposals to make permanent the R&D tax credit.

Expected Outcomes

Effective use of research support mechanisms that promote collaboration will lead to the creation and efficient use of knowledge to achieve national goals.

The outcomes from the new tax policies would be new research partnerships; new knowledge and ideas; new products, processes, and industries located in the United States; economic growth; and new jobs. The outcomes from these efforts would be the creation of new partnerships, new knowledge and ideas, achieving national goals in key policy areas, and the economic growth and jobs that result from new activity.

Improvements in university management of intellectual property will result in more effective dissemination of research results, generating economic activity and jobs.

Discussion

Intellectual property—the ideas and knowledge that are key to innovation—moves out of universities to business through a variety of important paths. Chief among these is the education of students who leave to work in businesses, bringing their new knowledge with them. In some cases, they are able to innovate within their new environments based on what they have learned; in others, they create start-ups that represent new business and, in some important cases, new industries. Other means by which new ideas are disseminated include publication of scholarly papers, faculty consulting, creation of spin-off companies by faculty, patenting and licensing, and business-university research partnerships. This recommendation is primarily focused on the last two of these.

Research outcomes can be deepened and multiplied through improvements in the dissemination, translation, and commercialization of research results. Society's problems are ever-more complex and need to be addressed by new learning and discovery. Industry-university-government engagement will take both prodding and resources to greatly expand. The most productive models of such engagement are interdisciplinary, flexible, and interconnected or networked—just like the problems that they need to address. Universities are not presently organized for this reality, and a deeper collaboration with industry and governments will provide further external pressure to make our institutions better able to address multidisciplinary societal problems. There is an equal responsibility for business to explore how new partnerships can benefit research, commercial innovation, and society.

To accomplish this, governments, industry, philanthropy, and academia should collaborate to enhance innovation and the dissemination of research results. Improvements in university management of intellectual property and technology transfer from university laboratories to industry and the marketplace and stronger university partnerships with industry, national laboratories, and philanthropy are key ingredients for ensuring that research leads to innovation and jobs. This is the point at which the strong investments in Recommendations 1 and 2 lead to the breakthroughs needed to power the economy, enhance our culture and society, and help us achieve national goals.

Over the last two decades, long-term changes in the structure of the national research enterprise that have affected the roles and partnerships that all actors play are as follows:

- *Corporate* practices for the funding and performance of basic research have shifted. Financial pressures have led to the disappearance of large industrial laboratories in many industries and, therefore, to new

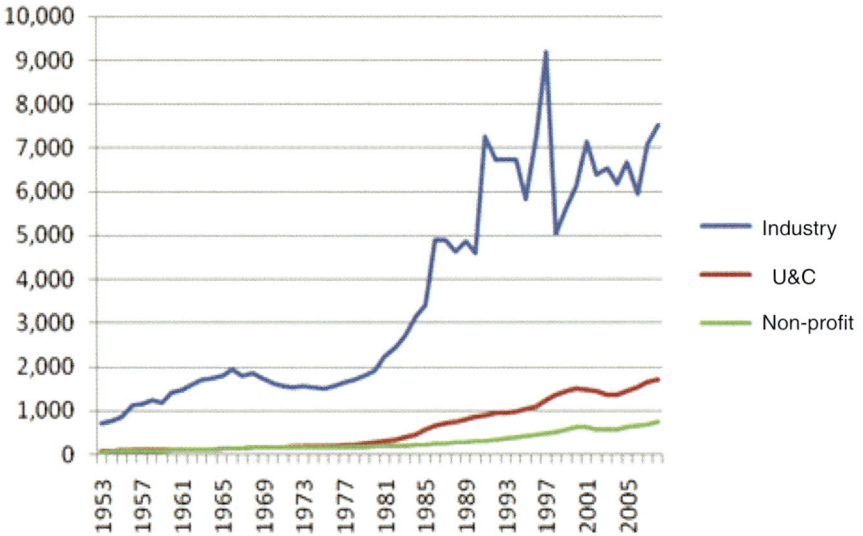

FIGURE 5-3.1 Industry-funded basic research by perfomer, 1953-2008 (millions of constant 2000 dollars).
Source: National Science Foundation, National Center for Science and Engineering Statistics, National Patterns of Research and Development, 2008 Data Update, Table 6. Available at: http://www.nsf.gov/statistics/nsf10314/content.cfm?pub_id=4000&id=2 (accessed April 22, 2012).

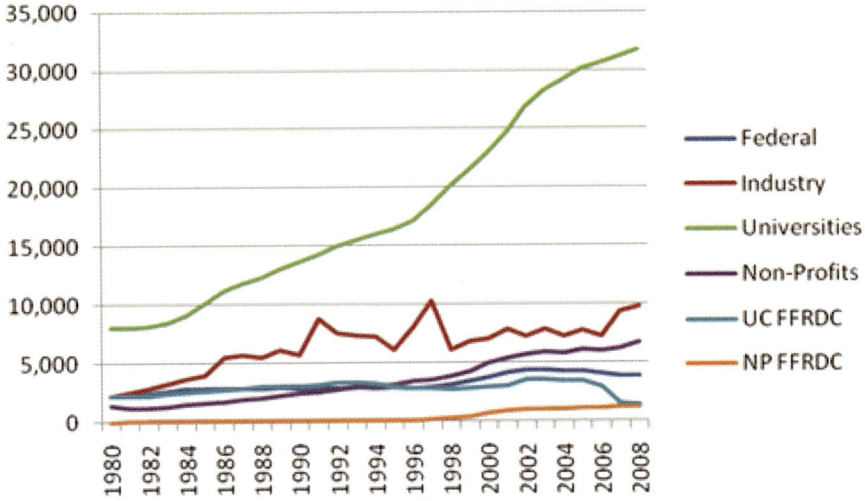

FIGURE 5-3.2 U.S. basic research by performing sector, 1980-2008 (millions of constant 2000 dollars).
Source: National Science Foundation, National Center for Science and Engineering Statistics, National Patterns of Research and Development, 2008 Data Update, Table 2, Available at: http://www.nsf.gov/statistics/nsf10314/content.cfm?pub_id=4000&id=2 (accessed April 22, 2012).

strategies for obtaining the productive knowledge that allows for innovation and the development of new processes and products. As seen in Figures 5-3.1 and 5-3.2, industry funding and performance of basic research has recently been wildly erratic, but over the long term, essentially flat. Meanwhile university-performed research and industry-funded university research have grown. Corporate funding for basic research has increased on campuses, creating both new opportunities for research and commercialization and challenges such as the management of conflict of interest.

  • The missions of *national laboratories*—particularly those that have historically been focused on nuclear weapons research—have also shifted since the end of the Cold War. Changes in mission may be accompanied by new partnerships between research universities and these laboratories, many of which are university-managed, to increase the productivity of both.

  • *Philanthropy* has played a strong role in the history of the American research university. Philanthropic funding continues to play a powerful role, both through charitable giving that strengthens institutions and through grants and gifts for facilities and lines of research. There was a significant decline in gifts during the recession, which added to the substantial challenge associated with declines in endowment value. The economy, endowments, and giving are all rebounding now, providing an opportunity to examine the best opportunities for philanthropic funding going forward.

Of particular note in these trends is the insufficiency of truly transformative R&D of the type that is usually attributed to the Advanced Research Projects Agency (ARPA) and Bell Laboratories in earlier decades and effective translational R&D capable of coupling fundamental scientific discovery with technological innovation and the marketplace, once characteristic of Bell Labs in industry or agricultural experiment stations in higher education.

Three areas provide opportunities for new approaches that may revitalize the U.S. research enterprise and enhance the contributions of academic research to meeting important national goals such as innovation and economic growth, national security, health, and energy. These areas are as follows:

1. Technology transfer from universities
2. Research-support mechanisms that promote collaboration and innovation
3. Incentives for industry participation in partnerships with universities

These practices can be broadly implemented, though the character of their application may diverge depending on differences among industries and fields (e.g., information technology, advanced materials, biomedical) in their traditional patterns of university-industry roles and collaboration.

First, patent reform can increase the effectiveness of technology transfer from universities to the marketplace. The enactment of patent reform in September 2011 through the America Invents Act is a start in overhauling the general patent system. A recent National Research Council (NRC) report evaluates more specifically the university technology transfer system established more than 30 years ago through the Bayh-Dole Act (P.L. 96-517, the Patent and Trademark Act Amendments of 1980). This system, in which universities control intellectual property (IP) that results from research supported by federal agencies, has been much more effective than the previous practice of government control. Faculty invention disclosures, patenting, licensing, and other metrics of commercialization have all increased, without serious interference in other university missions. But the NRC report identifies several areas where universities and the federal government could make significant improvements. For example, universities have uneven capabilities in the area of technology transfer, and there is a general need for universities to introduce more stakeholder involvement and accountability into the technology transfer system. The report suggests good practices for universities to follow in patenting, licensing, material transfer, and launching start-up companies based on university-developed technologies. In addition, the report recommends that universities take steps to streamline licensing negotiations with industry. Finally, the report calls for establishing an effective federal oversight framework with clear responsibilities and a supportive data collection system. During the course of this study, Congress passed and the President signed into law, on September 16, 2011, the America Invents Act, which overhauls the patent system, implementing many of the reforms recommended in the NRC report. This is a great step forward toward improving the flow of technological innovation.[20]

Second, the federal government can continue and expand support for collaborative research mechanisms that promote knowledge generation and transfer and innovation. Regarding research support mechanisms that promote collaboration and innovation, the committee reaffirms that universities remain the primary source of fundamental science and engineering discoveries and that federal research investments are necessary to sustain this knowledge generation. In addition to merit-reviewed grants to individual investigators, though, federal agencies support university research in a number of ways. NSF has several long-standing "centers" programs, such as the Science and Technology Centers, Materials Research Science and Engineering Centers, Engineering Research Centers, and Industry University Cooperative Research Centers. In order to provide the American research enterprise and industry with better balance and cohesive linkages among sectors, the federal government should continue to develop new research paradigms that address current shortcomings, applying these paradigms judiciously across fields and industries. Several federal agencies (DOE, Department of Commerce, NSF, and DOD) have already launched such programs that merit strong support from the federal government and more can be developed. Examples include innovation hubs focused on translational research (proposed by DOE and Commerce) and the ARPA-Energy and ARPA-Education organizations for transformational R&D (proposed by *Rising Above the Gathering Storm*

---

[20] See http://www.whitehouse.gov/the-press-office/2011/09/16/president-obama-signs-america-invents-act-overhauling-patent-system-stim (accessed September 19, 2011). National Research Council. Managing University Intellectual Property in the Public Interest. Washington, DC: National Academies Press, 2011. National Research Council. A Patent System for the 21st Century. Washington, DC: National Academies Press, 2006.

BOX 5-3.1
Further Initiatives Announced by the White House Today
to Move Ideas from Lab to Market, September 2011

Launch of new National Institutes of Health (NIH) center to assist biotech entrepreneurs: To help industry shorten the time needed and reduce costs for the development of new drugs and diagnostics, the NIH plans to establish a new National Center for Advancing Translational Sciences (NCATS). NCATS aims to help biomedical entrepreneurs by identifying barriers to progress and providing science-based solutions to reduce costs and the time required to develop new drugs and diagnostics. For example, as one of its initial activities, NCATS will partner with DARPA to support development of a chip to screen for safe and effective drugs far more swiftly and efficiently than current methods.

Development of a National Bioeconomy Blueprint: By January 2012, the Administration will develop a Bioeconomy Blueprint detailing Administration-wide steps to harness biological research innovations to address national challenges in health, food, energy, and the environment. Biological research lays the foundation of a significant portion of our economy. By better leveraging our national investments in biological research and development the Administration will grow the jobs of the future and improve the lives of all Americans. The Blueprint will focus on reforms to speed up commercialization and open new markets, strategic R&D investments to accelerate innovation, regulatory reforms to reduce unnecessary burdens on innovators, enhanced workforce training to develop the next generation of scientists and engineers, and the development of public-private partnerships.

University Presidents Commit to Commercialization Initiative: In coordination with the Administration, the Association of American Universities, and the Association of Public and Land-grant Universities, 135 university leaders committed to working more closely with industry, investors, and agencies to bolster entrepreneurship, encourage university-industry collaboration, and enhance economic development. Today, over 40 universities are answering the President's call to expand their commercialization programs and goals. These institutions include The Georgia Institute of Technology, which has outlined its expanded initiatives, as well as universities like the University of Virginia and Carnegie Mellon University, which are announcing plans today.

Coulter Foundation and NSF Launch a University Commercialization Prize with AAAS: This prize competition will be used to identify and promote incentives

and PCAST). Clusters of these initiatives should be launched at scale and adequately funded from multiple sources (federal, state, industry, universities). Box 5-3.1 outlines additional federal initiatives under way to move ideas from the laboratory to the market.

Third, the committee looked at incentives for industry participation in partnerships with universities viewing this as the critical area that requires additional action. Support for university research is covered in the current

to adopt best practices that improve university commercialization efforts. Supported by $400,000 in funding from the Wallace H. Coulter Foundation and NSF, the American Association for the Advancement of Science (AAAS) will lead the design and implementation of the prize in coordination with a diverse array of partner agencies, foundations, and organizations.

Developing University Endowments Focused on Lab to Market Innovations: Today, the Coulter Foundation is announcing that they have selected four new universities to participate in their Translational Research Partnership program—Johns Hopkins University, University of Louisville, University of Missouri and University of Pittsburgh. As part of the program, each university will create a $20 million endowment to foster research collaboration between biomedical engineers and clinicians, with the goal of developing new technologies to improve patient care and human health. Translational research moves new ideas and discoveries from university laboratories to new products and services that directly impact human health, often by creating startups or by partnering with established businesses.

New Tools and License Agreements for Start-Ups and Small Businesses: The National Institutes of Health (NIH) Office of Technology Transfer has developed new agreements for start-up companies to obtain licenses for early-stage biomedical inventions developed by intramural researchers at NIH or FDA. Companies that are less than 5 years old and have fewer than 50 employees will be eligible to use the new, short-term exclusive Start-Up Evaluation License Agreement and the new Start-Up Commercial License Agreement. These agreements allow a start-up company to take ideas sitting on the shelf, and attract additional investments to develop these NIH and FDA inventions into life-saving products.

New Help for Small Businesses: In addition, the USPTO, in collaboration with NSF and SBA, will pilot a program to assist SBIR grant recipients in taking advantage of the USPTO's small business programs and resources. The USPTO pilot will provide comprehensive IP support to, initially, 100 NSF SBIR grant recipients to take advantage of accelerated examination and benefits stemming from the America Invents Act and will engage external stakeholders to provide pro bono or low cost IP services to awardees.

Source: The White House, President Obama Signs America Invents Act, Overhauling the Patent System to Stimulate Economic Growth, and Announces New Steps to Help Entrepreneurs Create Jobs, September 16, 2011. Available at: http://www.whitehouse.gov/the-press-office/2011/09/16/president-obama-signs-america-invents-act-overhauling-patent-system-stim (accessed September 19, 2011).

federal R&D tax credit, but several factors prevent it from being utilized optimally. For example, the year-to-year renewal of the tax credit prevents companies from making longer commitments to university partnerships. To overcome this and other barriers, *we recommend the federal government institute new tax policies that create incentives for multiyear university-industry research and development collaboration.* These new policies, which may be created through tax credits, will be provided to businesses that invest in university-performed basic research. Research results that flow from these investments must be used in the development of U.S.-located economic activities so that the returns of the taxpayer investments are captured here to create economic growth and new jobs.

The National Academies report *Rising Above the Gathering Storm* strongly recommended strengthening and making permanent the research and experimentation tax credit, one of the most effective government tax incentives—clearly working as effectively as government spending on R&D in promoting research and development. Business accounts for about two-thirds of all R&D spending in the United States, providing laboratories and jobs for many of our scientists and STEM graduates. Although most business R&D is applied, the distinction between applied and basic is increasingly an artificial one, and business is the channel through which basic ideas developed in research universities reach the marketplace, often with the support of the R&D tax credit. Strengthening the R&D tax credit generally, particularly at a time when our incentives are declining relative to those of other countries, and creating specific opportunities within the credit to create productive research relationships between businesses and universities, will provide important additional tools for enhancing national innovation.

Finally, university management of intellectual property must be improved. The two main problems in this area are the amount of money that universities put into their technology-licensing offices and the institutional goals of the offices. First, much of the uneven approach to technology licensing results from the high cost of maintaining patents (about $20,000 per U.S. patent; more than $100,000 to protect foreign markets) until licensees are found, creating wide variations in approach depending on how much a university is willing to subsidize its licensing operations. University intellectual property policies should not only be simplified and streamlined but also better standardized across higher education, so that each negotiation between industry and university can move forward according to commonly accepted procedures. Second, a recent discussion of the trade-offs involved in institutional goals points out the near impossibility of satisfying the many competing goals of different stakeholders in the licensing process.[21] The focus of technology transfer should first be on economic stimulus and only secondarily on revenue return and support of faculty.

---

[21] Michael Sharer and Timothy L. Faley, The strategic management of the technology transfer function—Aligning goals with strategies and tactics, *les Nouvelles*, September 2008, p. 170.

Recommendation 4

Increase university cost-effectiveness and productivity in order to provide a greater return on investment for taxpayers, philanthropists, corporations, foundations, and other research sponsors.

Actors and Actions—Implementing Recommendation 4:

- *Universities*: The nation's research universities should set and achieve bold goals in cost-containment, efficiency, and productivity in business operations and academic programs. Universities should strive to constrain the cost escalation of all ongoing activities—academic and auxiliary—to the inflation rate or lower through improved efficiency and productivity. Beyond the implementation of efficient business practices, universities should review existing academic programs from the perspectives of centrality, quality, and cost-effectiveness, adopting modern instructional methods such as cyberlearning, and encouraging greater collaboration among research investigators and institutions, particularly in the acquisition and utilization of expensive research equipment and facilities.

- *University associations*: University associations should develop and implement more powerful and strategic tools for financial management and cost accounting that better enable universities to determine the most effective methods for containing costs and increasing productivity and efficiency. As part of this effort, they should develop metrics that allow universities to communicate their cost-effectiveness to the general public.

- *Universities, working together with key stakeholders*: Universities and key stakeholders should intensify efforts to educate key audiences about the unique character of U.S. research universities and their importance to state, regional, and national goals, including economic prosperity, public health, and national security.

Budget Implications

There may be an initial cost to institutions as they examine their operations in order to identify actions that will increase efficiency and as they invest in new infrastructure. In the long term, however, research universities will reap the rewards of these investments through greater productivity. Many institutions have already demonstrated that significant cost efficiencies are attainable. If research universities can take action, states and the nation will realize greater returns on their investments, and the savings associated with cost containment and greater productivity can then be deployed to other priorities such as constraining tuition increases (a major national concern), increasing student financial aid, or launching new programs.

Expected Outcomes

By increasing cost-effectiveness and productivity, institutions will realize significant cost savings in their operations that may be used to improve performance by shifting resources strategically and/or to reduce growth in their need for resources (e.g., tuition). There are many ways to do this, but one of the easiest is to implement a "priority fund" in which the base funding of ongoing activities is reduced by 1 percent or so each year (with the "savings" reallocated to new university priorities).

Discussion

Without compromising the quality of their core programs and activities, the nation's research universities should increase efficiency in their business operations, increase productivity and innovation in their academic programs, and report annually on their performance.

Revenue sources for U.S. research universities—and in particular for graduate education and research—have been constrained by the recent economic downturn and remain vulnerable for the near term: Federal appropriators have cut research funding as they negotiate how to reduce the federal debt, state appropriators have further cut already reduced support for higher education as their revenues have tightened and their policy priorities have shifted, corporate support has declined for both research and employee education, tuition increases are increasingly contested, gifts declined and endowments suffered during the financial collapse, and clinical income is threatened by new health legislation.

Consequently, most research universities have, along with other higher education institutions, faced budget crises that have necessitated emergency measures to balance their books through spending cuts and revenue enhancements, many of which work in the short term but are nonsustainable long-term strategies. Many institutions have increased tuition and fees, shifted enrollments toward higher-income or out-of-state students who pay higher tuitions, or increased enrollments while holding academic resources constant. Many have placed a freeze on hiring and salary increases, reduced benefits, instituted furloughs or laid off staff, or shifted to lower-cost, part-time instructors. Many have looked for one-time savings through cuts in administrative operations, academic programs, or student services. Table 5-4.1 displays the responses of presidents at public and private doctoral institutions to a question posed

TABLE 5-4.1 Strategies Deployed by Public and Private Doctoral Institutions to Address the Financial Consequences of the Economic Downturn (percentage that reported employing the strategy, Winter 2011)

Strategy Deployed to Address Financial Issues	Public Doctoral Institutions	Private Doctoral Institutions
Increased tuition by 5% or more for 2010-2011	59.3	17.2
Raised student fees for campus resources and services	47.5	6.9
Increases in endowment payout rates	0.8	13.8
Allowed the discount rate to rise to provide more financial aid	11.9	41.4
Budget cuts targeting selected administrative operations and services	57.8	69.0
Budget cuts targeting selected academic programs and activities	71.2	34.5
Budget cuts targeting selected student services	32.2	27.6
Budget cuts targeting varsity athletic programs	33.9	17.2
Across-the-board budget cuts	22.0	6.9
Hiring freeze for administrative positions	45.8	34.5
Hiring freeze for academic programs and departments	33.9	10.3
Increased proportion of part-time (versus full-time) faculty	27.1	6.9
Layoffs of administrative employees	50.8	37.9
Layoffs of clerical or custodial and support staff	39.0	34.1
Layoffs of instructors and academic staff members	32.2	3.4
Changes in benefit levels (e.g., health insurance, retirement)	30.5	20.7
Launching or expanding online education programs	45.8	20.7
Creation of new self-sustaining programs	45.8	34.5
Launching or expanding partnerships with other institutions	45.8	6.9
New alliances with corporate partners	39.0	10.3

Source: Kenneth C. Green with Scott Jaschik and Doug Lederman, Presidential Perspectives: The 2011 Inside Higher Ed Survey of College and University Presidents, *Inside Higher Ed*, 2011.

Projected Savings by Initiative

Projected Total Program Savings by Fiscal Year

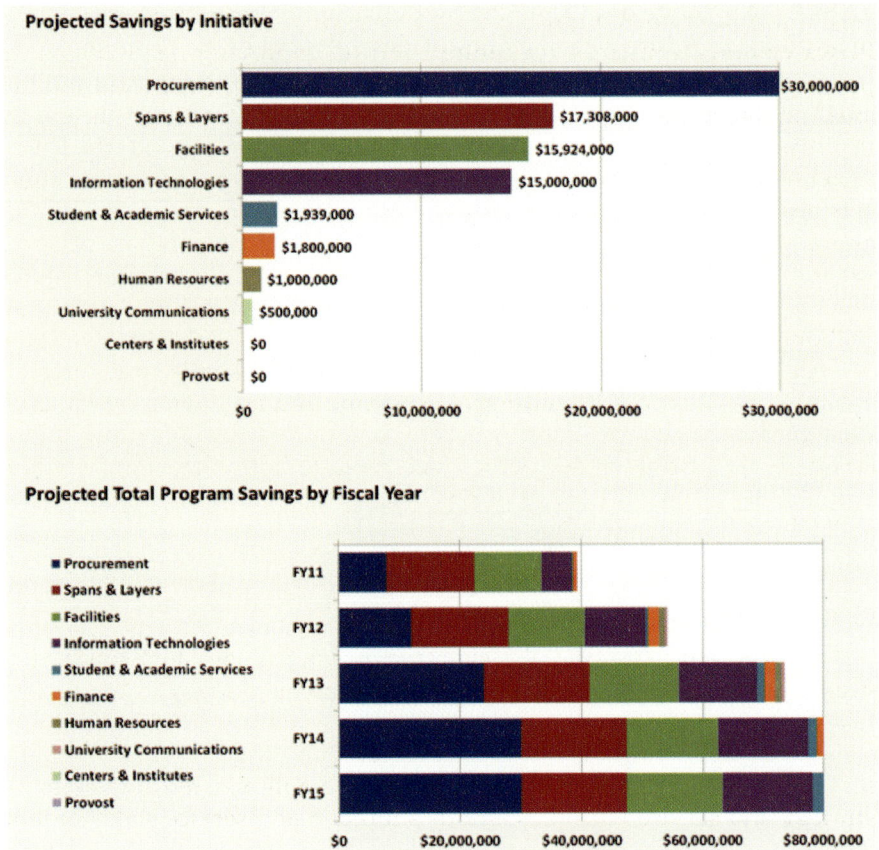

FIGURE 5-4.1 Cornell University, administrative streamlining program, projected savings by initiative, overall and by fiscal year, 2011-2015.
Source: http://asp.dpb.cornell.edu (accessed June 1, 2011).

by *Inside Higher Ed* about actions taken to address the current financial challenges.

Some institutions, however, have found that a thorough review of business operations can increase their overall efficiency and productivity by rationalizing their operations. For example, Cornell University; the University of California (UC), Berkeley; and the University of North Carolina (UNC) at Chapel Hill have each engaged Bain & Company, a management consulting firm, to examine ways to increase the efficiency of their administrative operations.[22] As shown in Figure 5-4.1, Cornell expects to

---

[22] Josh Keller, Universities can save millions by cutting administrative waste, panelists say, The Chronicle of Higher Education, July 25, 2010. Joe Wilensky, Update on budget cri-

save $75 million to $85 million over 5 years (FY 2011 to FY 2015) on its Ithaca campus, primarily by centralizing or improving negotiations in procurement or both ($30 million), reducing administrative layers and increasing direct reports per supervisor ($17.3 million), improving the use of facilities ($15.9 million), achieving efficiencies in information technology ($15 million), and achieving additional savings in student and academic services, finance, human resources, and communications. This amounts to annual savings of about 6 percent of Cornell's Ithaca campus base budget, excluding external research funding.[23] Meanwhile, UC Berkeley envisions savings of about $75 million annually and UNC Chapel Hill, about $66 million per year.[24]

All U.S. research universities should implement similar measures to ensure leaner and more productive academic and administrative operations in the long term. There is no single "magic bullet" for increasing efficiency and productivity, which will include both enhancing quality and improving cost control. Examples of efforts that are yielding results include the following:[25]

Strategic Planning

- Develop a strategic planning framework that lays out a university vision, supportive values, strategic goals, strategic initiatives, and progress indicators (University of Illinois).
- Conduct administrative unit reviews and high-level external assessments of critical campus-wide functions to optimize the alignment of strategy and service with the campus's mission and service stakeholders (University of California Davis).
- Review university spending to ensure that academic programs are fully aligned with institutional mission and core competencies. For some institutions, this may mean paring back the number of graduate

---

sis and "Reimagining Cornell" stresses that all options are on the table, Cornell University Chronicle Online, July 23, 2009. Available at: http://www.news.cornell.edu/stories/July09/ReimaginingUpdate.html (accessed April 18, 2012).

[23] Cornell University, Division of Planning and Budget, Administrative Streamlining Program (accessed February 22, 2011). Available at: http://asp.dpb.cornell.edu (accessed June 1, 2011).

[24] Kevin Kiley, Where universities can be cut, *Inside Higher Ed*, September 16, 2011.

[25] Cornell University, http://asp.dpb.cornell.edu (accessed June 1, 2011); University of Illinois, http://strategicplan.illinois.edu/planning_process.html (accessed September 11, 2011); Pennsylvania State University, http://strategicplan.psu.edu/StrategicPlancomplete.pdf (accessed September 11, 2011); University of Minnesota, http://www1.umn.edu/system-wide/strategic_positioning/initiatives_ttu/admin_background.html (accessed September 11, 2011); University of California, Davis, http://vision.ucdavis.edu/local_resources/docs/vision_of_excellence.pdf (accessed September 11, 2011). Kiley, Where universities can be cut.

programs to focus on strengthening those in which the institution meets critical local, regional, or national needs.

Culture

- Define and foster a culture that propels and reflects the university's aspiration through excellence, service, and continuous improvement (University of Minnesota).

People

- Implement voluntary separation programs for staff and faculty and rehire selectively and strategically (University of Illinois).
- Improve the strategic hiring of faculty by instituting review of all faculty hiring plans by the Office of the Provost (University of Illinois).
- Increase the number of staff in professional development and certification programs provided by the university, particularly in the areas of supervision, management, and leadership (University of California, Davis).
- Improve performance management systems so every employee understands the expectation to continuously upgrade skills and knowledge and regularly receives feedback on performance (University of Minnesota).
- Increase the use of part-time and part-year staff both to accommodate growing staff interest and to improve the efficiency of academic and administrative operations (Pennsylvania State University).
- Increase the number of reports per supervisor, eliminating about 300 supervisory positions (University of California, Berkeley).

Administration and Finance

- Recognize the university, its campuses, colleges, departments, and units as a single enterprise, establishing uniform standards and systems to reduce duplication of administrative processes and their associated support structures (University of Minnesota).
- Implement a new financial system that not only replaces aged technology but also overhauls university financial processes and reporting mechanisms, resulting in improvements in processes, quality and quantity of information, and cost-effectiveness (University of Minnesota).
- Consolidate administrative functions, such as payroll and accounts receivable, into a single university service center (University of Georgia System).

Information Technology

- Upgrade information technology (IT) systems to capitalize on the latest advances, eliminate redundancies, and achieve interoperability.
- Consolidate IT servers and establish centralized IT service centers, reducing IT staff by up to a third while maintaining service levels (University of Illinois).
- Improve the capacity, costs, accessibility, efficiencies, and cyber-safety of campus computing systems, as a resource for both academic and administrative excellence (University of California, Davis).

Health Care

- Encourage a shift from low (40 percent) to high (80 percent) use of generic medications to fill prescriptions in employee health care plans (University of Kentucky).
- Increase the creativity of health care programs through a variety of measures, including additional wellness education and incentives, differential rates for employees who continue to engage in higher health-risk behaviors and for those who utilize in-system providers as opposed to other health care professionals (Pennsylvania State University).

Energy Efficiency and Conservation

- Model energy efficiency and conservation in construction and maintenance operations and utilities consumption through pervasive and innovative application of green technologies (University of California, Davis).
- Improve environmental stewardship through programs such as use of biofuels in service fleet, adopt a new Leadership in Energy and Environmental Design (LEED) policy for all new buildings,[26] reduce greenhouse gas emissions, encourage bicycle use, and increase recycling (Pennsylvania State University).

Facilities

- Increase the effectiveness and efficiency of new construction, renovation, and maintenance projects as measured by timeliness, cost adherence, safety practices, and environmental certifications (University of California, Davis).

---

[26] Note: LEED certification costs about $100,000 and is only in part an economic model. Universities certainly should construct buildings to get the energy savings that would be paid back in energy cost savings over a reasonable period of time.

- Improve the use of campus facilities during the day by investing in a state-of-the-art master scheduling system that will better spread classes across the day between 9:00 a.m. and 6:00 p.m. and by exploring the offering of additional evening classes (Pennsylvania State University).
- Improve the use of campus facilities during the year by increasing the use of many university facilities that are now significantly underutilized during the summer months when students are away. By offering more courses during the summer, creating new summer programs, or allowing other organizations to use buildings during those months, universities may increase revenues without substantially increasing costs (Pennsylvania State University).

Instructional Productivity and Learning

- Use tuition policies to encourage increasing 4-year graduation rates (University of Texas System).
- Eliminate low-priority programs and reinvest the budget in higher-priority programs (Howard University, State University of New York (SUNY)–Albany, Washington State University).
- Implement transparent workload policies, while accounting for legitimate differences among disciplines, articulating a clear expectation that all faculty supported on general funds will participate fully in the instructional programs of their respective units and that those not engaged in highly productive programs of research will have higher instructional workloads (Pennsylvania State University).
- Achieve greater productivity in the classroom, particularly through the use of instructional technology, including blended and online learning. (The Open Learning Initiative at Carnegie Mellon University and the National Center for Academic Transformation provide important examples of how the use of technology and combinations of online and live instruction can dramatically reduce costs and improve learning in a variety of introductory and remedial classes. Stanford University recently ran an experiment that provided three online courses that enrolled 160,000 students, showing that there is a need, workable technology, and an opportunity for enhanced productivity.[27])

Accounting, Information, and Evaluation

- Develop metrics to assess faculty and department productivity (University of Texas System).

---

[27] See http://www.nytimes.com/2011/08/16/science/16stanford.html?_r=1 (accessed January 18, 2012).

- Develop the information and toll necessary to identify significant but currently unknown cost reductions.

On this latter point, a basic problem is that universities generally do not have the information and tools to identify significant reductions that are consistent with their agreed-upon outcomes. The core of what needs to be accomplished is to drive together the cost reductions with measurable outcome and quality improvements. To that end, there needs to be much better cost accounting; information data-informed decision making needs to be regularly used (i.e., the data must be collected and analyzed); and outcome measurements need to be agreed upon. Many of the outcome measurements must be developed by the individual institution because they measure what that institution seeks to achieve. This process causes fundamental questions to be raised and will make it possible to take steps otherwise impossible to understand and defend.

U.S. research universities should report annually to the public on their performance across their campuses to indicate how they have increased efficiency and productivity and met educational and research goals. They must show that they are good stewards of their resources, continuing to be fully transparent and accountable to the public and to policy makers through understandable performance measures. For example, the Association of Public and Land-grant Universities (APLU) and the American Association of State Colleges and Universities (AASCU) have been successful in developing the Voluntary System of Accountability (VSA) to enable universities to present clear, accessible, and comparable information on the undergraduate student experience to important constituencies through a common web report the College Portrait—so those constituents could better understand performance across institutions. Today, there are more than 300 institutions participating.[28] The development of similar or additional metrics on cost-effectiveness through VSA or another portal would enable institutions to provide the kind of information needed by policy makers, the public, families, and students to understand how institutions are utilizing their resources in a cost-effective manner.

Additional management and productivity issues are specific to academic health centers (AHCs), which have a rich history of an intricately entwined tripartite mission—education, research, and clinical care. These interactive missions have been a unique strength of the AHCs, as they have provided the underpinning for significant advances in biomedical discoveries and health care delivery. However, over the last four decades, the AHCs have relied on revenues from the clinical mission, with hos-

---

[28] See http://www.voluntarysystem.org/index.cfm?page=homePage (accessed January 17, 2012).

pital margins and physician practice plans, to sustain and expand their academic and research missions. It is estimated that the true cost of each medical student (i.e., the cost of training minus tuition recovery) requires subsidization of about $100,000, and as a whole, research grants require an investment of 30-40 percent by the university to cover the actual costs of conducting research.

With cuts in state appropriations to public universities, flattened federal budgets with lost spending power, increasing unfunded regulatory mandates, and mounting administrative burden, sponsored research funding at AHCs fails to recover the associated overhead costs incurred by universities. Meanwhile, clinical margins are in jeopardy. Managed care, changing payer mixes with increased Medicare and Medicaid patients, declining federal support for teaching hospitals, and complexity of care have contributed to strains on clinical revenues. Furthermore, the full impact of health care reform has yet to be realized by the AHCs. The net impact is unclear but, in general, the convergence of the current fiscal constraints puts the tripartite mission at risk. Erosion of the dollars typically used to fill funding gaps will require AHCs to work even more diligently to drive efficiencies, maximize productivity, diversify revenue sources, and enact a strategic approach to investing discretionary dollars across all three missions.

Recommendation 5

Create a "Strategic Investment Program" that funds initiatives at research universities critical to advancing education and research in areas of key national priority.

Actors and Actions—Implementing Recommendation 5:

- *Federal government*: The federal government should create a new "Strategic Investment Program" supporting initiatives that advance education and research at the nation's research universities. The program is designed to be a "living" program that responds to changing needs and opportunities. As such, it will be composed of term-limited initiatives requiring matching grants in critical areas that will change over time. The committee recommends the program begin with two 10-year initiatives: (1) an endowed faculty chairs program to facilitate the careers of young investigators and (2) a research infrastructure program initially focused on advancement of campus cyberinfrastructure, but perhaps evolving later to address as well emerging needs for physical research infrastructure as they arise. The federal investments in human capital and research infrastructure are intended for both public and private research universities. They require matching funds that different types of institutions may obtain from different sources. For example, public research universities may secure their matching funds from states sources, while private research universities may obtain their matches from private sources. However, the source that a particular institution taps for matching funds is not prescribed, so public and private institutions may draw from state support, philanthropy, business, or other sources for matching funds. While merit, impact, and need should continue to be important criteria for the awarding of grants, consideration should also be given to regional and/or cross-institutional partnerships, program focus, and opportunities for building significant research capacity, subject, of course, to the matching requirements for the federal grants.

- *Universities in partnership with state governments, business, philanthropy, and others*: Universities should compete for funding under these initiatives, bringing in partners—states, business, philanthropy, others—that will support projects by providing required matching funds.

Budget Implications

In addition to increases in federal funding for basic research (in Recommendation 1), the committee recommends federal support for these first two initiatives in the program that will cost $7 billion per year over the next decade. These funds will leverage an additional $9 billion per year through matching grants from other partners.

Expected Outcomes

This program develops and leverages the human-, physical-, and cyberinfrastructures necessary for cutting-edge research and advanced education. Of particular importance is the investment in rapidly evolving cyberinfrastructure that will increase productivity and collaboration in research, but may also provide opportunities to increase productivity in administration and education. Also of critical importance is the endowment of chairs, particularly for promising young faculty, during a time of serious financial stress and limited faculty retirements. This will ensure that we are building our research faculty for the future, as we can reap the rewards of their work over the long term.

Discussion

Research universities operate today in a mixed environment that presents both fiscal challenges and innovation opportunities. To keep these institutions at the leading edge of research and education, the federal government should create a new "Strategic Investment Program" to support initiatives that advance innovations in key areas that, as with NSF's Science and Technology Centers Program, eventually become self-sustaining. (See University of Illinois, http://strategicplan.illinois.edu/planning_process.html [accessed September 11, 2011] for an example of a strategic plan.) The first two initiatives should focus on (1) ensuring enhanced academic career opportunities for young faculty and (2) supporting investment in cyberinfrastructure that can increase the power of research and the productivity of institutional operations. These two initiatives are discussed below. The initiatives in the program should be term limited and change over time to reflect new needs and opportunities as they arise. This program should require matching funds from other stakeholders—states, business, philanthropic foundations, donors, and others—in order to ensure that the key parties that will benefit from these investments are contributing. Although the committee does not believe it appropriate to recommend a specific goal for the number of larger research universities that the nation should seek to maintain at world-class levels, the importance of advanced education and research to regional economic development suggests the need for a broader geographical distribution of research capacity than currently exists. Hence, we suggest that in addition to the usual criteria of merit, impact, and need used to determine research awards, some consideration be given to criteria such as program focus and opportunities for building significant research capacity and excellence. In particular, we would note that many universities that currently do not possess the resources or scale to become one of the larger research universities have demonstrated the capacity to mount high-quality research and graduate programs in more narrowly defined areas. By focusing resources, these institutions have managed to create peaks of excellence that can make significant contributions in particular areas of research and scholarship and have and can provide leadership to state and regional economic development. Such efforts should be supported as otherwise appropriate.

Faculty Chairs

To rebuild and sustain the faculties of research universities in key strategic areas during a period of serious financial stress, the federal government should launch an initiative under the Strategic Investment Program that provides matching grants to establish endowments for research faculty positions. Each faculty chair would be supported by a $3 million endowment, consisting of a $1 million grant from the federal government distributed through a competitive process based on research excellence and graduate student productivity, and a required $2 million matching grant from private, state, or institutional resources. A total federal program of \$2 billion per year would establish 2,000 new chairs each year, contributing significantly to the research and graduate education capacity of America's research universities.

Replenishing the faculties of the nation's research universities will bring new perspectives, capabilities, and energy. It would support young and mid-career scholars and investigators engaged in teaching and research who are often at the most creative point in their careers.[29] Yet many research universities, particularly public institutions now experiencing serious reductions in state appropriations, are limited in their ability to add faculty members at this time by serious financial constraints. Furthermore, the recent recession has shaken the confidence of senior faculty enrolled in defined contribution retirement programs, delaying their decisions to retire; consequently, our institutions have a rapidly aging and heavily tenured faculty cadre without the turnover necessary to open up positions for new junior faculty hires. Consequently, as shown in Figure 5-5.1, the age distribution of faculty is skewed toward the older end of the distribution, particularly in the humanities, social and behavioral sciences, and biological sciences. In the short term, this creates a bottleneck to refreshing the faculty. In the biomedical sciences, as shown in Figure 5-5.2, it has increased the average age at which an investigator receives a first NIH research grant to over 43 years old.

To address this current challenge, a federal program of matching grants to establish endowments for the support of junior and mid-career faculty positions would open faculty lines that will help build our nation's faculties for the long term. There are other important reforms that may also be employed, but chief among them is the creation or strengthening of large, multiyear awards for early- and mid-career faculty (see Box 5-5.1). The use of chaired professorships has been very successful in building academic programs at many institutions and may be adapted specifically to the development of early-career faculty.

Examples of successful faculty development programs can be seen in a variety of places and times. In the late 1960s, for example, New York State established a program to award five Albert Einstein Chairs in Science and five Albert Schweitzer Chairs in the Humanities to institutions within the state. The awards were made competitively and available to both private and public institutions. While not explicitly stated, the

---

[29] Recent research provides hard evidence for this position. Pierre Azoulay, Joshua S. Graff Zivin, and Gustavo Manso, Incentives and creativity: evidence from the academic life sciences, *The RAND Journal of Economics* 42:3 (September 1, 2011): 527-554. This article showed that promising biomedical researchers who were appointed as HHMIs (Howard Hughes Medical Institute Investigators) did more innovative research than similar researchers who did not have such long-term support.

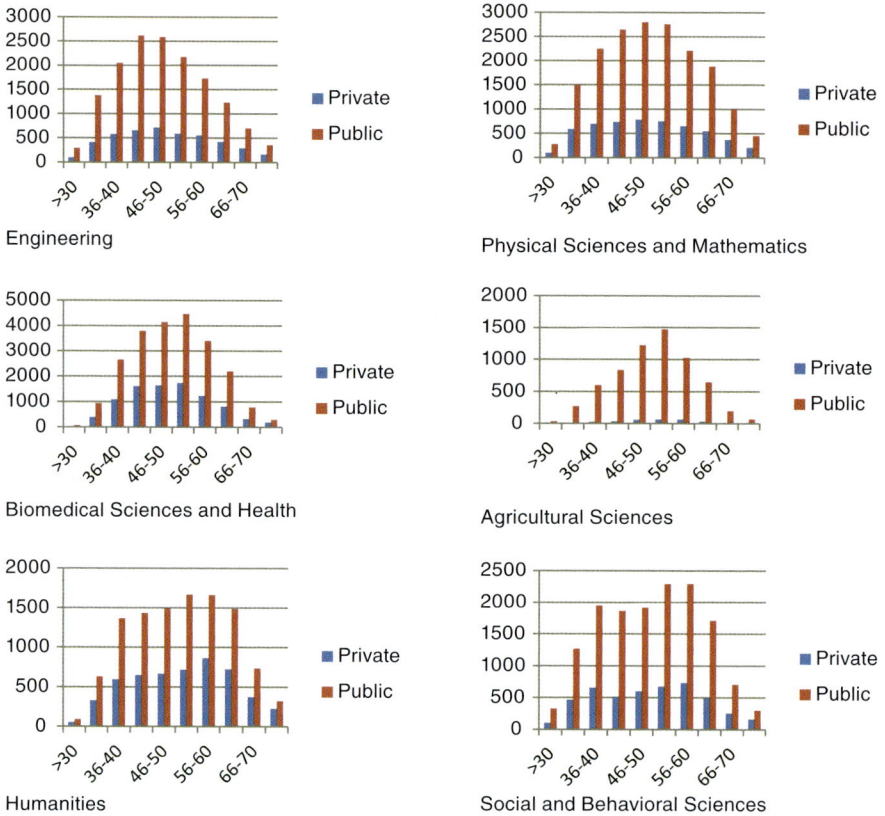

FIGURE 5-5.1 Age distribution of faculty in doctoral programs, by control (public, private), 2006.
Source: National Research Council, A Data-Based Assessment of Research-Doctorate Programs (Washington, DC: National Academies Press, 2011). Available at: http://www.nap.edu/rdp/ (accessed April 22, 2012).

program expected that new faculty hired with these awards would be recruited from institutions outside of New York State, since one of the goals was to build New York institutions. The 10 SUNY institutions receiving the awards benefited by hiring scholars who then served a focal point for building academic programs, attracting permanent and visiting faculty, and organizing international conferences. Similarly, in the 1980s, private foundations provided funding for regents chairs at the University of Texas at Austin, which used the program to create prestigious faculty positions, attract outstanding scholars to the university from around the world, and grow academic programs at the institution. In 1998, as a final example,

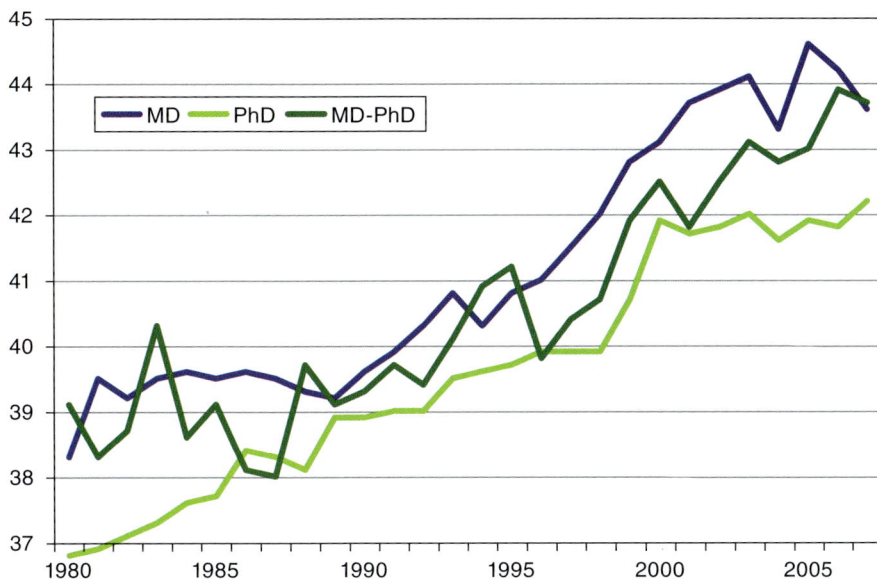

FIGURE 5-5.2 Average age of first-time R01-equivalent principal investigators, National Institutes of Health, by degree, 1980-2007.
Source: Sally Rockey, Deputy Director for Extramural Research, National Institutes of Health, Presentation to NRC Committee on Research Universities, November 22, 2010.

the University of Kentucky created its Endowment Match Program, more popularly known as the Bucks for Brains, or B4B, Program, in order to attract top researchers to Kentucky universities. B4B has required the universities to match the state funding through donations from philanthropists, corporations, foundations, and others, and the public and private funds have been invested to produce earnings that fund faculty positions, programs, or scholarships. During the program, the number of endowed chairs and professorships in Kentucky increased from 108 in 1997 to 523 in 2006. At the same time, extramural research and development grants at the Universities of Kentucky and Louisville more than tripled.[30]

A national program that has built faculty, programs, and institutions in the global competition for talent is the Canada Research Chairs Program created by the Canadian government in 2000. The program

---

[30] Kentucky's Bucks for Brains Initiative: The Vision, the Investment, the Future, 1997-2007. Available at: http://cpe.ky.gov/NR/rdonlyres/CA48D119-0E78-41BB-9D05-1FFB BA0CF7C5/0/BucksForBrains10YearReport.pdf (accessed September 13, 2011).

BOX 5-5.1
Supporting Early-Career Faculty, Recommendations
from the American Academy of Arts and Sciences

Today's early-career faculty will be responsible for our country's future science and technology discoveries and for the education of our future Ph.D.-level scientists and engineers. Yet they face greater obstacles than their more senior colleagues in securing research grants to inaugurate what should be one of the most productive stages of their careers. Time spent submitting repeated grant applications is a distraction from the research endeavor itself and poorly utilizes the potential of this highly creative resource. Federal research-funding agencies, universities, and private foundations play an important role in nurturing early-career faculty and should take the following steps to support these researchers:

Recommendations for Federal Agencies
- Create or strengthen existing large, multiyear awards for early-career faculty.
- Pay special attention to early-career faculty during merit reviews of regular grant programs.
- Adopt career-stage appropriate expectations for grant funding.
- Provide seed funding for early-career faculty to enable them to explore new ideas for which no results have yet been achieved.
- Develop policies responsive to the needs of primary caregivers, such as grant extensions or other appropriate support mechanisms.

Recommendations for Universities
- Develop or strengthen mentoring programs to encourage early-career faculty.
- Reconsider promotion and tenure policies for early-career faculty.
- Address the needs of primary caregivers.

Recommendations for Private Foundations
Historically, private foundations have played a pivotal role in filling the gap in funding for early-career researchers through dedicated programs. These initiatives are exceedingly valuable, but they can produce windfall effects. Private foundations should spread the wealth and cap the number of start-up and first awards made to a single investigator.

Source: American Academy of Arts and Sciences, Advancing Research in Science and Engineering: Investing in Early-Career Scientists and High-Risk, High-Reward Research (Cambridge, MA: American Academy of Arts and Sciences, 2008). Available at: http://www.amacad.org/AriseFolder/ariseReport.pdf (accessed September 19, 2011).

provided two types of awards: Tier 1 Chairs for experienced researchers and Tier 2 Chairs for junior faculty with acknowledged research potential. The program allocated $900 million between 2000 and 2005 to create 2,000 university chairs with an additional $250 million in infrastructure funding from the Canada Foundation for Innovation. Under the program, institutions were given 3 years to fill a chair, and the goal was to have all 2,000 chairs awarded by the 2007-2008 academic year. An evaluation of the program at the end of 2004 showed that, as of August of that year, funding had been used to create 1,282 chairs for researchers at 64 institutions.

Given the perceived success of the program, the government announced in 2010 the availability of $275.6 million to fund 310 additional chairs. The 2004 evaluation found the program to be successful in leveraging additional research funding and increasing research productivity. Further, while most of the awards under the program were made to faculty within the nominating institution, 364, or 29 percent, came from outside Canada. Almost all (84 percent) of the non-Canadian awardees indicated that the chairs program was influential in making their decision to join a Canadian institution. Tier 1 Chairs were awarded for 7 years and were renewable, but Tier 2 Chairs are for 5 years and are renewable once. The latter restriction was found to be a problem, since funds for the holding of these chairs may not be available after 10 years.

Creating a similar program in the United States, focused on the creation of endowed positions awarded through a national competition, would address the lack of research career opportunities for early- and mid-career scientists and ensure the existence of a research workforce for the future. There are successful young faculty programs such as the Presidential Early Career Award for Scientists and Engineers, NSF Faculty Early Career Development Program, and the NIH Pathway to Independence Award (see Box 5-5.2). Each of these programs awards support to an individual, and while that individual enhances the research program at the institution where they are employed or choose to be employed, this is not a position that the institution can use to build its programs. One additional advantage to endowed junior faculty positions over the above existing programs is the availability to support faculty in the humanities as well as in science and engineering. We believe it is the institutions' responsibility to identify how best to allocate such positions across fields. These chairs would be handled like other university-endowed chairs, designed to support tenure-track faculty with both teaching and research obligations, and held in perpetuity. Whether faculty members would have fixed-term or lifetime appointments to the chairs would be addressed in the implementation phase through the proposals submitted by the institution.

Endowed junior faculty positions would be institution based and

---

BOX 5-5.2
NIH New Investigators Program: Pathway
to Independence Award (K99/R00)

The new Pathway to Independence Award program will provide a unique opportunity for highly promising candidates to obtain two forms of support from a single NIH award. The support is interconnected and combines an initial mentored research phase followed by the scientist's first independent research support.

The initial 1-2 year mentored phase allows investigators to complete their supervised research work, publish results, and search for an independent research position.

The independent phase provides up to 3 years of support and allows successful awardees who are appointed to an independent assistant professor (or equivalent) position to continue to work toward establishing research independence and to prepare an application for NIH Research Project R01 grant support. The R01 is the primary mechanism for investigator-initiated funding. Facilities and administrative (F&A) costs for this independent phase will be reimbursed at the extramural sponsoring institution's current rate.

The Pathway to Independence Award is a relatively new initiative that will augment, but not replace, existing NIH programs that provide mentored research and career development experiences for new investigators. Every NIH Institute and Center is contributing to the support of this program.

Source: National Institutes of Health. New Investigators Program: Pathway to Indendendence Award. Available at: http://grants.nih.gov/grants/new_investigators/QsandAs.htm#1586 (accessed September 12, 2011).

---

once funded would remain with the institution and could be offered to any faculty members with the field specified for the position. A faculty member would hold the position for an initial 5-year term and would be renewable for an additional 5 years. At the end of the initial appointment or the renewal period, the faculty member would transition into a regular faculty slot. The allocation of federal grants to create these chairs should be merit driven, based on quality of proposals as well as the impact of the grant (e.g., the size of the graduate program or importance of the research area). But we also believe that the need of the institution for such endowed chairs should be a criterion, since well-endowed universities already have ample numbers of such positions, while less-wealthy institutions have serious needs.

Cyberinfrastructure

The National Academies report *Rising Above the Gathering Storm* recommended a $500 million federal investment in research infrastructure. Through the American Recovery and Reinvestment Act of 2009, the National Science Foundation and the National Institutes of Health made significant investments in research infrastructure during fiscal years 2009 and 2010. For example, NSF's Academic Research Infrastructure Program: Recovery and Reinvestment and NIH's Research and Research Infrastructure "Grand Opportunities" programs each provided $200 million in grants. These kinds of investments in research infrastructure are important. An area of investment that has the potential for significantly increasing productivity is cyberinfrastructure.

The federal government, philanthropy, and industry should focus one of its first two initiatives under the Strategic Investment Program on cyberinfrastructure necessary for cutting-edge research and advanced education. Rapidly evolving cyberinfrastructure (hardware, software, networks, and technical staff) will energize the conduct of research, collaboration and facilities sharing among elements of the national research enterprise (e.g., research universities, national agencies and laboratories, and industrial R&D activities), productivity enhancement through emerging IT-based paradigms (e.g., data centers, cloud computing, simulation), and progressive and innovative education (e.g., technology-enabled learning, cyberlearning).

It is increasingly clear that research in nearly all fields has entered a new era in which the discovery, application, and sharing of new knowledge rely fundamentally on advances in information technology.[31] There are numerous examples of how IT-intensive research is transforming many disciplines. Some individual experiments, such as CERN's Large Hadron Collider in physics and the Panoramic Survey Telescope and Rapid Response System in astronomy, generate enormous amounts of data that must be managed and analyzed. Climate research involves collecting and integrating disparate streams of data from observing systems in space, on land, and in the ocean. Advanced analytics and modeling increase the effectiveness and efficiency of enterprises in a service economy by mining large datasets and modeling effective practices. In biomedical research, advances are increasingly driven by patterns in data.[32] In the

---

[31] Tony Hey, Stewart Tansley, and Kristin Tolle, The Fourth Paradigm: Data-Intensive Scientific Discovery. Redmond, WA: Microsoft Research, 2009, available at: http://research.microsoft.com/en-us/collaboration/fourthparadigm/.

[32] National Research Council, Steps Toward Large-Scale Data Integration in the Sciences: Summary of a Workshop. Washington, DC: National Academies Press, 2010.

humanities, arts, and social sciences, digitization and a variety of new IT-enabled tools are opening new possibilities for research.[33]

A recent NRC report, *Transforming Combustion Research Through Cyberinfrastructure*, concluded, "The trends in continued use of fossil fuels and likely use of alternative combustion fuels call for more rapid development of improved combustion systems. New engines that are based on more predictive understanding of combustion processes must be designed for new fuel streams. A cyberinfrastructure (CI) that facilitates the timely dissemination of research results, experimental and simulated data, and simulation tools throughout the combustion community and extends into the engineering design process is necessary for shortening the time lines for combustion research (CR), development, and engineering. The current pace is rate-limited—by isolation, replication, and the reliance on experimentation, which is inherently slower than computer simulation. . . . A combustion CI will speed up the process of generating and testing designs and predictions preceding full-scale experimentation."[34]

In recent years, research universities, federal agencies, private foundations, and industry have launched a variety of programs to build a modern cyberinfrastructure—the research environments required for this new era of IT-intensive discovery. Federal agencies have made investments in domain-specific capabilities, such as the Bioinformatics Research Network supported by the National Institutes of Health. To coordinate and support the development of cyberinfrastructure resources broadly across the sciences and engineering, the National Science Foundation established the Office of Cyberinfrastructure in 2006. Within the higher education community itself, the Internet2 consortium leverages the capabilities of its members (primarily universities but also including industry and others) to develop and deploy advanced networking capabilities, which are a key component of cyberinfrastructure.

Although these and many other efforts have been valuable in enabling researchers to make crucial progress in ushering in twenty-first-century eScience, a significantly larger-scale national effort is urgently needed. In April 2011 the NSF's Advisory Committee for Cyberinfrastructure (ACCI) released six task force reports to explore long-term cyberinfrastructure needs in campus bridging, cyberlearning and workforce development, data and visualization, grand challenges, high performance computing, and software for science and engineering. The ACCI task force reports

---

[33] Burton, Orville Vernon, and Simon Appleford. 2009. Cyberinfrastructure for the Humanities, Arts, and Social Sciences. Research Bulletin, Issue 1. Boulder, CO: EDUCAUSE Center for Applied Research.

[34] National Research Council, Transforming Combustion Research Through Cyberinfrastructure, Washington, DC: National Academies Press, 2011.

identify many pressing long-term needs in cyberinfrastructure and contain a number of specific recommendations.[35]

The ACCI Task Force on Grand Challenges found that cyberscience and engineering (CS&E) has emerged as a distinct field and has become so important to advances across science and engineering that traditional mechanisms for NSF support, characterized by ad hoc, cross-directorate initiatives, should give way to a more permanent structure.[36] The task force also concluded that greater cooperation between agencies is required to ensure efficient progress in developing particular areas of CS&E—such as high-performance computing—and building a framework for multiagency support for specific grand challenges. The report also emphasizes the importance of training, education, and knowledge of how diverse communities can work together to build and upgrade cyberinfrastructure.

A comprehensive, sustained, and evolving cyberinfrastructure will support the fundamental requirements for the key activities of simulation and prediction, data mining, data management, online instruments and facilities, and interdisciplinary and interinstitutional collaboration. This capability is essential to the conduct of transformative research and associated education, and critical to the future well-being of the nation. To greatly enhance intellectual collaboration, productivity, and efficiency, much of this infrastructure should be shared across the national research enterprise (research universities, national laboratories, and industry R&D) and take advantage of rapidly evolving architectures, such as massive data centers, cloud services, and ultra-high-speed connectivity.

To realize this vision, the committee recommends that the federal government launch a national program to provide grants (with incentives for matching investments from institutions, industry, and the states) necessary to bring the cyberinfrastructure characterizing American research universities—and the broader national research enterprise—to the levels required for the conduct of world-class research, education, and collaboration. This necessary investment in cyberinfrastructure on campuses will also enable significant innovation gains and cost reductions in research and education, as it will expand that which has occurred through applications in business and industry. The program may also allow or even encourage joint efforts of institutions to spread the cost, build economies of scale, and share innovations.

---

[35] National Science Foundation, Advisory Committee on Cyberinfrastructure Task Force Reports. March 2011. Available at: http://www.nsf.gov/od/oci/taskforces/index.jsp.

[36] The ACCI Task Force defines grand challenges as science and engineering problems requiring breakthroughs in some combination of key areas, such as high-performance computing, computational models and algorithms, data management and visualization, software, and collaboration among diverse fields. National Science Foundation, Advisory Committee on Cyberinfrastructure Task Force Reports.

Recommendation 6

The federal government and other research sponsors should strive to cover the full costs of research projects and other activities they procure from research universities in a consistent and transparent manner.

Actors and Actions—Implementing Recommendation 6:

- *Federal government—research sponsors*: The federal government and other research sponsors should strive to support the full cost, direct and indirect, of research and other activities they procure from research universities so that it is no longer necessary to subsidize these sponsored grants by allocating resources (e.g., undergraduate tuition and patient fees for clinical care) away from other important university missions. Both sponsored research policies and cost recovery negotiations should be developed and applied in a consistent fashion across all federal agencies and academic institutions, public and private.

Budget Implications

Federal coverage of a higher portion of indirect costs would, at the margins, shift part of federal research funding from direct to indirect costs, so there will be no net change in cost to the federal government.

Expected Outcomes

This change will allow our research universities to hold steady or reduce the amount of their funding from other sources, such as tuition revenue or patient clinical fees, that they have had to provide for research procured by the federal government, amounts that have increased over the past two decades. Consequently, they will be able to use the flexibility this provides to allocate their resources from other sources more strategically for their intended purpose.

Discussion

In addition to a stable overall budget environment, a commitment from federal and other research sponsors to pay a fair share of the costs of research performed at universities would be an important step in strengthening U.S. research universities for leadership in the 21st century. Specifying the full costs of research and the appropriate contribution of sponsors has been a topic of debate, and occasional contention, particularly between research universities and the federal government, for several decades.

One perennial focus has been the ability of universities to recover the full and significant indirect costs of research from sponsors. The direct costs of research are those that can be attributed to a specific project, such as researcher salaries, travel, and the costs of laboratory materials. Indirect costs include outlays for facilities and administration (F&A), library costs, and other elements that support multiple projects or an institution's entire research program.

There is ample support for the proposition that appropriately defined indirect costs of research incurred by universities should be fully recoverable. Indirect costs are *real* costs of research. For example, to launch a research project, laboratories and other facilities need to be built and maintained. In addition, existing evidence indicates that the indirect cost rates of research universities are comparable to those of government and industry labs, and perhaps slightly lower.[37] Sponsors are getting good value for their investments.

To be sure, there are countervailing views. Sponsors might argue that universities should make some contribution to research efforts because they reap rewards, too, including ownership of intellectual property, prestige for programs and schools, and enhanced recruitment of students and faculty. Parts of the philanthropic community, in particular, might see themselves as providing risk capital for the research enterprise. It is particularly difficult for these donors to understand indirect costs and the differences among different institutions in the levels of these costs. Furthermore, public concerns about rising tuition levels and medical costs, driven in part by declining support from state and federal government, will place many research universities in very awkward positions if they continue to be forced by research sponsors to utilize these sources to also subsidize the costs of sponsored research grants from public or private sources.

Naturally, federal agencies have an interest in maximizing the impact of taxpayer investments in research and have established mechanisms aimed at ensuring that indirect costs are justified, well-defined, and limited. Partly responding to a rise in F&A charges as a percentage of total award amounts during the 1970s and 1980s, the Office of Management and Budget established a cap of 26 percent on administrative costs in

---

[37] Arthur Anderson, The Costs of Research: A Report to the National Academies' Government-University-Research Roundtable, 1996.

1991.[38] The Department of Defense and the Department of Health and Human Services (DHHS) are charged with negotiating F&A rates with research universities and other recipients. Institutions are regularly audited to make sure they are adhering to sound financial management practices and appropriately recovering indirect costs; universities found to have recovered costs inappropriately are required to reimburse the government.[39]

Current policies and practices related to indirect cost recovery are causing significant problems for universities that are becoming more serious over time. First, the effective indirect cost recovery rates of many universities fall below the rates negotiated with DOD or DHHS.[40] For example, under some programs, such as NIH career awards and training grant programs, U.S. Department of Agriculture project grants, and U.S. Agency for International Development programs, F&A cost recovery is capped at lower rates by statute or by agency policy (OSTP, 2000). Similarly, agencies may formally request or favorably consider proposals that specify an indirect cost recovery rate below the institution's negotiated rate. Second, during the two decades that OMB's 26 percent cap on administrative cost recovery has been in effect, an increasing load of federal regulations and requirements have been added to research grants, raising the real costs of compliance borne by the institutions. These requirements in the context of the cap represent a significant unfunded mandate.

University contributions to research procured by the federal government and other sponsors are significant and growing. A report released in 2000 estimated that universities themselves were providing between $700 million and $1.5 billion to cover F&A costs in addition to those that the federal government covered.[41] Since that time, institutions have reported that the costs of regulatory compliance in research programs have

---

[38] U.S. Office of Management and Budget, Circular A-21: Cost Principles for Educational Institutions, May 20, 2004. Available at: http://www.whitehouse.gov/omb/circulars_a021_2004.

[39] Government Accountability Office. National Institutes of Health Extramural Research Grants: Oversight of Cost Reimbursements to Universities (GAO-07-294R). January, 2007. Washington, DC. Available at: http://www.gao.gov/new.items/d07294r.pdf.

[40] Government Accountability Office. University Research: Policies for the Reimbursement of Indirect Costs Need to Be Updated (GAO-10-937). September 2010. Washington, DC. Available at: http://www.gao.gov/new.items/d10937.pdf.

[41] Charles A. Goldman, Traci Williams, David M. Adamson, and Kathy Rosenblatt. Paying for University Research Facilities and Administration. Santa Monica, CA: RAND Corporation, 2000. Available at: http://www.rand.org/pubs/monograph_reports/MR1135-1.html

increased dramatically, in one case quadrupling between 2000 and 2010.[42] As shown in Table 5-6.1, institutional spending on university-performed R&D increased by 44 percent from 2004 to 2009, while R&D expenditures overall increased 27 percent and federally funded R&D expenditures increased about 18 percent. The pattern can also be seen in Figure 5-6.1 and the conclusion is the same: The institutional contribution to research has been growing faster than federal funding. To be sure, some of this may result from aggressive construction in anticipation of larger grant revenue, but a substantial portion of it stems from the increasing institutional subsidy for sponsored research. The institutional contribution must be funded through other sources, chiefly tuition, state appropriations, or private donations: As state appropriations and donations have declined in the recent recession and its aftermath, it is hardly fair to ask students and families to shoulder an ever-increasing share of these costs with tuition and fees already rising steeply.

While the basic principle that sponsors should pay for the full costs of research is straightforward, identifying and adopting the specific steps needed to realize it is more complex. There are several options that the committee discussed and should be carefully considered by OMB and others.

First, OMB could adjust its 26 percent cap on indirect cost recovery to account for the increasing costs of grant administration and regulatory compliance. This approach would be opposed by some out of concern that it would, in a flat-budget environment, represent a shift of federal expenditures from direct to indirect costs.[43] For this approach to be effective, the necessary additional funding would need to be appropriated, implementation would need to be gradual, and adjustment of the cap would need to be based on a rigorous analysis of actual costs.

A second approach would be the adoption of a flat F&A rate for all federal agencies and universities that would eliminate the negotiation of individual rates and the associated auditing. This approach would carry some advantages. It would increase certainty and reduce costs. Negotiating a standard rate across all federal agencies and institutions would create a level playing field for public-private competition for research grants. In the current economic climate, most universities cannot afford the current subsidy they are required to make for federal research grants

---

[42] Association of American Universities, Association of Public and Land-grant Universities, and Committee on Government Relations. Regulatory and Financial Reform of Federal Research Policy Recommendations to the NRC Committee on Research Universities. January 21, 2011. Available at: http://www.aau.edu/policy/reports_presentations.aspx.

[43] Talman, William T. Letter from the President of the Federation of American Societies for Experimental Biology to Charles O. Holliday, Jr., Chair of the National Research Council Committee on Research Universities. March 14, 2011.

TABLE 5-6.1 Science and Engineering Research and Development Expenditures at Universities and Colleges: FY 2004-2009 (Millions of current dollars)

Source of funds and character of work	2004	2005	2006	2007	2008	2009	Percent change 2008-2009	Percent change 2004-2009
All R&D expenditures	43,258	45,799	47,751	49,493	51,934	54,935	5.8	27.0
Source of funds								
Federal government	27,644	29,209	30,128	30,443	31,281	32,588	4.2	17.9
State and local government	2,879	2,940	2,962	3,143	3,452	3,647	5.7	26.7
Industry	2,129	2,291	2,402	2,670	2,865	3,197	11.6	50.2
Institutional funds	7,753	8,266	9,062	9,705	10,408	11,198	7.6	44.4
Other	2,852	3,093	3,196	3,533	3,928	4,305	9.6	50.9
Character of work								
Basic research	31,968	34,367	36,076	37,725	39,408	40,955	3.9	28.1
Applied research and development	11,290	11,432	11,674	11,768	12,526	13,980	11.6	23.8

S&E = science and engineering.
NOTE: Because of rounding, detail may not add to total.
SOURCE: National Science Foundation, National Center for Science and Engineering Statistics, Academic Research and Development Expenditures, Fiscal Year 2009, Tables 1 and 2, available at: http://www.nsf.gov/statistics/nsf11313/content.cfm?pub_id=4065&id=2 (accessed April 22, 2012).

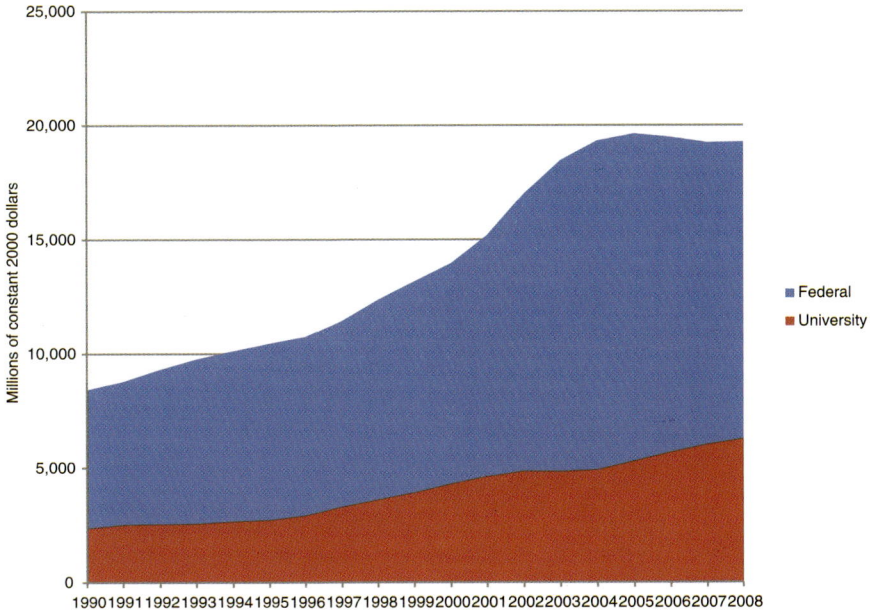

FIGURE 5-6.1 Federal and university funding for university-performed basic research, 1990-2008 (millions of 2000 constant dollars).
Source: National Science Foundation, National Center for Science and Engineering Statistics, National Patterns of R&D Resources, 2008 Data Update, Table 6. Available at: http://www.nsf.gov/statistics/nsf10314/content.cfm?pub_id=4000&id=2 (accessed September 4, 2011).

because of inadequate indirect cost recovery and excessive cost-sharing requirements. In reality, for all but the wealthiest private institutions, this subsidy today must come from the tuition dollars paid by students or the clinical fees paid by patients. It is no longer politically tolerable either at the institutional or federal level for undergraduates and patients to pay for federal research. The flat-rate approach would also involve some complications in implementation. For example, the facilities costs of different types of institutions vary widely. A variation on the flat-rate approach that could address variations in facilities costs is to limit the flat rate to the nonfacilities administrative costs.

A third approach would be to allow researchers to account for some portion of the time clerical and administrative staff spend on administrative and compliance tasks as direct costs. This approach would provide faculty with more flexibility, and allow any cost savings realized from the rationalization of regulatory requirements discussed below to flow directly to research support. The disadvantage is that the true magnitude of indirect costs might grow in an opaque way over time, leading to lower productivity in research activity.

Notwithstanding the difficulty in reaching consensus on a specific approach to ensure that federal agencies and other research sponsors pay the full costs of research, there are areas where positive steps can clearly be made. Therefore, the committee recommends that

- OMB should fully enforce existing cost-reimbursement rules and prohibit federal agencies from practices and policies inconsistent with federal cost principles. Some agencies establish rates for specific programs that are significantly lower than the 26 percent cap.
- OMB should ensure that rate-setting practices by government negotiators are consistent and fair across all institutions. When different agencies negotiate rates, there can be inconsistent outcomes that are not fair to institutions.[44]

The committee realizes that such harmonization among agencies may require statutory change, but also notes that a great deal can be achieved in the meantime by funding agencies working with OMB and with research institutions.

Another relevant aspect of policy toward research funding is the use of voluntary or mandatory cost-sharing provisions in federal grants, in which the grantee is to assume some of the direct costs of a project. The National Science Foundation has adopted a new policy based on a National Science Board report of several years ago.[45] The new policy eliminates voluntary cost sharing, and limits mandatory cost sharing to a set of programs where a financial commitment from the institution is seen as necessary for the project to succeed, or those involving partnerships with industry or state governments. Adopting this approach across all agencies, and adding a provision that exempts research universities from the mandatory cost-sharing requirements imposed on industry, would deliver significant benefits to institutions.[46]

The steps recommended here would not, by themselves, ensure that private foundations, companies, and other research sponsors pay the full costs of research. The committee expects that the adoption of this principle and its implementation on the part of the federal government will

---

[44] AAU, APLU, and COGR, Recommendations to the NRC Committee.

[45] National Science Board. Investing in the Future: NSF Cost Sharing Policies for a Robust Federal Research Enterprise. Arlington, VA: National Science Foundation, 2009. Available at: http://www.nsf.gov/pubs/2009/nsb0920/nsb0920.pdf.

[46] AAU, APLU, and COGR, Recommendations to the NRC Committee.

have a positive impact on the willingness of nonfederal sponsors to do likewise.

Recommendation 7

Reduce or eliminate regulations that increase administrative costs, impede research productivity, and deflect creative energy without substantially improving the research environment.

Actors and Actions—Implementing Recommendation 7:

- *Federal government (OMB, Congress, agencies), state governments*: Federal and state policy makers and regulators should review the costs and benefits of federal and state regulations, eliminating those that are redundant, ineffective, inappropriately applied to the higher education sector, or impose costs that outweigh the benefits to society.
- *Federal government*: The federal government should also harmonize regulations and reporting requirements across federal agencies so universities can maintain one system for all federal requirements rather than several, thereby reducing costs.

Budget Implications

While the staff time to review regulatory and reporting requirements has a small, short-term cost, the savings to universities and federal and state governments over the long term will be substantial. Quantifying the burdens is difficult, so it is not feasible to estimate the savings in advance of a review, but we believe they could run into the billions of dollars over the next decade.

Expected Outcomes

Reducing or eliminating regulations can reduce administrative costs, enhance productivity, and increase the agility of institutions. We agree with the conclusion of the AAU, APLU, and Council on Governmental Relations (COGR) that "minimizing administrative and compliance costs ultimately will also provide a cost benefit to the federal government and to university administrators, faculty, and students by freeing up resources and time to directly support educational and research efforts."[47] With greater resources and freedom, they will be better positioned to

---

[47] AAU, APLU, and COGR, Recommendations to the NRC Committee.

respond to the needs of their constituents in an increasingly competitive environment.

Discussion

The federal government—OMB, in conjunction with other federal agencies—should review the regulatory and reporting requirements it imposes on U.S. higher education institutions with the aim of eliminating those that are redundant, ineffective, onerous, or inappropriately applied to the higher education sector. Additions to the reporting or regulatory obligations of universities should be implemented only in light of an OMB cost-benefit analysis and should be accompanied by additional funding to support the higher resulting indirect and administrative costs.

As academic research activities have grown and become more complex, they have become subject to a broad array of regulations. Although state and local governments, as well as universities themselves, promulgate regulations affecting research, federal regulations are the main focus here because they constitute the predominant source of the research-related regulatory burden of universities. (State regulations and requirements were addressed in Recommendation 2.)

The vast majority of federal regulations are aimed at addressing legitimate issues and risks, and compliance and regulatory oversight are essential to the conduct of federally supported research. AAU, APLU, and COGR affirm that "research universities strongly support the objectives of accountability, transparency, and implementation of important policy and regulatory requirements."[48]

However, the sheer growth of requirements from many federal agencies, a substantial percentage of which were created with other types of organizations (e.g., industry) in mind, has raised the effort and costs necessary for compliance to a significant, unreasonable degree. AAU, APLU, and COGR argue that "in this environment, universities are often forced to institute one agency's compliance requirements across an entire campus, even where they don't make sense, and to sift through each agency's specific rules and develop different compliance mechanisms all aimed at the same ultimate purpose." They continue, noting that the uneven and unsynchronized implementation of regulations and reporting across many federal agencies create "a compliance miasma."[49]

AAU, APLU, and COGR note, "It is a growing fiscal challenge for universities to manage unfunded mandates as institutional budgets are being reduced, administrative cost reimbursements are being suppressed, and

---

[48] Ibid.
[49] Ibid.

cost-sharing requirements are increasing."[50] While observing that compliance is difficult to measure, they provided the following as examples of the increasing costs of regulatory compliance:

- One public university in the Northeast noted that the costs of managing its Sponsored Project Administration cost pool increased from $3.5 million in FY 2005 to nearly $6 million in FY 2010. Another, a private institution in the Midwest, estimated that its costs had increased from $4.2 million in 2002 to $7.3 million in 2008. A prominent medical school in the Southeast saw its compliance and quality assurance costs increase from approximately $3 million in 2000 to $12.5 million in 2010.
- For that same prominent Southeastern medical school, compliance and quality assurance costs exhibited a cumulative growth rate of more than 300 percent between 2001 and 2010, while sponsored expenditures increased by only 125 percent during that same time.

Reviewing federal regulatory and reporting requirements will ensure both that important regulations are effectively enforced and that universities can use federal research funding efficiently and productively. In addition, efforts should be made to shift, where possible, from compliance-driven requirements to incentives for best practices. Most of the cost in compliance (for example, human subjects or animal treatment) is not the actual compliance. Rather, it is in maintaining, checking, and double-checking the bullet-proof audit records required. This is because it is an entirely compliance-driven regime, where the penalties of even a single infraction can be severe. By contrast, in a best-practices regime, an institution would be allowed a (limited) set of trade-offs between the cost of actual compliance and the cost of audit-proof documentation. An example is the system by which ISO-9000 certification is awarded. Firms are scored by whether their processes are up to best practices (with a percentage score allowing some variance), not audited at the single-incident level.

The current efforts on the part of the Obama administration to address the broad issue of regulatory reform are encouraging.[51] The process put in place by Executive Order 13563, Improving Regulation and Regulatory Review, will hopefully lead to a lowering of regulatory burdens in areas relevant to universities. The ultimate results of this process and impacts on research universities should be evaluated at the appropriate time. A special effort focused on the regulatory burdens on research uni-

---

[50] Ibid.

[51] Barack Obama. Executive Order 13563: Improving Regulation and Regulatory Review. January 18, 2011. Available at: http://www.gpo.gov/fdsys/pkg/FR-2011-01-21/pdf/2011-1385.pdf.

BOX 5-7.1
AAU-APLU-COGR Recommendations for Regulatory Reform

(1) *Harmonize regulations and information systems between agencies and statutes where reasonable and eliminate unnecessary duplication and redundancy.* University research is funded by 25 different federal agencies, each with a unique approach to regulatory implementation. While regulations concerning areas like human subject protections, animal welfare, export controls, select agents, responsible conduct of research, and financial conflicts of interest all serve important public policy goals, unique interpretations and implementations across agencies are difficult to manage, create inefficiencies, and increase costs. Additional challenges occur when rules applicable to grants (established by OMB) are inconsistent with rules applicable to contracts (established under the Federal Acquisition Regulations Councils).

(2) *Eliminate regulations which do not add value or enhance accountability.* At least two requirements, Effort Reporting and Cost Accounting Standards, neither add value nor enhance accountability. As characterized by the Federal Demonstration Project, Effort Reporting "is based on effort which is difficult to measure, provides limited internal control value, is expensive, lacks timeliness, does not focus specifically on supporting direct charges, and is confusing when all forms of remuneration are considered." Cost Accounting Standards require institutions to disclose in writing accounting policies that are already documented in other institutional systems. Both of these regulations could be eliminated without any detriment to the accountability or oversight of the research enterprise. As other valueless regulations are indentified, there should be a formal process in which each can be reviewed and made eligible for elimination.

(3) *Provide targeted exemptions for research universities similar to protections provided for small entities under the Regulatory Flexibility Act (RFA).* The RFA requires agencies to prepare and publish a regulatory flexibility analysis describing the impact of a proposed rule on small entities. In addition, agencies are encouraged to facilitate participation of the affected entities by holding conferences and public hearings on the proposed rule. The RFA encourages tiering of government regulations or the identification of "significant alternatives" designed to make proposed rules less burdensome. The law could be amended to include organizations engaged in conducting federally sponsored research. For example, the Chemical Facilities and Anti-Terrorism Standards (CFATS) capture universities in the same class with chemical manufacturers and industrial agricultural corporations, requiring identical policy and procedure implementation and reporting. In a similar vein, the cumbersome export controls promulgated by the Departments of State and Commerce, even while currently undergoing much needed revision, fail to recognize the fundamental difference between the physical export of very sensitive technologies to a foreign country and the legitimate sharing of information at U.S. universities between U.S. researchers and foreign nationals.

(4) *Ensure that regulations are meeting their goals in terms of performance, rather than simply in terms of process.* Research universities support the objectives of implementing important policy and regulatory requirements—research institutions take their stewardship responsibilities seriously. However, when imple-

mentation of regulation is premised on overly prescriptive measures issued by agencies, and subject to audit by federal and local auditors, institutional management of regulation becomes grossly complex and expensive. "Performance-based regulatory compliance" focuses on regulatory outcomes (e.g., research animals are treated in a humane manner) rather than intermediate measurements (e.g., all holding areas must meet specific dimensions). A regulatory approach that is based on performance-based standards offer[s] universities greater flexibility to achieve regulatory goals and results in a more rational and cost-effective regulatory infrastructure.

(5) *Extend coverage provided under the Unfunded Mandates Reform Act (UMRA) to research universities and allow institutions to better account for new regulatory costs, and to charge these costs to federal awards.* It is often not a single regulation that creates compliance challenges, but the stacking of regulations over time. Agencies rarely reevaluate, eliminate, or redesign regulatory schemes to reduce the burden of compliance (the Environmental Protection Agency's development of Subpart K of the hazardous waste regulations is a notable exception). The UMRA requires Congress and agencies to give special consideration to the costs and regulatory impact of new regulations on state and local governments, as well as on tribal entities. Extending coverage to universities would result in agencies being more responsive to the cost burdens of new requirements.

Additionally, the Paperwork Reduction Act (PRA) requires that all proposed regulations be analyzed for the paperwork that they require, and that paperwork be reduced to a minimum. Regulations creating new paperwork requirements must be cleared by OMB. Unfortunately, agency projections of the paperwork burden are often underestimated and do not recognize how new reporting requirements will be paid for. (American Recovery and Reinvestment Act reporting requirements and the recently proposed NIH reporting requirements related to financial conflicts of interest are two notable examples.) Suggestions by federal officials that indirect cost reimbursements will pay for new regulatory costs fail to recognize that the 26 percent administrative cap precludes additional recovery of these costs. In situations when new requirements are not effectively controlled to minimize cost burden, institutions should be allowed to establish a cost reimbursement mechanism in which the incremental costs can be recovered as a direct charge to the federal award.

(6) *Simplify sub-recipient monitoring requirements.* Sub-recipient monitoring requirements continue to expand under both regulatory and statutory mandates. While there may be value to monitoring sub-recipients that are not established recipients of federal funding, to monitor sub-recipients (e.g., other research universities) that regularly receive federal awards is a wasteful exercise and should be eliminated. A monitoring requirement that would apply only to those sub-recipients that are not federal awardees would be a logical improvement.

(7) *Reinforce the original intent of the Single Audit Act.* Research universities spend significant money on an annual basis to complete their A-133 audit as required under the Single Audit Act. Results of the A-133 audit provide assurance to Federal agencies that an institution's internal controls, oversight, and compliance infrastructure are adequate to manage federal funds. While agencies should conduct program expenditure audits in those situations deemed necessary, many

continued

BOX 5-7.1 Continued

agency audits and reviews are duplicative of the audit work completed in the A-133 audit. All agency audits and reviews should be subject to pre-approval by the federal ombudsman (see Recommendation 10) to determine which aspects of a proposed audit or review are duplicative of the A-133 audit. Those aspects of the proposed audit or review that are duplicative should be eliminated from the scope of the audit.

(8) *Prohibit voluntary committed cost sharing across the Federal government and create a mandatory cost sharing exemption for research universities.* Based on a 2009 recommendation by the National Science Board (NSB), the National Science Foundation (NSF) has implemented a new policy that prohibits voluntary cost sharing on all NSF programs. The NSF policy should be implemented by all agencies that fund research since such cost sharing inappropriately imposes additional costs on universities and frequently is not truly voluntary. The 2009 NSB recommendation encourages mandatory cost sharing requirements only for a small subset of NSF programs—specifically, programs where it has been determined that an institutional commitment is critical to long-term program success, as well as programs built on partnerships with industry and state and local governments. Programs sponsored by other agencies should be subject to similar scrutiny before mandatory cost sharing can be imposed. For example, the Department of Energy has a long history of requiring a mandatory cost share commitment with its industry partners. While this may be an appropriate expectation of for-profit industry enterprises, to require the same commitment from university partners ignores both the public policy role and the nonprofit status of research universities. Exempting research universities from mandatory cost sharing requirements would be an important step forward.

versities might still ultimately be needed. Fortunately, organizations and institutions that can help facilitate the necessary dialog among research universities and federal sponsors, such as the Federal Demonstration Partnership, are already in existence.

The problem of excessive regulatory burdens is itself an issue that puts a drag on the efficiency of all university research. The committee received testimony on many specific regulations and issues, several of which will be mentioned here by way of example. The full list of recommendations suggested by AAU, APLU, and COGR are provided in Box 5-7.1.[52] The committee endorses this list as a basis for discussions moving forward.

In some cases, experts have identified regulations that do not add value or help ensure accountability, and have proposed alternative ap-

---

[52] AAU, APLU, and COGR, Recommendations to the NRC Committee.

(9) *Establish protocols to address statutorily-mandated regulatory concerns.* When new laws are passed by Congress to achieve important public policy goals, unintended regulatory burden can be an unfortunate by-product. When statutorily-mandated requirements create unintended regulatory burdens for universities, a fast-track approach to amending the law would be a useful tool that could help to minimize burdensome regulations.

(10) *Designate a high level official within OMB's Office of Regulatory Affairs (OIRA) to serve as a Federal Ombudsman, responsible for addressing university regulatory concerns and for seeking ways to increase regulatory efficiency.* This individual should be empowered with broad responsibilities to manage and minimize regulatory burdens applicable to research universities and institutions. The ombudsman would assist in harmonizing and streamlining federal regulations, and would also have responsibility for reviewing specific "simplification requests." Under the auspices of the National Science and Technology Council (NSTC), the ombudsman—along with a designated representative from OSTP—should lead an interagency group charged with regularly reviewing regulations affecting research universities. This interagency group could be organized as a new subcommittee of the National Science and Technology Council (NSTC) Committee on Science, or as part of the existing Research Business Models Subcommittee. Through an application process, research universities or university associations could submit proposals to "fix" or eliminate rules that either add no value or promote inefficiency and excessive regulatory burden.

Source: AAU, APLU, and COGR, Regulatory and Financial Reform of Federal Research Policy Recommendations to the NRC Committee on Research Universities, January 21, 2011.

proaches. For example, effort reporting is the current mechanism used to support salary, wage, and related charges to federal contracts and grants.[53] Because effort is difficult to measure, the reporting mechanism is of little value as an internal financial control for the institution, while compliance is expensive and the reports are untimely from the standpoint of agency oversight. (Box 5-7.2 provides data collected by AAU, APLU, and COGR on the costs of effort reporting.) The current requirement puts a considerable burden on universities, with very little, if any, value to the federal sponsors or to the performing institutions. The committee

---

[53] Federal Demonstration Partnership. Payroll Certifications: A Proposed Alternative to Effort Reporting. January 3, 2011. Available at: http://sites.nationalacademies.org/PGA/fdp/PGA_055834

BOX 5-7.2
Estimating the Cost of Effort Reporting

Some specific compliance areas have relatively large costs associated with them. For example, virtually every institution that responded to our request for information identified effort reporting as an area that has had significant cost and productivity implications. Effort reporting requires significant faculty and staff time, which was difficult for many universities to quantify.

Effort reporting also requires administrative time. One public university in the Midwest told us that nine separate full-time employees (FTEs) spend approximately one quarter of their time each year monitoring certifications, at a total estimated cost per year of $117,000. Another public university, this one in the West, estimated its annual central administrative cost was $320,000, with an additional department administrative staff and faculty cost of $241,000.

For many schools, effort reporting also required the development or purchase, and the continuing maintenance of, specialized software systems. A public university in the Midwest reported that the last estimate to purchase necessary software from an external vendor was over $500,000, exclusive of all the implementation and training costs devoted to it. A public university in the West estimated the cost of its system at $435,000 annually. System implementation for a private university in the South cost $443,000.

One private university in the Midwest estimated that on its campus there are over 6,000 effort reports completed three times per year, resulting in more than 18,000 effort reports processed per year overall. Estimating that 60-90 minutes were spent on each effort report—including issuing instructions, completion by faculty and staff, administrative review, tracking, and storing—yields a conservative estimate of 20,000 hours per year spent on this process. Several universities reported that overall they spent in the range of $500,000 to nearly $1 million annually on effort reporting alone.

Source: AAU, APLU, and COGR, Regulatory and Financial Reform of Federal Research Policy Recommendations to the NRC Committee on Research Universities, January 21, 2011.

---

therefore recommends that effort reporting be eliminated or significantly modified.

In other areas, such as human subjects protection, animal welfare requirements, export controls, management and use of select agents, responsible conduct of research, and financial conflicts of interest, differing implementations and interpretations across agencies can cause inefficiencies in ensuring compliance and raise costs.[54] Standardized approaches to these across agencies would ease compliance burdens on universities significantly. (See further detailed suggestions in Table 5-7.1.)

---

[54] AAU, APLU, and COGR, "Recommendations to the NRC Committee TEXT MISSING

Further measures aimed at lowering and eliminating regulatory burdens on universities on a continuing basis should be considered. These measures would include the designation of a high-level ombudsman in the OMB's Office of Information and Regulatory Affairs who would be charged with overseeing and regularly reviewing regulations affecting research universities and institutions, perhaps as part of an interagency effort under the National Science and Technology Council. Institutions could apply to the ombudsman to fix or eliminate inefficient regulations that do not add value.[55]

During the course of this study, the committee received substantial testimony concerning the increasingly burdensome administrative and regulatory requirements associated with federally sponsored research imposed upon both institutions and investigators (including the statement that the majority of primary investigator time on NIH grants is now spent on project administration). Clearly this not only drives up university administrative costs, it also erodes research effort.

Recommendation 8:

Improve the capacity of graduate programs to attract talented students by addressing issues such as attrition rates, time to degree, funding, and alignment with both student career opportunities and national interests.

Actors and Actions—Implementing Recommendation 8:

- *Research universities*: Research universities should restructure doctoral education to enhance pathways for talented undergraduates, improve completion rates, shorten time-to-degree, and strengthen the preparation of graduates for careers both in and beyond the academy.
- *Research universities, federal agencies*: Research universities and federal agencies should ensure, as they implement the above measures, that they improve education across the full spectrum of research university graduate programs, because of the increasing breadth of academic and professional disciplines necessary to address the challenges facing our changing world, including the physical, life, social, and behavioral sciences; engineering; the arts and humanities; and the professions.
- *Federal government*: The federal government should significantly increase its support for graduate education through balanced programs of fellowships, traineeships, and research assistantships provided by all science agencies dependent upon individuals with advanced training.

---

[55] Ibid.

TABLE 5-7.1 AAU-APLU-COGR Suggestions for Easing Compliance Burden on Research Universities

This table lists remedies for some examples of regulatory burdens faced by our institutions. This is by no means a comprehensive list. Columns in the table represent types of suggested remedies for regulatory issues. Rows in the table represent categories of regulation. Note that most categories require a mix of regulatory remedies.

	Exempt Universities or Eliminate	Harmonize/Avoid Duplication and Redundancy	Tier to Risk	Focus on Performance, Not Process	Better Synch with University R&D
Human Subjects		Harmonize human subjects protections between the Office of Human Research Protections (OHRP) and the Food and Drug Administration (FDA).	Tier human subjects research for exemption from IRB Review (e.g., social science research vs. clinical trials).		
		Eliminate Health Insurance Portability and Accountability Act (HIPAA) from research, or harmonize HIPAA regulations with OHRP regulations.			

Animal Research			Consult on whether the Animal Enterprise Terrorism Act (AETA) provides sufficient protection for animal researchers.	
Export Controls	Eliminate new regulations requiring deemed export certification for certain visa applications (I-129 form).	Harmonize ITAR, EAR, and OFAC controls.	Tier export control lists to risk, removing much of what is currently on these lists or reclassify to lower their control levels.	For purposes of enforcement of deemed export control laws, require that individuals have knowledge or intent that controlled information will be exported or transmitted without proper authorization.
Effort Reporting	Eliminate effort reporting.			

continued

TABLE 5-7.1 Continued

	Exempt Universities or Eliminate	Harmonize/Avoid Duplication and Redundancy	Tier to Risk	Focus on Performance, Not Process	Better Synch with University R&D
Financial Reporting	Expanded Form 1099 Reporting Requirements will create an additional burden on financial reporting.		Sub-recipient monitoring; modify requirement so that grantees would no longer be required to monitor sub-recipients who regularly receive Federal awards.		Federal Funding Accountability and Transparency Act (FFATA): Raise subreporting threshold from $25,000 to the simplified acquisition threshold, use OMB definition of "subcontract" (which eliminates procurements), and only report first tier. FFATA: makes reporting annual or eliminate more onerous requirements for universities.

		Change timing of Quarterly Cash Transactions Report- revised timing has put a stain on reporting resources, and it's not clear how the government benefits from getting the data 2 weeks earlier. The old 45-day timing has been around for at least 20 years.
Conflict of Interest/ Research Integrity	Eliminate negative patent reports, which require form completion even when there are no intellectual property concerns.	Direct OSTP to convene agencies to develop a conflict of interest policy like the Misconduct in Science Policy, which articulates general goals and objectives.
Select Toxins and Agents	Develop a tiered list and associated requirements, as has been documented by the American Society of Microbiology.	

continued

TABLE 5-7.1 Continued

	Exempt Universities or Eliminate	Harmonize/Avoid Duplication and Redundancy	Tier to Risk	Focus on Performance, Not Process	Better Synch with University R&D
Hazardous Materials	CFATS: wherever possible, create an exception for research laboratories.		CFATS: tier chemicals of interest to risk when exemption isn't possible.		Examine and consider university facilities as different from large chemical facilities: design alternative approaches in light of these differences.

Source: AAU, APLU, and COGR, Recommendations to the NRC Committee on Research Universities

- ***Employers***: Business, government agencies, and non-profits that hire master's- and doctorate-level graduates should more deeply engage programs in research universities to provide internships, student projects, advice on curriculum design, and real-time information on employment opportunities.

Budget Implications

Increasing the number of federal fellowships and traineeships to support 5,000 new graduate students per year in science and engineering would amount to $325 million in year one, climbing to a steady state expenditure of $1.625 billion per year. This funding is not designed to increase the overall numbers of doctoral students per se, but to provide incentives for students to pursue areas of national need and to shift support from the research assistantship to mechanisms that strengthen doctoral training. At the same time that the committee recommends increased federal funding for graduate education, the implementation of other aspects of our recommendation will also save money for the federal government, universities, and students. Reducing attrition and time-to-degree in doctoral programs, for example, will increase the cost-effectiveness of federal and other investments in this area.

Expected Outcomes

Improving pathways will ensure that we draw strongly from among the "best and brightest" for our nation's future doctorates in science and engineering fields that are critical to our nation's future.

Improving completion rates and shortening time-to-degree to an optimal length is the right thing to do for students and also increases cost-effectiveness, ensuring good stewardship of resources from the federal government and other sources.

Strengthening preparation of doctorates for a broad range of careers, not just those in academia, assists the students in their careers, and also assists employers who need their staff to be productive in the short term. This benefits new doctorates, employers, and society.

Discussion

Doctoral education in the United States represents the world's leading effort for producing the next generation of faculty and researchers. By uniquely combining graduate education and research in the same place and at the same time, our universities have created a research and training system that is one of the nation's greatest strengths—and the envy of the rest of the world. Many countries globally are now moving to the U.S. model as they reform their own programs. Yet two sets of challenges now pressure us to reform key aspects of the process and substance of doctoral education to ensure that it remains vital, productive, and world class. The first are financial pressures on universities that call simultaneously for process improvements and additional financial support. The second are challenges and opportunities for realigning graduate education with labor markets to ensure students are trained for the careers they will have in academia, industry, government, or nonprofits. Many young people who imagine research careers also imagine careers as teachers in colleges and universities. Academic careers have become less attractive as salaries decline and permanent faculty positions become rarer. This affects the quality of those who choose research careers. The modern research enterprise requires a different mix of training levels and personnel capabilities than in previous generations. Then, the model was that every graduate student should be capable of becoming a Ph.D. and postdoc; every postdoc capable of becoming a junior faculty member; every junior faculty member, tenurable somewhere; every tenured faculty member capable of being an independent principal investigator. That is just not true anymore.

Response to Financial Pressures

Significant financial pressures on research universities impinge on their ability to provide support to doctoral students. Private institutions experienced falling endowment values during the recent recession. As we move out of that recession, these resources are rebounding, but political pressure on private institutions has forced them to increase spending rates from endowments for need-based financial aid for undergraduates, which is critically important but reduces resources for graduate education.[56] Meanwhile, public research universities have seen even greater pressure with deep cuts in state support for higher education compounded by substantial political pressure to use remaining resources to accommodate increases in undergraduate enrollments. For public and private institutions, these pressures result in reallocation of budgets that make support for graduate education extremely vulnerable, especially given the high mobility of doctorate recipients that creates incentives for states to underinvest in graduate education. Universities and governments must work together to place graduate education on a more solid financial foundation by improving the resource base for doctoral education, increasing the efficiency of doctoral education, and ensuring that doctoral programs are effectively meeting goals.

---

[56] The average discount rate for freshman in Fall 2008 was 42 percent, the highest ever.

Institutional Response

Given constraints on resources, institutions must become more efficient in educating graduate students. Two measures of this efficiency are completion rates and time-to-degree. By encouraging talented students to complete and to do so within a reasonable amount of time, institutions can save resources and propel graduates into early productive careers. The Council of Graduate Schools (CGS) has collected data on degree completion and attrition at 29 institutions in 23 fields across engineering, the sciences, and the humanities for students who began study in the early 1990s. As shown in Figure 5-8.1, the findings from this study show that after 10 years the overall completion rate for these programs was 57 percent, with a high of 64 percent in engineering and a low of 49 percent in the humanities. The flatness of the curves in this figure after about 8 years demonstrates that few students are likely to complete the degree after this point in time, at which about 50 percent have completed, the majority of those who will. While completion is not a measure of attrition, since students may eventually complete after 15 or 20 years, CGS data also show that the 10-year attrition rate averages about 31 percent in STEM fields and 30 percent overall. The highest attrition occurs in the physical sciences and mathematics at 37 percent, a level largely attributable to the attrition rate of more than 50 percent in computer science.[57]

To be sure, attrition rates owe at least in part to the difference in the required talents and preferences for success in graduate versus undergraduate education and the fact that most university departments and students cannot easily determine suitability before admission. Unless advance training for research occurs early in a student's undergraduate experience to allow sorting before attending a graduate program, there is bound to be a high rate of attrition; this situation has been true for many decades. Furthermore, completion statistics mask some clearly good outcomes for some noncompleters. Conservatively, half of the noncompleters studied in the CGS Ph.D. Completion Project left with a master's degree awarded before they reached candidacy, and for many that was their original intended outcome. Still, given financial realities, it is clear that there are opportunities for improvement in completion statistics at the doctoral level, and it is incumbent upon doctoral programs to examine ways to reduce attrition, particularly for students who are prepared, talented, and otherwise eager to continue.

Hand in hand with the low completion rates are long times-to-degree, shown over time in Figure 5-8.2. In 2008, median duration between

---

[57] Council of Graduate Schools. Ph.D. Completion and Attrition: Analysis of Baseline Program Data from the Ph.D. Completion Project. Washington, DC: Council of Graduate Schools, 2008.

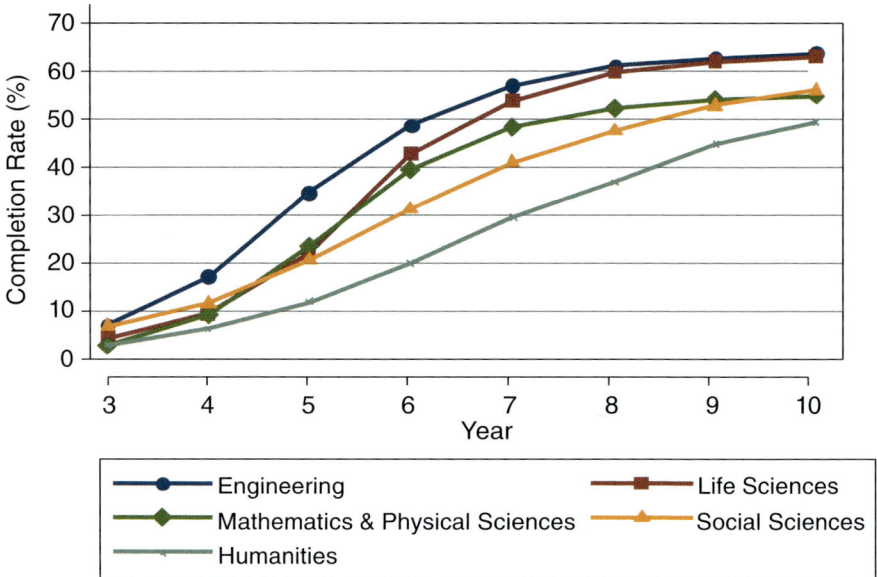

FIGURE 5-8.1 Average cumulative 10-year completion rates for cohorts entering doctoral study from 1992-1993 through 1994-1995, by broad field and year.
Source: Council of Graduate Schools. *Ph.D. Completion and Attrition: Analysis of Baseline Program Data from the Ph.D. Completion Project.* Washington, DC: Council of Graduate Schools, 2008.

starting graduate school and completing a doctorate was 7.7 years. This varied by field: 6.7 years in physical sciences, 6.7 years in engineering, 6.9 years in life sciences, 7.7 years in social sciences, and 9.3 years in the humanities.[58] These times-to-degree seem to match the completions data, as about 50 percent of the students complete in about 7 years. It also suggests that there is very little completion after 10 years and that attrition is near 40 percent for most fields.

Excessive attrition rates and time-to-degree represent inefficiencies in the current model of graduate education and incur considerable waste of both human capital and financial resources. Timely completion may be supported through a variety of means, including improved academic advising and mentoring, increased information about career opportunities, closer tracking of student progress, and activities to promote social integration within a department. Another aspect to the CGS study was

---

[58] National Science Foundation, Doctorate Recipients from U.S. Universities: Summary Report 2007-08. Arlington, VA: National Science Foundation, December 2009 (NSF 10-309), Table 18.

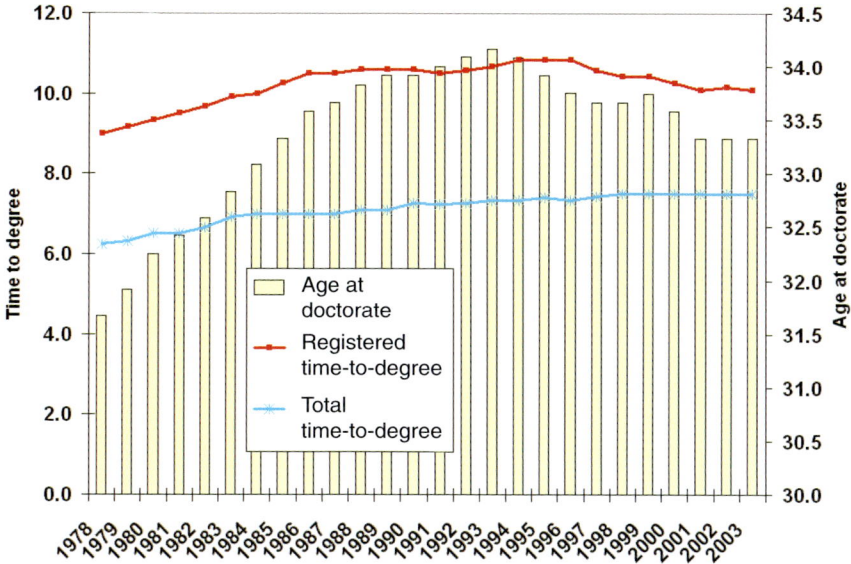

FIGURE 5-8.2 Average time-to-degree and age-at-degree for science and engineering Ph.D. recipients: 1978-2003.
Source: Mark C. Regets, Senior Analyst, National Science Foundation, National Center for Science and Engineering Statistics, Presentation to Committee on Research Universities, September 22, 2010. (Data from NSF/NCSES, Survey of Earned Doctorates.)

the development of interventions or best practices that could increase the completion rate. These included the following:

- *Selection and admissions* policies to create a better "fit or match" between a prospective student and a specific program
- *Mentoring and advising*, from student orientation to career guidance
- *Financial support* in a form to optimize completion and enhance academic and social integration
- *Program environment* that supports networks and support services
- *Research experience* at the pregraduate level and exposure to different research options in the program
- *Curricular and administrative processes and procedures* that provide support at different stages in graduate study and at the critical dissertation phase

These practices are particularly important for underrepresented minorities in doctoral programs, since they represent a growing segment of the graduate application pool and, by CGS data, their completion rates are as much as 10 percent lower than white students.

Instituting these and other interventions to increase completion rates and reduce time-to-degree will require a different structure for graduate education, one that focuses on a programmatic commitment to student success and on preparing doctoral graduates for 21st-century careers. While the research and educational mission of universities is somewhat blurred at the doctoral level, it is important to students that they have clear objectives; only in this way will students be able to reach their full potential as researchers and contributors to the nation's wealth.

A final note on doctoral education: The recent National Research Council Assessment of Research Doctorate Programs collected and analyzed data that provide a starting point for thorough institutional review of doctoral programs. These reviews should focus on how to strengthen programs that are viable and well targeted; right-size or redirect programs that are viable but need to be reoriented to meet current needs; or even eliminate programs that are not viable, as they do not meet goals or do not serve a current need.

Concerns about the length of time in training apply as well to postdoctoral study. Many postdoctoral fellows working in larger laboratories are engaged in interesting and productive work contributing to the science of their fields. This training allows them to mature as investigators and, eventually, move on to research positions in industry, faculty positions in research universities, or faculty positions in other higher education institutions. However, the uncertainty of and long time-to-career outcomes creates a strong disincentive to American college graduates to enroll in doctoral programs. Doctorates, mainly in the biomedical sciences, are experiencing long periods in training with little expectation of finding an academic research position that utilizes the training they received as a graduate student and a postdoctorate fellow. To shorten the postdoctoral period, many institutions have imposed time limits of usually 5 years, and once reached, these researchers either move on to another position or they find employment outside of research. Long postdoctoral appointments and poor prospects for a research career also deter newly awarded doctorates who are not electing the additional training; they select alternate career paths, possibly outside of their field of study. This may be viewed as an inefficient use of talent in the educational system.

Efforts are being made to address these concerns, such as the NIH Pathway to Independence Award Program. This program provides 5 years of funding for transition from a postdoctoral appointment to a research position at an institution or organization. The program will keep the career path open for the most promising researchers; however, it is limited to a few hundred individuals, and a portion of the several thousand other postdoctorates will not find the research positions they trained for. Aside from the long periods in postdoctoral positions, these positions do not pay well, benefits given to regular institutional employees are not available, and the positions could be terminated at any time. A mechanism is needed for postdoctorates to continue their work in a research position that carries some job security and a reasonable salary level. Such positions as research faculty exist in educational institutions, but it is typically more economical for principal investigators to use lower-paid postdoctorates for the research. The NRC Research Associateship Programs provide an alternative career track for postdoctorates who work in national laboratories and often continue in these as permanent employees. These programs may serve as an example of innovation in this area.

To address these concerns, we await the final report of the National Academies' committee that is currently undertaking, under the auspices of the Committee on Science, Engineering, and Public Policy (COSEPUP), an update of the report *Enhancing the Postdoctoral Experience for Scientists and Engineers.* That report played a key role in elevating the visibility of issues in postdoctoral training and, as a consequence, many institutions created postdoctoral offices and undertook reforms. The update will provide new recommendations based on current data.

Federal Response

While institutions are increasing efficiency, the federal government must also increase its support of graduate education, particularly for students in doctoral programs. Since the current financial climate facing American research universities makes it increasingly difficult for institutions to reallocate funds for this purpose (e.g., from undergraduate tuition revenues or endowment income), maintaining graduate enrollments and program quality in critical areas will require a significant increase in federal support for graduate education. As shown in Table 5-8.1, the number of federally supported, full-time graduate students in science and engineering peaked at almost 84,000 and has since declined to just above 78,000. It is critical at this time that the federal government compensate for this decline by committing to 5,000 new fellowships or traineeships. By providing multiple-year support, the federal government can signal to prospective students that they will have sufficient support to pursue advanced degrees, thereby enhancing the ability of graduate programs to attract the most outstanding undergraduates.

A program to increase federal support for doctoral students would also benefit from a review of the proper "package" of support for doctoral students during their time in graduate school. (See Box 5-8.1 for defini-

TABLE **5-8.1** Percentage of Full-Time Science, Engineering, and Health Graduate Students by Source of Support, Federal Agencies in 1988, 1998, and 2008

	2003	2004	2005	2006	2007	2008
Number federally supported	81,761	83,816	83,723	83,962	81,859	78,464
Percent federally funded	20.6	20.8	20.6	20.0	18.7	17.5
Percent nonfederal support[±]	45.5	45.1	45.1	45.0	45.4	45.7
Percent no support	33.9	34.1	34.3	35.0	35.9	36.8

Source: National Science Foundation, National Center for Science and Engineering Statistics, Graduate Students and Postdoctorates in Science and Engineering, Fall 2008, Table 38. Available at: http://www.nsf.gov/statistics/nsf11311/content.cfm?pub_id=4072&id=2 (accessed, September 9, 2011).

BOX 5-8.1
Mechanisms of Support in Doctoral Education: Definitions

Fellowships are competitive awards, often from a national competition, obtained by students for financial support of their graduate studies. They are often portable and generally have few or no requirements for work, allowing the student to focus on doctoral study.

Traineeships are educational awards that an institution provides to students. Often funded by federal agencies, these awards typically support the student within an institutional program that includes activities and instruction to recipients beyond coursework and research.

Research assistantships are given to students whose assigned duties are devoted primarily to research, typically under the guidance of a principal investigator.

Teaching assistantships are given to students whose assigned duties are devoted primarily to teaching.

Other mechanisms of support include work-study programs, business or employer support, and support from foreign governments that is not in the form of a previously mentioned mechanism.

Self-support is derived from any loans obtained (including federal loans) or from personal or family contributions.

Source: National Science Board, Science and Engineering Indicators; National Science Foundation, National Center for Science and Engineering Statistics, Survey of Graduate Students and Postdoctorates in Science and Engineering (GSS). Available at: http://nsf.gov/statistics/srvygradpostdoc/surveys/srvygradpostdoc_2009.pdf (accessed, September 19, 2011).

---

tions of support mechanisms.) This review would examine the ways in which different mechanisms support both progress to the degree and experiences within the program. It may conclude that a shift in the support of graduate education away from research and teaching assistantships to multiple-year fellowships and traineeships is warranted, returning to a more balanced system of graduate student support similar to that of the 1960s. As seen in Figure 5-8.3, the shift from traineeships and fellowships to research assistantships began in the mid-1980s and increased rapidly in the early part of this century with the doubling of the NIH budget. In contrast to today's graduate student support dominated by teaching and research assistantships that have as primary objectives providing low-cost support for the teaching and research enterprise, fellowships and traineeships have a primary objective of graduate student education.

Arguments for maintaining the proportion of support provided by different mechanisms focus on research efficiency and student eligibility. The shift of graduate support from traineeships and fellowship in the 1960s to research grants was driven by the dramatic increase in research

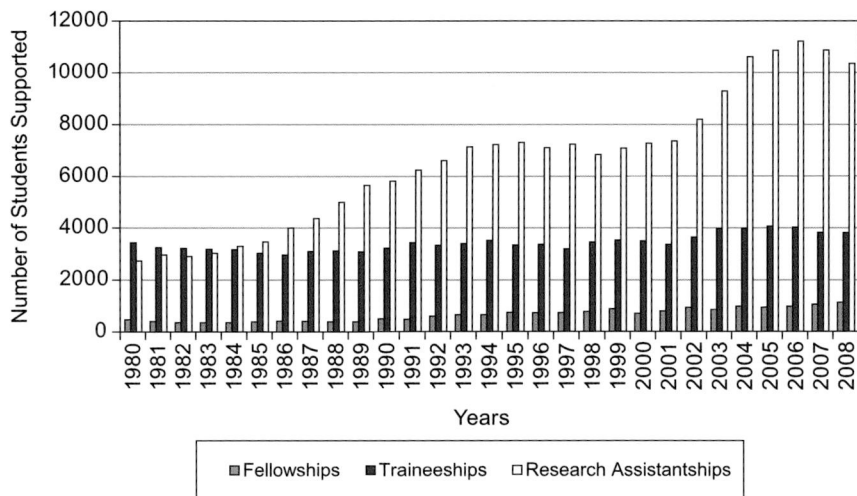

FIGURE 5-8.3 NIH graduate support, by mechanism, 1980 to 2008.
Source: National Research Council, Research Training in the Biomedical, Behavioral, and Clinical Research Sciences, Washington, DC: National Academies Press, 2011, Figure 3-16. Available at: http://books.nap.edu/catalog.php?record_id=12983 (accessed April 22, 2012).

grants and the need for individuals to do the research. The current system is very efficient at producing the research, but possibly at the expense of students who might seek research projects that suit their career goals. The shift to research assistantships also correlated with increases in non-U.S. citizens who are not eligible for traineeships that NIH restricts to U.S. citizens.

However, the downside to the current reliance on research assistantships in the natural sciences is that students on research grants are not necessarily provided with the kinds of programmatic commitment to success, alignment with 21st-century careers, and professional development activities (such as Responsible Conduct of Research) that are components of training grants. The NIH recognizes there may be problems with the current structure of support for graduate students and postdoctorates and has established a task force that will provide analysis of "the current composition and size of the workforce to understand the consequences of current funding policies on the research framework" to the Advisory Committee to the Director.

Alignment with Careers

The scientific workforce needs of our nation's employers have evolved over the last several decades with changes in the work of science-based industries, government agencies, and non-profits. This highly trained, scientific and technical workforce has matured to include both more doctoral-level researchers and more staff who have both deep training in science at the graduate level and critically important skills in project or process management, sales, regulation, and similar areas. Consequently, as shown in Figure 5-8.4, there has been an increase in new doctorates who work outside of academia and, in Figure 5-8.5, the number of master's programs focused on providing professional skills to students with advanced scientific training at the master's level. Yet most research uni-

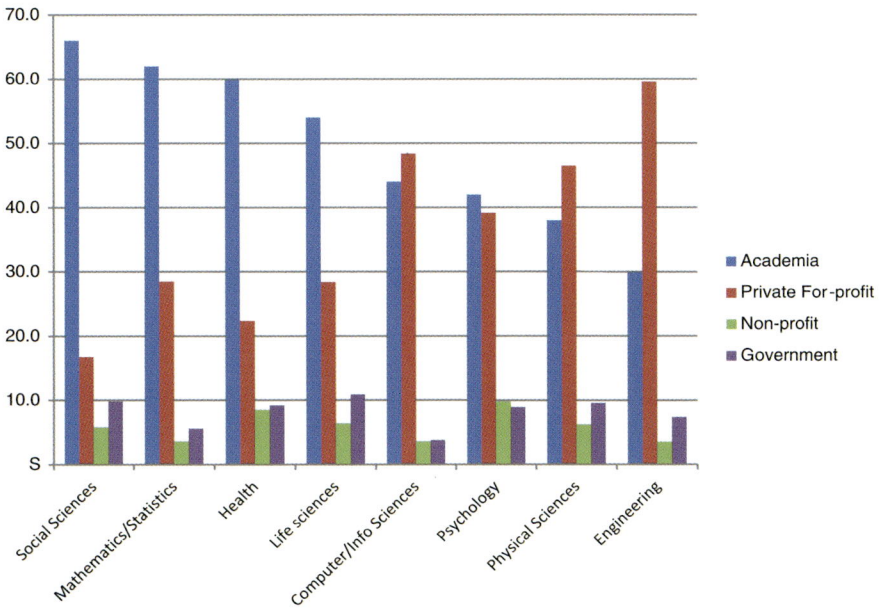

FIGURE 5-8.4 Work sector of Ph.D.'s, by Field, 2006.
Note: Academia includes 4-year and other educational institutions. Private, Non-Profit includes self-employed. Government includes federal, state, and local government.
Source: National Science Foundation, National Center for Science and Engineering Statistics, Survey of Doctorate Recipients, 2006, in Characteristics of Doctoral Scientists and Engineers in the United States, 2006, Table 12. Available at: http://www.nsf.gov/statistics/nsf09317/content.cfm?pub_id=3920&id=2 (accessed April 22, 2012).

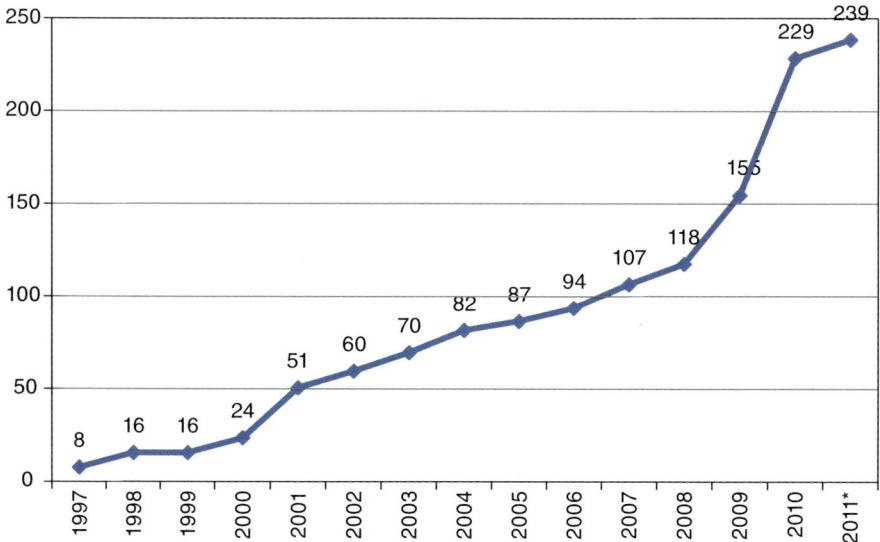

FIGURE 5-8.5 Total number of professional science master's programs in U.S. universities, 1997-2011.
Source: Council of Graduate Schools, Professional Science Master's Initiative.

versities have not adequately adapted to the new realities of these labor markets.

Doctoral Careers

First, job markets and careers for doctoral scientists and engineers have shifted since 1990, with more than 50 percent of new doctorates now working outside of academe. This shift has led to conversations about re-forming doctoral education to better position new Ph.D.'s for the careers they will have by providing more information about career options and by providing opportunities to acquire, in addition to the knowledge of one's field, skills that are useful for academic positions (teaching, grant writing, publishing, presentations) and positions in government, business, or non-profits (oral and written communication, project management, regulatory compliance, business ethics, and innovation.)[59]

---

[59] William G. Bowen and Neil L. Rudenstine, In Pursuit of the PhD. Princeton: Princeton University Press, 1992. National Academy of Sciences, National Academy of Engineering, and Institute of Medicine, Reshaping the Graduate Education of Scientists and Engineers. Washington, DC: National Academy Press, 1995. Chris M. Golde, At Cross Purposes: What the Experiences of Today's Doctoral Student Reveal about Doctoral Education. Released January 16, 2001. Available at: http://www.phd-survey.org/report (accessed September 19,

TABLE 5-8.2 Percent of Doctoral Programs that Track
the Career Outcomes of Their Graduates, by Field,
2006

Broad Field	Percent of Programs that Collect Student Data
Agricultural sciences	72.1
Biological and health sciences	77.9
Engineering	60.0
Physical and mathematical sciences	79.0
Social and behavioral sciences	82.7
Humanities	82.7

Source: National Research Council, A Data-Based Assessment of
Research-Doctorate Programs (Washington, DC: National Academies
Press, 2011). Available at: http://www.nap.edu/rdp/.

Few incentives, internal or external, motivate graduate programs
to align doctoral education with evolving employment opportunities,
whether regional or national in scope. In most universities, the size of doctoral programs is driven by a range of factors, including its research and
undergraduate teaching missions (and the need for university teaching
and research assistants), without much thought to labor market trends.
At a minimum, research universities must require their doctoral programs
to track their graduates. The NRC's Assessment of Research Doctorate
Programs, as shown in Table 5-8.2, found that between 60 and 83 percent
of doctoral programs were tracking their graduates as of 2006, though
many programs that only ask for first employment may have responded
affirmatively to this question. It is likely that the percentage of programs
and institutions that track students out to 10 years or more is much lower.
Tracking data are a crucial starting point for understanding both the careers of program graduates and how programs should be better aligned
to support those careers. With greater self-understanding, programs can
then also increase interaction with current and prospective employers
to better inform the content of their programs and develop internship

2011). Carnegie Foundation, Carnegie Initiative on the Doctorate. Available at: http://www.
carnegiefoundation.org/previous-work/professional-graduate-education (accessed, September 19, 2011). The Pew Charitable Trust, Re-envisioning the Ph.D. Available at: http://
depts.washington.edu/envision/index.html (accessed September 19, 2011). Woodrow
Wilson National Fellowship Foundation, The Responsive Ph.D. Available at: http://www.
woodrow.org/responsivephd/ (accessed September 19, 2011).

opportunities for students with employers in industry, government, and non-profits.

Master's Education

The shift has at the same time also led to important experiments in science master's education that have successfully trained students both more deeply in science and more broadly in the job skills they need in business, governments, and non-profits. Improving graduate education will help programs respond to the job market through new thinking about the curriculum and better communication between universities and employers. Addressing these concerns can also increase the appeal of graduate education to U.S. students who currently may be turned off at present by uncertainties in the length of time and outcomes of graduate education.

At the master's level, the National Academies' report *Science Professionals: Master's Education for a Competitive World* argued that "strengthened master's education in the natural sciences will produce professionals who bring scientific knowledge and also anticipate, adapt, learn, and lead where and when needed in industry, government, and nonprofit organizations." Indeed, the report found that "exciting experiments in master's education over the last decade—the Master of Biosciences (MBS) program at the Keck Graduate Institute of Applied Life Sciences and the Professional Science Master's (PSM) initiative seeded by the Alfred P. Sloan Foundation—have shown that graduate education in these fields can prepare students for advanced science-based work in a way that is highly desired by employers."[60] These students become professionals with both scientific knowledge and workplace skills for the practical application of that knowledge—that is, a new kind of scientist with multidisciplinary skills and experiences." Graduates of PSM programs are in demand by banks, insurance and financial companies needing financial mathematicians; a maturing biotechnology industry needing middle managers with advanced scientific knowledge and broader business skills; computer services corporations that require technical employees with business and customer skills; and state and federal agencies needing science- and technology-savvy staff with interdisciplinary training.[61]

The national capacity for interdisciplinary, employer-focused professional science master's programs is likely far higher than at present. The number of PSM programs has now grown, from 1997 to 2011, to 239 nationwide. The America COMPETES Act of 2007 authorized the National

---

[60] National Research Council, Science Professionals: Master's Education for a Competitive World. Washington, DC: National Academies Press, 2008, p. 2.
[61] Ibid., p. 3.

Science Foundation to create a new program of grants to 4-year institutions for the creation or expansion of science master's programs and the American Recovery and Reinvestment Act (ARRA) of 2009 provided 1 year of appropriations for this program, which was able to fund 21 grants out of 214 applications. There is room for further effort.

Consequently, the Commission of the Future of Graduate Education in the United States, in its report *The Path Forward: The Future of Graduate Education in the United States*, recommended that "the federal government should authorize a new federal competitive grant program across agencies to build capacity at universities to inspire innovation in master's degree programs and responsiveness to workforce needs." The report suggests that "universities would propose innovative new master's programs or reinvigoration of existing programs, including professional master's programs." Furthermore, "each successful program would be required to demonstrate maintenance of enrollment, completion rates, and job placement outcomes, as well as ongoing involvement by employers to ensure that programs produce graduates for local, state, regional, and national workforce needs. Programs will be required to secure at least two thirds of program funding from sources other than the federal government."[62]

Recommendation 9

Secure for the United States the full benefits of education for all Americans, including women and underrepresented minorities, in science, mathematics, engineering, and technology.

Actors and Actions—Implementing Recommendation 9:

- *Research universities*: Research universities should engage in efforts to improve education for all students at all levels in the United States by engaging in outreach to K–12 school districts and undertaking efforts to improve access and completion in their own institutions.

- *Research universities*: Research universities should assist efforts to improve teacher education and preparation for K–12 STEM education and improve undergraduate education, including persistence and completion in STEM.

- *Federal government, states, local school districts, industry, philanthropy, universities*: All stakeholders should take action—urgent, sus-

---

[62] Council of Graduate Schools and Education Testing Service, Commission on the Future of Graduate Education in the United States, The Path Forward: The Future of Graduate Education in the United States, April 2010. Available at: http://www.fgereport.org/rsc/pdf/CFGE_report.pdf (accessed February 12, 2011).

tained, comprehensive, intensive, and informed—to successfully increase the participation and success of women and underrepresented minorities across all academic and professional disciplines and, especially, in science, mathematics, and engineering education and careers.

Budget Implications

Increasing federal support for programs that enable the participation and success of women and underrepresented minorities in STEM disciplines has already been stated as a priority by both the America COMPETES Act and the Office of Science and Technology Policy. The committee supports the investments recommended for these purposes by these efforts.

Expected Outcomes

Our people are our greatest asset. Improving the educational success of our citizens at all levels improves our democracy, culture and society, social mobility, and both individual and national economic success. As career opportunities in science, technology, engineering, and math continue to expand at a rapid pace, recruiting more underrepresented minorities and women into STEM careers and ensuring that they remain in the pipeline is essential and strategic not only for meeting the workforce needs of an increasingly technological nation but also for obtaining the intellectual vitality and innovation necessary for economic prosperity, national security, and social well-being that such diversity brings.

Discussion

Research universities should become more fully engaged in the effort to improve the nation's educational systems and academic careers for all students and at all levels, but particularly in science, technology, engineering, and mathematics, and particularly for women and underrepresented minorities. Especially given the uncertainty in the future participation of international students and scholars in U.S. doctoral education, discussed in Recommendation 10, it is critical that we also address the need to develop a more robust domestic talent pool. For each of the topics discussed below, we cannot stress enough the importance of a commitment from institutional leadership to achieving these goals and to creating an environment conducive to achieving them. To engage faculty interest, clear goals must first be articulated at the top, so that there is a broad commitment by the research university—including, in particular, its research, graduate, and professional education programs (not just its school of education)—to addressing the challenges facing K–12 education, as well as continuing to give a high priority to undergraduate education, particularly in STEM disciplines.

Research Universities and Educational Reform

Research universities have an obligation to play a key role in reforming and improving education in the United States in general, a critical goal for our nation as we seek to bolster our global competitiveness, grow our economy, and improve the lives of individuals and families. To advance this effort, research universities and their faculty can pursue several avenues that will have broad benefits. First, they may expand their outreach programs to assist public schools, particularly those that have large numbers of disadvantaged students. Faculty can assist in the development of high-quality educational curricula. Universities may join with business and others to establish high-quality learning environments as a top national priority. Second, they must also help meet the national goals of increasing college degree attainment. Here they have much work to do. In most states, the share of undergraduate students at public research universities that come from these underrepresented groups (people of color, students from relatively lower-income families, first-generation students) is less than the share of undergraduate students at public institutions in general. Our research universities must turn this around.

In *Coming to Our Senses*, the College Board elaborated common-sense strategies for helping to accomplish goals for improving access and persistence rates, including the following:[63]

- *Clarify and simplify the admissions process* to encourage more first-generation students to apply.
- *Provide more need-based grant aid while simplifying and making financial aid processes more transparent* to minimize student debt, and at least keep pace with inflation; make financial aid processes more transparent and predictable; and provide institutions with incentives to enroll and graduate more low-income and first-generation students.
- *Keep college affordable* by controlling college costs, using available aid and resources wisely, and insisting that state governments meet their obligations for funding higher education.
- *Dramatically increase college completion rates* by reducing dropouts,

---

[63] College Board, Coming to Our Senses. Available at: http://advocacy.collegeboard.org/sites/default/files/coming-to-our-senses-college-board-2008.pdf (accessed September 19, 2011).

easing transfer processes, and using "data-based" approaches to improve completion rates at both 2- and 4-year institutions.

Research universities must participate in this effort, supporting these goals and strategies.

Research Universities and STEM Education

A recent PCAST report stressed the importance of STEM education: "The success of the United States in the 21st century—its wealth and welfare—will depend on the ideas and skills of its population. These have always been the nation's most important assets. As the world becomes increasingly technological, the value of these national assets will be determined in no small measure by the effectiveness of science, technology, engineering, and mathematics (STEM) education in the United States. STEM education will determine whether the United States will remain a leader among nations and whether we will be able to solve immense challenges in such areas as energy, health, environmental protection, and national security."[64]

Research universities have an important, perhaps even more critical, role to play here. *Rising Above the Gathering Storm*, for example, recommended that the nation "annually recruit 10,000 science and mathematics teachers by awarding 4-year scholarships and thereby educating 10 million minds." (Box 5-9.1 describes this recommendation in detail.) Research universities can be very instrumental in this vein by expanding their efforts to train qualified K–12 teachers in STEM disciplines by developing and replicating successful science teacher-training programs, such as UTeach, raising very substantially the quality of the teaching workforce. The Association of Public and Land-Grant Universities has developed the Science and Mathematics Teacher Imperative (SMTI) that also helps these institutions undertake this effort.[65] SMTI is driven by the commitments of 125 university presidents in 43 states whose institutions presently prepare more than 8,000 science and mathematics teachers annually, and there are hopes to link this to the new Undergraduate STEM Education Initiative just launched by the Association of American Universities, discussed below.

Research universities, along with our nation's liberal arts colleges that

---

[64] President's Council of Advisors on Science and Technology, Prepare and Inspire: K–12 Education in Science, Technology, Engineering, and Mathematics (STEM) for America's Future. Available at: http://www.whitehouse.gov/sites/default/files/microsites/ostp/pcast-stemed-report.pdf (accessed September 19, 2011).

[65] See http://www.aplu.org/smti (accessed September 19, 2011).

BOX 5-9.1
Gathering Storm Recommendation:
"10,000 Teachers, 10 Million Minds."

Annually recruit 10,000 science and mathematics teachers by awarding 4-year scholarships and thereby educating 10 million minds. Attract 10,000 of America's brightest students to the teaching profession every year, each of whom can have an impact on 1,000 students over the course of their careers. The program would award competitive 4-year scholarships for students to obtain bachelor's degrees in the physical or life sciences, engineering, or mathematics with concurrent certification as K–12 science and mathematics teachers. The merit-based scholarships would provide up to $20,000 a year for 4 years for qualified educational expenses, including tuition and fees, and require a commitment to 5 years of service in public K–12 schools. A $10,000 annual bonus would go to participating teachers in underserved schools in inner cities and rural areas. To provide the highest-quality education for undergraduates who want to become teachers, it would be important to award matching grants, on a one-to-one basis, of $1 million a year for up to 5 years, to as many as 100 universities and colleges to encourage them to establish integrated 4-year undergraduate programs leading to bachelor's degrees in the physical and life sciences, mathematics, computer sciences, or engineering *with teacher certification*. The models for this action are the UTeach and California Teach program.

Source: National Academy of Sciences, National Academy of Engineering, and Institute of Medicine, Rising Above the Gathering Storm: Energizing and Employing America for a Brighter Economic Future, 2007.

---

prepare a disproportionate share of those who go on to earn doctorates in science and engineering, must also continue to invest in and enhance undergraduate STEM education to ensure that students are prepared for the twenty-first-century economy, for study at the graduate level, and for the life-long learning process that will be needed to be successful after graduation. As recommended in the National Academies' *Expanding Underrepresented Minority Participation: America's Science and Technology Talent at the Crossroads*, there are many well-documented approaches to strengthening our STEM pipeline (for all students, including minorities), including summer science programs that engage high school students, undergraduate research experiences, improved academic mentoring, career counseling, peer study groups, and activities designed to promote social integration.[66] It is also important to address financial concerns that may pose a disincentive to study in STEM fields. These could be addressed through a range of

---

[66] National Academy of Sciences, National Academy of Engineering, and Institute of Medicine, Expanding Underrepresented Minority Participation: America's Science and Technology Talent at the Crossroads. Washington, DC: National Academies Press, 2010.

options, including the scholarship program recommended by *Rising Above the Gathering Storm* or other means, such as loan forgiveness for those who continue in STEM careers.

Reforming the first 2 years of undergraduate STEM education is critical. A new study by the President's Council of Advisors on Science and Technology recommends the following:

- Catalyze widespread adoption of empirically validated teaching practices;
- Advocate and provide support for replacing standard laboratory courses with discovery-based research courses;
- Launch a national experiment in postsecondary mathematics education to address the math preparation gap;
- Encourage partnerships among stakeholders (high school and college; 2-year and 4-year institutions; majority- and minority-serving institutions; academia and business) to diversify pathways to STEM careers; and
- Create a presidential council on STEM education with leadership from the academic and business communities to provide strategic leadership for transformative and sustainable change in STEM undergraduate education.[67]

As the first two items suggest, we need a strategic focus on reshaping first-year courses in the sciences. For far too long, they have been large lecture courses used to "weed out" students. The focus must be shifted to student learning, support, and encouragement.

We are also looking forward to a new 5-year initiative of the Association of American Universities to improve undergraduate STEM education. This initiative will develop an analytical framework for assessing and improving the quality of STEM teaching and learning, particularly in the first 2 years of college. It will establish a demonstration program at a subset of AAU institutions to implement the framework; explore mechanisms that institutions and departments can use to train, recognize, and reward faculty members who want to improve the quality of their STEM teaching; and work with federal agencies to develop mechanisms for rewarding and promoting these efforts as well.[68]

---

[67] President's Council of Advisors on Science and Technology, Engage to Excel: Producing One Million Additional College Graduates with Degrees in Science, Technology, Engineering, and Mathematics, February 2012. Available at: http://www.whitehouse.gov/sites/default/files/microsites/ostp/pcast-engage-to-excel-final_feb.pdf (accessed February 22, 2012).

[68] See http://www.aau.edu/policy/article.aspx?id=12588 (accessed September 19, 2011).

Women and Underrepresented Minorities in STEM

A recent study by the National Academy of Engineering recommended that "all participants and stakeholders in the science and engineering community (industry, government, institutions of higher education, professional societies, and others) should place a high priority on encouraging women and underrepresented minorities to pursue careers in STEM fields and on facilitating their participation and success, addressing field-specific issues evidenced by differential rates of completion by gender and race or ethnicity among STEM fields. Increasing diversity will not only increase the size and quality of our scientific and engineering workforce, but it will also introduce diverse ideas and experiences that can stimulate creative approaches to solving difficult challenges. Although this is likely to require a significant increase in investment from both public and private sources, increasing diversity of our scientific and engineering workforce is clearly vital to the future of the nation."[69]

First, research universities must work to increase the success of women in STEM by examining ways to increase their success as faculty. COSEPUP's *Beyond Bias and Barriers: Fulfilling the Potential of Women in Academic Science and Engineering* found that while there are increasing numbers of women entering the STEM pipeline, their loss from that pipeline was not due to lack of talent, but rather a consequence of unintentional biases and outmoded institutional structures that are hindering the access and advancement of women. [70] Noting that "the United States can no longer afford the underperformance of our academic institutions in attracting the best and brightest minds to the science and engineering enterprise," the report recommended "transforming institutional structures and procedures to eliminate gender bias" and the following actions:

- *Trustees, university presidents, and provosts* should provide clear leadership in changing the culture and structure of their institutions to recruit, retain, and promote women—including minority women—into faculty and leadership positions.
- *Deans and department chairs and their tenured faculty* should take responsibility for creating a productive environment and immediately implement programs and strategies shown to be successful in minimizing the effect of biases in recruiting, hiring, promotion, and tenure.
- *University leaders should work with their faculties and department*

---

[69] National Academy of Engineering, Engineering Research and America's Future: Meeting the Challenges of a Global Economy. Washington, DC: National Academies Press, 2005.

[70] National Academy of Sciences, National Academy of Engineering, and Institute of Medicine, Beyond Bias and Barriers: Fulfilling the Potential of Women in Academic Science and Engineering. Washington, DC: National Academies Press, 2007.

chairs to examine evaluation practices to focus on the quality of contributions and their impact.

- *Professional societies and higher education organizations* have a responsibility to play a leading role in promoting equal treatment of women and men and to demonstrate a commitment to it in their practices.

- *Federal funding agencies and foundations* should ensure that their practices—including rules and regulations—support the full participation of women and do not reinforce a culture that fundamentally discriminates against women.

- *Federal agencies* should lay out clear guidelines, leverage their resources, and rigorously enforce existing laws to increase the science and engineering talent developed in this country.

Of particular importance in driving cultural changes, research universities should conduct regular audits of institutional culture and practices regarding gender in the faculty so that issues can be brought to light and acted upon. The report provides a model for doing so.

More recently, the National Academies' *Gender Differences at Critical Transitions in the Careers of Science, Engineering, and Mathematics Faculty* found that while there has been some improvement for women at key career transition points at research universities, underrepresentation of women continues (see Figure 5-9.1) and important actions remain to be undertaken. Importantly, and in response to the kinds of audits recommended in *Beyond Bias and Barriers*, some research universities have made progress in hiring and advancing women. *Gender Differences*, through surveys of departments and faculty of research universities, found that women who applied for STEM faculty positions were at least as likely as men to be hired. The report also found that women who came up for tenure review were also at least as likely as their male counterparts to be granted tenure. This is good news, to be sure, but it does not free research universities, their leadership, and programs of responsibility. Two key areas that all of these actors must continue to act on are (1) recruitment, so that the numbers of women in the hiring pool can be increased, and (2) retention, so that the numbers of women who eventually do come up for tenure review also grow and begin to match the overall numbers of women who are coming up in the pipeline.[71]

As we cannot detail here all that must be undertaken to increase the success of women in STEM, we strongly recommend key actors pay care-

---

[71] National Research Council, Gender Differences at Critical Transitions in the Careers of Science, Engineering, and Mathematics Faculty. Washington, DC: National Academies Press, 2010.

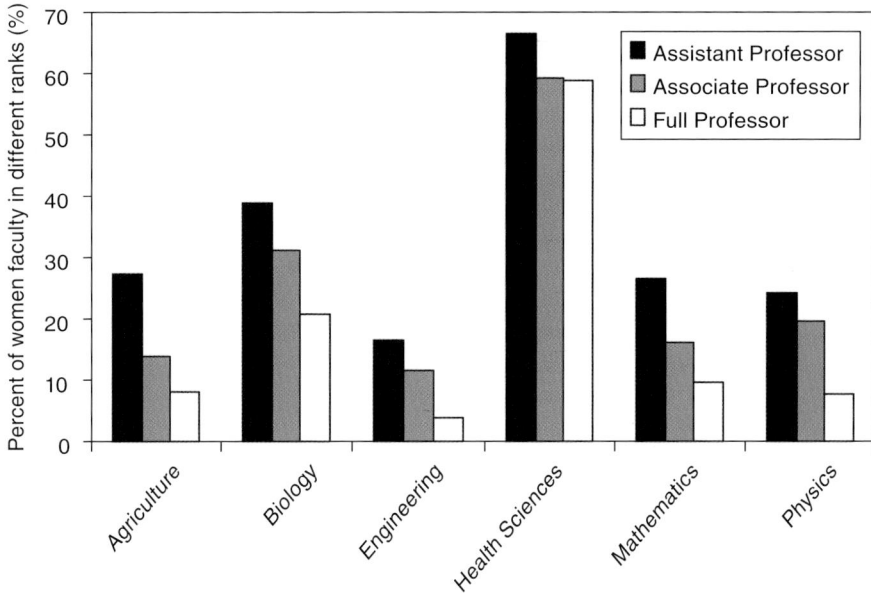

FIGURE 5-9.1 Representation of women in faculty positions at Research I institutions by rank and field in 2003.
Source: National Research Council. Gender Differences at Critical Transitions in the Careers of Science, Engineering, and Mathematics Faculty. Washington, DC: National Academies Press, 2010. Table S-1.

ful attention to the detailed actions provided in the important reports discussed on how to achieve these broad goals.

Research universities also have, along with a range of other actors, a strong role to play in increasing the participation and success of underrepresented minorities in STEM. While African Americans, Hispanics, and Native Americans comprise 27 percent of the U.S. population, they represent just 9 percent of the college-educated U.S. science and engineering workforce. And what makes this especially worrisome, the groups that are most underrepresented in science and engineering are the fastest-growing groups in the country. As seen in Figure 5-9.2, these groups will comprise about 45 percent of the U.S. population.

The National Academies' *Expanding Underrepresented Minority Participation* argues that underrepresentation of this magnitude is due to increasing underproduction of underrepresented minority scientists and engineers at every level. This report notes that in 2007, as shown in Figure 5-9.3, "underrepresented minorities comprised 38.8 percent of K–12 public enrollment, 33.2 percent of the U.S college age population, 26.2

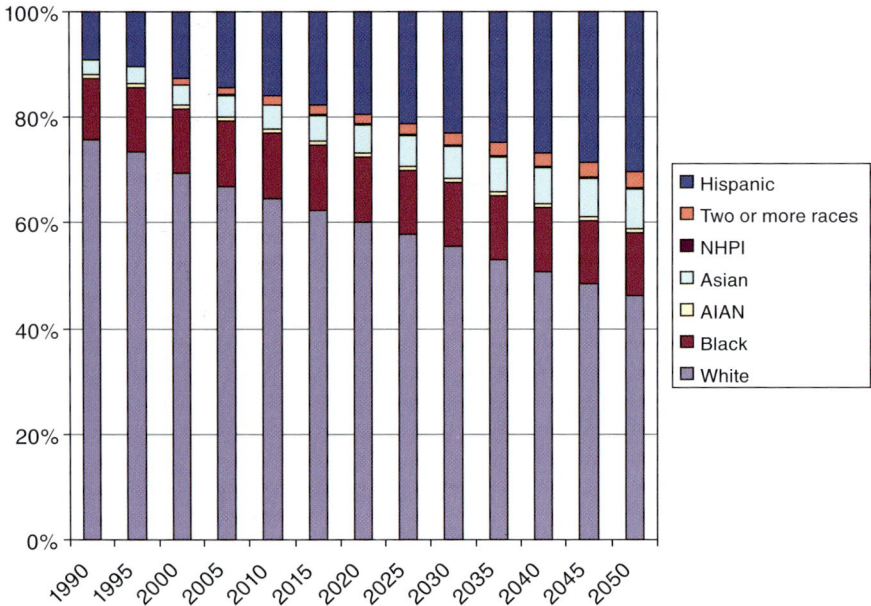

FIGURE 5-9.2 U.S. population by race/ethnicity, 1990-2050 (2010-2050 projected)
Source: United States Census Bureau.

percent of undergraduate enrollment, and 17.7 percent of those earning science and engineering bachelor's degrees. In graduate school, underrepresented minorities comprise 17.7 percent of overall enrollment, but are awarded just 14.6 percent of S&E master's degrees and a miniscule 5.4 percent of S&E doctorates."[72]

Expanding Underrepresented Minority Participation examines how students become scientists and engineers and the problems of underrepresentation across the entire educational pathway from preschool to graduate school. Based on this assessment, the report outlined six principles for action: [73]

1. The problem is *urgent* and will continue to be for the foreseeable future.
2. A successful national effort to address underrepresented minority participation and success in STEM will be *sustained*.
3. The potential for losing students along all segments of the path-

---

[72] National Academy of Sciences et al., Expanding Underrepresented Minority Participation, p. 38.
[73] Ibid., pp. 7-8.

way from preschool through graduate school necessitates a *comprehensive* approach that focuses on all segments of the pathway, all stakeholders, and the potential of all programs, targeted or nontargeted.

4. Students who have not had the same level of exposure to STEM and to postsecondary education require more *intensive* efforts at each level to provide adequate preparation, financial support, mentoring, social integration, and professional development.

5. A *coordinated* approach to existing federal STEM programs can leverage resources while supporting programs tailored to the specific mis-

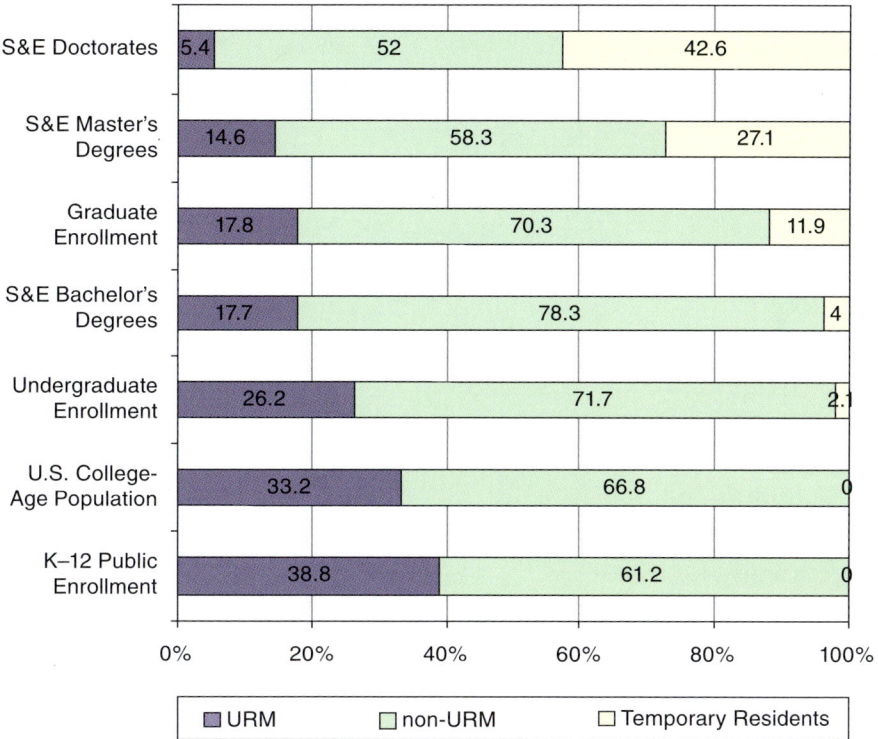

FIGURE 5-9.3 Enrollment and degrees, by educational level, race/ethnicity, and citizenship, 2007.
Sources: U.S Department of Education, National Center for Education Statistics, Digest of Education Statistics, 2008, Table 41; National Science Foundation, National Center for Science and Engineering Statistics, Women, Minorities, and Persons with Disabilities, Tables A-2, C-6, E-3, and F-11; National Science Foundation, National Center for Science and Engineering Statistics, Science and Engineering Degrees, 1966-2006, Table 3.

sions, histories, cultures, student populations, and geographic locations of institutions with demonstrated success.

6. Evaluation of STEM programs and increased research on the many dimensions of underrepresented minorities' experience in STEM help ensure that programs are well *informed*, well designed, and successful.

Box 5-9.2 outlines the six broad recommendations from the report that address important issues across the educational pathway of laying an academic foundation in reading and arithmetic, preparation in science and mathematics, motivation for STEM education careers, access to and affordability of higher education, and academic and social integration. We strongly recommend that K–12 and higher education institutions as well as other actors pay careful attention to the detailed actions provided in this significant report on how to achieve these broad recommendations.

As a priority for the short term, the report recommended the nation

---

BOX 5-9.2
Broad Recommendations Across STEM Educational Pathways
Outlined in *Expanding Underrepresented Minority Participation*

1. *Pre-School through Grade 3 Education:* Prepare America's children for school through pre-school and early education programs that develop reading readiness, provide early mathematics skills, and introduce concepts of creativity and discovery.

2. *K–12 Mathematics and Science:* Increase America's talent pool by vastly improving K–12 mathematics and science education for underrepresented minorities.

3. *K–12 Teacher Preparation and Retention:* Improve K–12 mathematics and science education for underrepresented minorities overall by improving the preparedness of those who teach them those subjects.

4. *Access and Motivation:* Improve access to all post-secondary education and technical training and increase underrepresented minority student awareness of and motivation for STEM education and careers through improved information, counseling, and outreach.

5. *Affordability:* Develop America's advanced STEM workforce by providing adequate financial support to underrepresented minority students in undergraduate and graduate STEM education.

6. *Academic and Social Support:* Take coordinated action to transform the nation's higher education institutions to increase inclusion of and college completion and success in STEM education for underrepresented minorities.

Source: National Academy of Sciences, National Academy of Engineering, and Institute of Medicine, Expanding Underrepresented Minority Participation: America's Science and Technology Talent at the Crossroads (Washington, DC: National Academies Press, 2011).

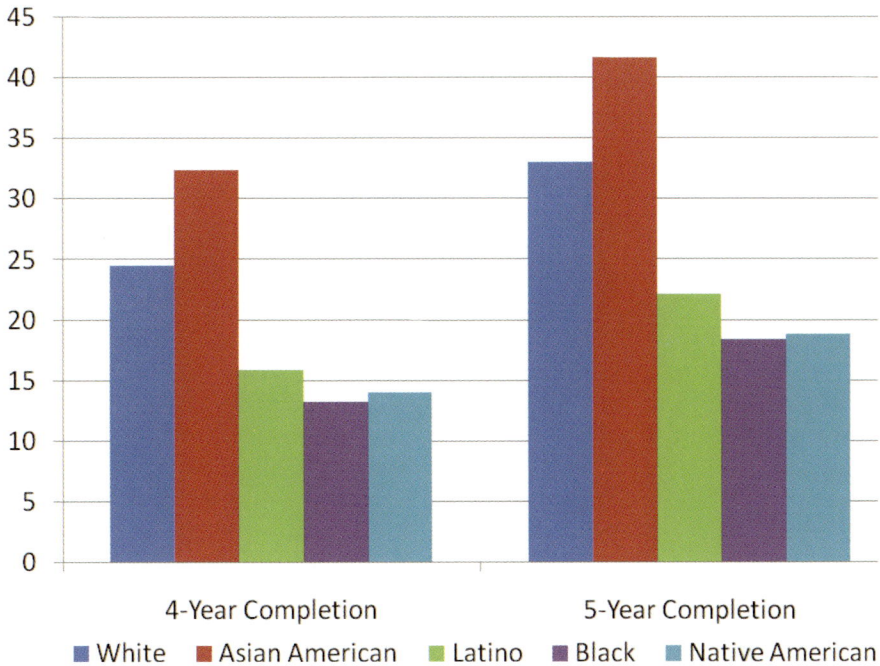

FIGURE 5-9.4 Percentage of 2004 freshmen at 4-year institutions who aspire to STEM majors who then completed STEM degrees in 4 and 5 years, by race/ethnicity.
Source: University of California Los Angeles, Higher Education Research Institute, Degrees of Success: Bachelor's Degree Completion Rates among Initial STEM Majors, January 2010. Available at: http://www.heri.ucla.edu/nih/downloads/2010%20-%20Hurtado,%20Eagan,%20Chang%20-%20Degrees%20of%20Success.pdf (accessed April 22, 2012).

focus on undergraduate completion in STEM. Citing new data from the Higher Education Research Institute at UCLA, displayed in Figure 5-9.4, the report argues that the nation needs to take action to address significantly lower 4- and 5-year completion rates in STEM of underrepresented minorities relative to those of whites and Asian Americans. Since underrepresented minorities who matriculate at 4-year institutions aspire to a STEM degree as their peers, these lower completion rates represent both a challenge and an opportunity if we can implement actions that we know from experience work in sustaining the persistence and completion of underrepresented students.

Expanding Underrepresented Minority Participation, therefore, recommended policies and programs that seek to increase undergraduate retention and completion of underrepresented minorities in STEM through strong academic, social, and financial support. It strongly recommends financial support from the federal government for underrepresented minorities that allows them to focus on and succeed in STEM by joining it to programs that simultaneously integrate academic, social, and professional development. It also recommends a federal program modeled on the NSF's ADVANCE Program that would fund efforts to change institutional cultures in colleges and universities so that they are more supportive of underrepresented minorities.

The report concludes by arguing that all of the nation's higher education institutions—including research universities—must play a role in implementing this priority action. It argued that while diversity of institutions is an asset, "currently, only a small number of institutions" are playing the role that all must play. It notes that these institutions "are diverse and can be found among all institutional types and categories; they are successful because they are doing something special to support the retention and completion of underrepresented minority undergraduates in the natural sciences and engineering. Their actions can be replicated and when they are, with a focus on both numbers and quality, it will pay off significantly."[74] The report identifies the importance of leadership in creating a positive institutional environment for minority integration and success; practical steps that can be taken to increase the completion of minorities (making student success a priority, tracking student achievement, identifying choke points such as course availability, and improving course transfer); key elements for successful program development (resources and sustainability, coordination and integration, focus on the pipeline and transition points, program design execution, and evaluation); and proven, intensive interventions for underrepresented minorities in STEM (summer programs, research experiences, professional development activities, academic support and social integration, and mentoring).

Recommendation 10

Ensure that the United States will continue to benefit strongly from the participation of international students and scholars in our research enterprise.

Actors and Actions—Implementing Recommendation 10:

- *Federal government*: Federal agencies should ensure that visa processing for international students and scholars who wish to study or

---

[74] Ibid., p. 8.

conduct research in the United States is as efficient and effective as possible, consistent also with homeland security considerations.

• *Federal government*: As we benefit from the contributions of highly skilled, foreign-born researchers, the federal government should also streamline the processes for non-U.S. doctoral researchers to obtain permanent residency or U.S. citizenship in order to ensure that a high proportion remain in the United States. The United States should consider taking the strong step of granting residency (a Green Card) to each non-U.S. citizen who earns a doctorate in an area of national need from an accredited research university. The Department of Homeland Security should set the criteria for and make selections of areas of national need and of the set of accredited institutions in cooperation with the National Science Foundation and the National Institutes of Health.

• *Federal government*: Engage in the proactive recruitment of international students and scholars.

Budget Implications

There is no additional cost.

Expected Outcomes

The United States has benefited significantly over the last half-century and more from highly talented individuals who have come to the United States from abroad to study or conduct research. Today, there is increasing competition for these individuals as students or researchers both in general and from their home countries. It is in the interest of the United States to attract and keep individuals who will create new knowledge and/or convert it to new products, industries, and jobs in the United States.

Discussion

The federal government should also strongly encourage the continued study and work of international graduate students and postdoctoral scholars in U.S. science and engineering through improvements in visa, residency, and citizenship processes. As James Duderstadt has noted, "Aging populations, out-migration, and shrinking workforces are seriously challenging the productivity of developed economies throughout Europe and Asia. Yet, here the United States stands apart because of another important demographic trend: immigration. As it has been so many times in its past, America is once again becoming a highly diverse nation of immigrants, benefiting immensely from their energy, talents, and hope."[75] In fact, today, one-quarter or more of new high-tech companies launched in the United States are founded by immigrants.[76] Attracting such talent to the United States is particularly important in knowledge-intensive, high-skill areas such as science and technology. Here, American research universities are extraordinary assets, since the world-class quality of their programs attract the best and brightest from around the world as students and faculty. The attractiveness of U.S. research universities for non-U.S. doctoral students and researchers is still a relative strength of American research universities. As seen in Figure 5-10.1, temporary residents earn a significant percentage of doctorates from U.S. institutions in key fields, including 27 percent in the life sciences, 42 percent in the physical sciences, and 55 percent in engineering. Moreover, this has been a significant benefit to U.S. research universities and, by extension, to the United States generally, as we have often drawn the very best students from overseas. These highly trained individuals are the best affirmation of U.S. academic leadership, and many of them are the sparks for continued domestic innovation and economic growth in our highly competitive global community.

However, trends can reverse. In the late 1990s, doctoral students from Taiwan and South Korea, the leading countries of origin, peaked both in number and in the percentage that stayed in the United States following degree receipt. That is, fewer came and of those who did, an increasing proportion returned home due to increases in opportunities there. They were replaced by India and China as the leading countries of origin.[77] As the growing strength of Ph.D. programs, research opportunities, and

---

[75] James J. Duderstadt, Higher Education in the 21st Century: Global Imperatives, Regional Challenges, National Responsibilities, and Emerging Opportunities, September 1, 2007. Available at: http://milproj.ummu.umich.edu/pdfs/2008/Glion%20VI%20 Globalization.pdf (accessed March 22, 2012).

[76] Vivek Wadhwa, AnnaLee Saxenian, Ben Rissing, and Gary Gereffi, America's new immigrant entrepreneurs: Part I (January 4, 2007). *Duke Science, Technology & Innovation Paper No. 23*. Available at: SSRN: http://ssrn.com/abstract=990152. This report found that 25.3 percent of the engineering and technology companies started in the United States from 1995 to 2005 had at least one foreign-born founder. *The "New American" Fortune 500, A Report by the Partnership for a New American Economy*, June 2011, available at: http://www. renewoureconomy.org/2011_06_15_1, found that close to "20 percent of the newest Fortune 500 companies—those founded over the 25-year period between 1985 and 2010—have an immigrant founder." *American Made: The Impact of Immigrant Entrepreneurs and Professionals on U.S. Competitiveness*, A joint study by National Venture Capital Association, Stuart Anderson (National Foundation for American Policy), and Michaela Platzer (Content First, LLC) (available at : http://www.nvca.org/index.php?option=com_content&view=article&id=25 4&Itemid=103), found that "40 percent of U.S. publicly traded venture-backed companies operating in high-technology manufacturing today [2005] were started by immigrants."

[77] Peter H. Henderson et al., Doctorate Recipients from United States Universities: Summary Report 1995. Washington, DC: National Academy Press, 1996.

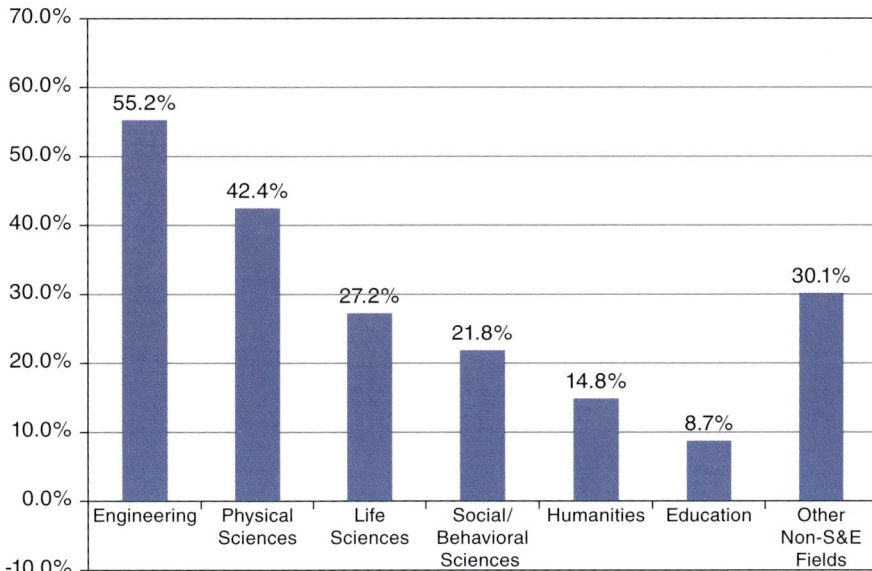

FIGURE 5-10.1 Doctorate awards to temporary visa holder by major field of study, 2009.
Source: National Science Foundation, National Center for Science and Engineering Statistics, Doctorate Recipients from U.S. Universities, 2009, (NSF 11-306). Arlington, VA: National Science Foundation, December 2011. Table 20. Available at: http://www.nsf.gov/statistics/nsf11306/ (accessed December 10, 2011).

incentives increase in India and China over the next decade, will future trends for their students follow the pattern we have seen for South Korea and China? How long will it take to see this trend play out? Recent trends in the number of international graduate student applications, admissions, and enrollment can be seen in Figure 5-10.2, and the number of doctorates awarded to non-U.S. students on temporary visas can be seen in Figure 5-10.3. These trends show significant oscillation and uncertainty about future directions.

The United States should make enhancements to immigration policy that would encourage talented international graduates from programs in science and engineering to remain in the United States and allow the country to benefit from the investment in their graduate education. *Rising Above the Gathering Storm* addressed this issue head-on by arguing for improvements in visa processing for international students and scholars; providing a 1-year automatic visa extension to international students who receive doctorates or the equivalent in science, technology, engineering, mathematics, or other fields of national need at qualified U.S. institutions

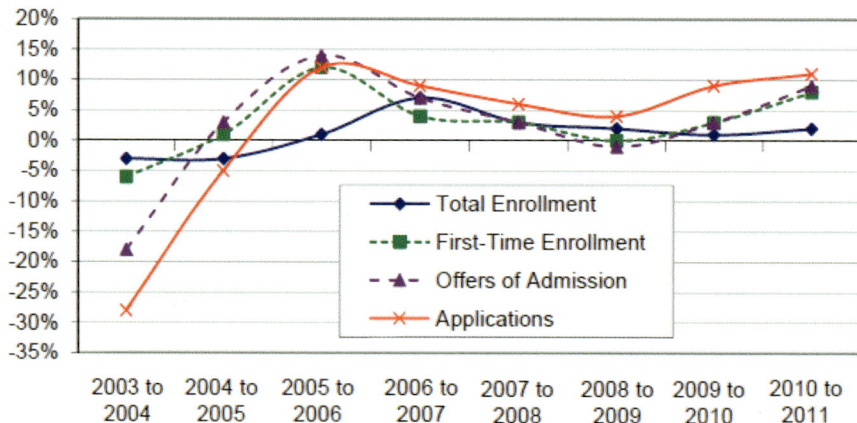

FIGURE 5-10.2 Year-to-year percentage change in international student participation in U.S. graduate education, 2003 to 2004 through 2009 to 2010.
Source: Council of Graduate Schools, Findings from the 2011 CGS International Graduate Admissions Survey, Phases III: Final Offers of Admission and Enrollment, November 2011. Available at: http://www.cgsnet.org/ckfinder/userfiles/files/R_IntlEnrl11_III.pdf (accessed April 22, 2012).

to remain in the United States to seek employment; instituting a new skills-based, preferential immigration option; and reforming the system of "deemed exports" (see Box 5-10.1).

Yet current immigration policies continue to seriously constrain the valuable flow of international talent so critical to the economic prosperity of our nation.

- The process of obtaining most classes of temporary visas needed to come to the United States contains costs, delays, and uncertainties, though this has improved since *Rising Above the Gathering Storm* was published.
- There are application fees and separate wait times for obtaining an interview and a determination. Around one-quarter of those who apply for student visas are rejected. While this rate is believed to be much lower for accepted applicants to research universities, it is still reported as an issue. While some rejections and delays are due to security concern, most are because the student was unable to prove that they have no intent to stay in the United States.
- An increasing number of international conferences have been placed and held outside of the United States to avoid visa problems. The

need to recruit internationally and to have frequent visits from foreign researchers has also made this a factor in the placement of some research laboratories.

- Stories of faculty and students being stranded abroad with visa problems, whether common or rare, become oft-repeated horror stories that affect decisions of others to come to the United States.
- Restrictions on what research may be undertaken by foreign students and scholars in the United States affect both decisions to come to the United States and decisions whether to stay—this has improved since publication of *Rising Above the Gathering Storm*, but restrictions remain.
- Foreign researchers are sometimes excluded from a research activity due to rules, or uncertainty about the rules, that pertain to sensitive areas, restricted exports, or the terms of a specific research grant.
- While allowed to work as research assistants on federal grants,

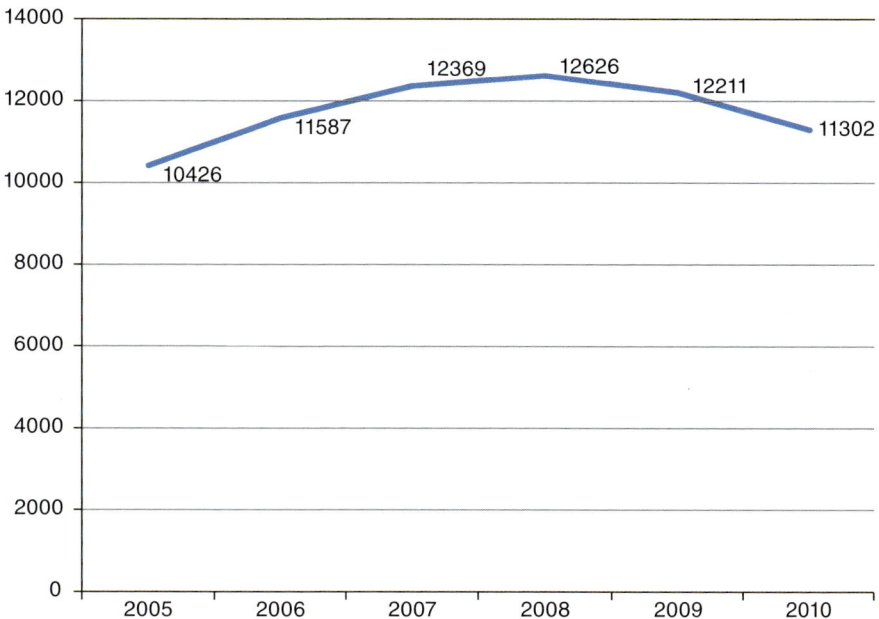

FIGURE 5-10.3 Science and engineering doctorates awarded by U.S. institutions to non-U.S. citizens on temporary visas.
Source: National Science Foundation, National Center for Science and Engineering Statistics, Numbers of Doctorates Awarded in the United States Declined in 2010 (NSF 12-303), November 2011. Available at: http://www.nsf.gov/statistics/infbrief/nsf12303/ (accessed December 10, 2011).

BOX 5-10.1
Rising Above the Gathering Storm,
Recommendations on Immigration

Action C-4: Continue to improve visa processing for international students and scholars to provide less complex procedures and continue to make improvements on such issues as visa categories and duration, travel for scientific meetings, the technology alert list, reciprocity agreements, and changes in status.

Action C-5: Provide a 1-year automatic visa extension to international students who receive doctorates or the equivalent in science, technology, engineering, mathematics, or other fields of national need at qualified U.S. institutions to remain in the United States to seek employment. If these students are offered jobs by U.S.-based employers and pass a security screening test, they should be provided automatic work permits and expedited residence status. If students are unable to obtain employment within 1 year, their visas would expire.

Action C-6: Institute a new skills-based, preferential immigration option. Doctoral-level education and science and engineering skills would substantially raise an applicant's chances and priority in obtaining U.S. citizenship. In the interim, the number of H-1B visas should be increased by 10,000, and the additional visas should be available for industry to hire science and engineering applicants with doctorates from U.S. universities.

Action C-7: Reform the current system of "deemed exports." The new system should provide international students and researchers engaged in fundamental research in the United States with access to information and research equipment in U.S. industrial, academic, and national laboratories comparable with the access provided to U.S. citizens and permanent residents in a similar status. It would, of course, exclude information and facilities restricted under national-security regulations. In addition, the effect of deemed-exports regulations on the education and fundamental research work of international students and scholars should be limited by removing from the deemed-exports technology list all technology items (information and equipment) that are available for purchase on the overseas open market from foreign or U.S. companies or that have manuals that are available in the public domain, in libraries, over the Internet, or from manufacturers.

Source: National Academy of Sciences, National Academy of Engineering, and Institute of Medicine. 2007. Rising Above the Gathering Storm: Energizing and Employing America for a Brighter Economic Future.

---

foreign students are not usually eligible for federal fellowships and traineeships.

•   Many job opportunities after graduation are restricted to U.S. citizens. Application for U.S. citizenship usually requires 5 years after receiving a Green Card. Time as a student or with a temporary work visa does not count.

Put in the simplest of terms, the United States must address these issues both to ensure that we can capitalize on the flow of international students and scholars and to provide our nation with the talent we need as we make progress on our goals listed under Recommendation 9 in increasing the participation of women and underrepresented minorities in key fields. First, we must ensure that visa, residency, and citizenship processes are as efficient as possible. Second, we must reform the temporary work authorization visa process (H-1B visas). Third, we must, as a priority, be more proactive, both by recruiting students, postdoctorates, and scholars and by following the practice of other nations such as Canada in encouraging the immigration of international students by attaching a Green Card to every doctorate in science and engineering.

6
Conclusion

During past eras of challenge and change, our national leaders have acted decisively to create innovative partnerships to enable its universities to enhance American security and prosperity.

While engaged in the Civil War, Congress passed the Morrill Land-Grant Act of 1862 to forge a partnership between the federal government, the states, higher education, and industry aimed at creating universities capable of extending educational opportunities to the working class while conducting the applied research to enable American agriculture and industry to become world leaders. The results were the green revolution in agriculture that fed the world, an American manufacturing industry that became the economic engine of the twentieth century and the arsenal of democracy in two world wars, and an educated middle class that would transform the United States into the strongest nation on Earth.

In the next century, emerging from the Great Depression and World War II, Congress acted once again to strengthen this partnership by investing heavily in basic research and graduate education to build the world's finest research universities, capable of providing the steady stream of well-educated graduates and scientific and technological innovations central to our robust economy, our vibrant culture, our vital health enterprise, and our national security in a complex, competitive, and challenging world. This expanded research partnership enabled America to win the Cold War, put a man on the Moon, and develop new technologies such as computers, the Internet, Global Positioning Systems, and new medical procedures and drugs that have contributed immensely to national prosperity, security, and public health.

Today, our nation faces new challenges, a time of rapid and profound economic, social, and political transformation driven by the growth in knowledge and innovation. A decade into the 21st century, a resurgent America must stimulate its economy, address new threats, and position itself in a competitive world transformed by technology, global competitiveness, and geopolitical change. In this milieu, educated people, the knowledge they produce, and the innovation and entrepreneurial skills they possess, particularly in the fields of science and engineering, have become the keys to America's future.

It is essential as a nation to reaffirm and revitalize the unique partnership that has long existed among the nation's research universities, federal government, states, and business and industry. The actions recommended will require significant policy changes, productivity enhancement, and investments on the part of each member of the research partnership. Yet they also comprise a fair and balanced program that will generate significant returns to a stronger America.

Bibliography

Al Saud, King Abdullah Bin Abdulaziz. Message on the Creation of King Abdullah University of Science and Technology. Available at: http://www.kaust.edu.sa/about/kingsmessage.html.

America Creating Opportunities to Meaningfully Promote Excellence in Technology, Education, and Science Act, Public Law No. 110-69.

American Academy of Arts and Sciences. Advancing Research in Science and Engineering: Investing in Early-Career Scientists and High-Risk, High-Reward Research. Cambridge, MA: American Academy of Arts and Sciences, 2008. Available at: http://www.amacad.org/AriseFolder/ariseReport.pdf.

Anderson, Arthur. 1996. The Costs of Research: A Report to the Government-University-Industry Research Roundtable.

Association of American Universities. 2011. Recommendations to the National Research Council Committee on Research Universities, February 2.

Association of American Universities, Association of Public and Land-grant Universities, and Council on Government Relations. 2011. Regulatory and Financial Reform of Federal Research Policy Recommendations to the NRC Committee on Research Universities. January 21. Available at: http://www.aau.edu/policy/reports_presentations.aspx.

Azoulay, Pierre, Joshua S. Graff Zivin, and Gustavo Manso. 2001. Incentives and creativity: evidence from the academic life sciences, *The RAND Journal of Economics* 42(3):527-554 (September 1).

Boston Consulting Group and National Association of Manufacturers. 2009. International Innovation Index. Available at: http://www.bcg.com/media/pressrelease details.aspx?id=tcm:12-8040.

Bowen, William G., and Neil L. Rudenstine. 1992. In Pursuit of the PhD. Princeton: Princeton University Press.

Burton, Orville Vernon, and Simon Appleford. 2009. Cyberinfrastructure for the Humanities, Arts, and Social Sciences. Research Bulletin, Issue 1. Boulder, CO: EDUCAUSE Center for Applied Research. Available at: http://net.educause.edu/ir/library/pdf/ERB0901.pdf.

Bush, Vannevar. Science: The Endless Frontier : A Report to the President. 1945. Washington, DC: U.S. Government Printing Office. Available at http://www.nsf.gov/about/history/nsf50/vbush1945.jsp.

Cole, Jonathan. 2009. The Great American University: Its Rise to Preeminence, Its Indispensable National Role, and Why it Must be Protected. New York: Public Affairs.

Cole, Jonathan. 2010. Can American research universities remain the best in the world? The Chronicle of Higher Education, January 3.

College Board. 2008. Coming to Our Senses. Available at: http://advocacy.collegeboard.org/sites/default/files/coming-to-our-senses-college-board-2008.pdf.

Council of Graduate Schools. 2008. Ph.D. Completion and Attrition: Analysis of Baseline Program Data from the Ph.D. Completion Project. Washington, DC: Council of Graduate Schools.

Council of Graduate Schools. 2011. Findings from the 2011 CGS International Graduate Admissions Survey, Phases III: Final Offers of Admission and Enrollment. Washington, DC: Council of Graduate Schools, November. Available at: http://www.cgsnet.org/ckfinder/userfiles/files/R_IntlEnrl11_III.pdf.

Council of Graduate Schools and Education Testing Service, Commission on the Future of Graduate Education in the United States. 2010. The Path Forward: The Future of Graduate Education in the United States, April. Available at: http://www.fgereport.org/rsc/pdf/CFGE_report.pdf.

Courant, Paul N., James J. Duderstadt, and Edie N. Goldenberg. 2010. Needed: A national strategy to preserve public research universities. The Chronicle of Higher Education, January 3.

Desrochers, Donna M., and Jane V. Wellman. Trends in College Spending, 1999-2009, Where does the money come from? Where does it go? What does it buy? A report of the Delta Cost Project. Available at: http://www.deltacostproject.org/resources/pdf/Trends2011_Final_090711.pdf.

Duderstadt, James J. 2000. A University for the 21st Century. Ann Arbor, MI: The University of Michigan Press.

Duderstadt, James J. 2007. Higher Education in the 21st Century: Global Imperatives, Regional Challenges, National Responsibilities, and Emerging Opportunities. September 1. Available at: http://milproj.ummu.umich.edu/pdfs/2008/Glion%20VI%20Globalization.pdf.

Duderstadt, James J., and Farris W. Womack. 2003. The Future of the Public University in America: Beyond the Crossroads. Baltimore, MD: The Johns Hopkins University Press.

Ernst, Dieter. China's Innovation Policy is a Wake-Up Call for America. East-West Center, Analysis from the East-West Center, No. 100, May 2011. Available at: http://www.eastwestcenter.org/fileadmin/stored/pdfs/api100.pdf.

European Higher Education Area. Available at: http://www.ehea.info/.

Federal Demonstration Partnership. 2011. Payroll Certifications: A Proposed Alternative to Effort Reporting. January 3. Available at: http://sites.nationalacademies.org/PGA/fdp/PGA_055834.

Friedman, Thomas. 2006. The World is Flat: A Brief History of the Twenty-First Century, Release 2.0. New York: Farrar, Straus, and Giroux.

Gerald, Danette, and Kati Haycock. 2006. Engines of Inequality: Diminishing Equity in the Nation's Premier Public Universities. Washington, DC: The Education Trust. Available at: http://www.edtrust.org/sites/edtrust.org/files/publications/files/EnginesofInequality.pdf.

Golde, Chris M. 2001. At Cross Purposes: What the Experiences of Today's Doctoral Student Reveal about Doctoral Education. January 16. Available at: http://www.phd-survey.org/report.

Goldin, Claudia, and Lawrence F. Katz. 2008. The Race Between Education and Technology. Cambridge, MA: Harvard University Press.

Goldman, Charles A., Traci Williams, David M. Adamson, and Kathy Rosenblatt. Paying for University Research Facilities and Administration. Santa Monica, CA: RAND Corporation, 2000. Available at: http://www.rand.org/pubs/monograph_reports/MR1135-1.html.

Government Accountability Office. National Institutes of Health Extramural Research Grants: Oversight of Cost Reimbursements to Universities (GAO-07-294R). Washington, DC: GAO, January, 2007. Available at: http://www.gao.gov/new.items/d07294r.pdf.

Government Accountability Office. University Research: Policies for the Reimbursement of Indirect Costs Need to Be Updated (GAO-10-937). Washington, DC: GAO, September 2010. Available at: http://www.gao.gov/new.items/d10937.pdf.

Graham, Hugh Davis, and Nancy Diamond. 1997. The Rise of American Research Universities: Elites and Challengers in the Postwar Era. Baltimore: The Johns Hopkins University Press.

Green, Kenneth C., with Scott Jaschik and Doug Lederman. 2011. Presidential Perspectives: The 2011 Inside Higher Ed Survey of College and University Presidents. Inside Higher Ed. Available at: http://inpathwaysnet/presidentialperspective2011.pdf.

Henderson, Peter H., et al. 1996. Doctorate Recipients from United States Universities: Summary Report 1995. Washington, DC: National Academy Press.

Hey, Tony, Stewart Tansley, and Kristin Tolle. 2009. The Fourth Paradigm: Data-Intensive Scientific Discovery. Redmond, WA: Microsoft Research. Available at: http://research.microsoft.com/en-us/collaboration/fourthparadigm/.

Huiyao, Wang. China's National Talent Plan: Key Measures and Objectives. Brookings Institution: Available at: http://www.brookings.edu/~/media/Files/rc/papers/2010/1123_china_talent_wang/1123_china_talent_wang.pdf.

Information Technology and Innovation Foundation and European-American Business Council. The Atlantic Century II, July 2011. Available at: http://www.itif.org/files/2011-atlantic-century.pdf.

INSEAD. Global Innovation Index Report, 2009-2010. Available at http://www.management.se/2010/08/30global-innovation-index2009-2020-from-insead/.

Keller, Josh. 2010. Universities can save millions by cutting administrative waste, panelists say, The Chronicle of Higher Education, July 25.

Kerr, Clark. 2002. The Gold and the Blue: A Personal Memoir of the University of California, 1949-1967, Volume Two: Political Turmoil. Berkeley: University of California Press, p. 92.

Kiley, Kevin. 2011. Where universities can be cut, Inside Higher Ed, September 16, 2011.

National Academy of Engineering. 2005. Engineering Research and America's Future: Meeting the Challenges of a Global Economy. Washington, DC: National Academies Press.

National Academy of Engineering. Grand Challenges of Engineering. Available at: http://www.engineeringchallenges.org/.

National Academy of Sciences, National Academy of Engineering, Institute of Medicine. 1993. Science, Technology, and the Federal Government: National Goals for a New Era. Washington, DC: National Academy Press.

National Academy of Sciences, National Academy of Engineering, Institute of Medicine. 1995. Reshaping the Graduate Education of Scientists and Engineers. Washington, DC: National Academy Press.

National Academy of Sciences, National Academy of Engineering, Institute of Medicine. 2002. Observations on the President's Fiscal Year 2003 Federal Science and Technology Budget. Washington, DC: National Academies Press.

National Academy of Sciences, National Academy of Engineering, and Institute of Medicine. 2007. Beyond Bias and Barriers: Fulfilling the Potential of Women in Academic Science and Engineering. Washington, DC: National Academies Press.

National Academy of Sciences, National Academy of Engineering, and Institute of Medicine. 2007. Rising Above the Gathering Storm: Energizing and Employing America for a Brighter Economic Future. Washington, DC: National Academies Press.

National Academy of Sciences, National Academy of Engineering, and Institute of Medicine. 2010. Expanding Underrepresented Minority Participation: America's Science and Technology Talent at the Crossroads. Washington, DC: National Academies Press.

National Academy of Sciences, National Academy of Engineering, and Institute of Medicine, Members of the "Rising Above the Gathering Storm" Committee. 2010. Rising Above the Gathering Storm Revisited: Rapidly Approaching Category 5, Prepared for the Presidents of the National Academy of Sciences, National Academy of Engineering, and Institute of Medicine. Washington, DC: National Academies Press.

National Association of College and University Business Officers. Educational Endowments Earned Investment Returns Averaging 11.9% in FY 2010. Available at http://www.nacubo.org/Documents/research/2010NCSE_Full_Data_Press_Release_Final.pdf.

National Governors Association. Higher Education's Contribution to Economic Growth Strategies. Available at http://www.nga.org/cms/home/nga-center-for-best-practices/center-issues/page-ehsw-issues/col2-content/main-content-list/higher-educations-contribution-t.html.

National Institutes of Health. New Investigators Program: Pathway to Independence Award. Available at: http://grants.nih.gov/grants/new_investigators/QsandAs.htm#1586.

National Research Council. 1995. Allocating Federal Funds for Science and Technology. Washington, DC: National Academy Press.

National Research Council, 2008. Science Professionals: Master's Education for a Competitive World. Washington, DC: National Academies Press.

National Research Council. 2010. Gender Differences at Critical Transitions in the Careers of Science, Engineering, and Mathematics Faculty. Washington, DC: National Academies Press.

National Research Council. 2010. Steps Toward Large-Scale Data Integration in the Sciences: Summary of a Workshop. Washington, DC: National Academies Press.

National Research Council. 2010. The Dragon and the Elephant: Understanding the Development of Innovation Capacity in China and India. Washington, DC: National Academies Press.

National Research Council. 2011. A Data-Based Assessment of Research-Doctorate Programs. Washington, DC: National Academies Press. Available at: http://www.nap.edu/rdp/.

National Research Council. 2011. A Data-Based Assessment of Research-Doctorate Programs in the United States. Washington, DC: National Academies Press.

National Research Council. 2011. Managing University Intellectual Property in the Public Interest. Washington, DC: National Academies Press.

National Research Council. 2011. Measuring the Impacts of Federal Investments in Research: A Workshop Summary. Washington, DC: National Academies Press.

National Research Council. 2011. Research Training in the Biomedical, Behavioral, and Clinical Research Sciences. Washington, DC: National Academies Press.

National Research Council. 2011. Transforming Combustion Research Through Cyberinfrastructure. Washington, DC: National Academies Press.

National Science and Technology Council, Subcommittee on Social, Behavioral, and Economic Sciences. 2009. Social, Behavioral, and Economic Research in the Federal Context. January. Available at http://www.nsf.gov/sbe/prospectus_v10_3_17_09.pdf.

National Science Board. 2004. Science and Engineering Indicators. Two Volumes (volume 1, NSB 04-01; volume 2, NSB 04-01A). Arlington, VA: National Science Foundation, 2004.

National Science Board. 2009. Investing in the Future: NSF Cost Sharing Policies for a Robust Federal Research Enterprise (NSB0920). Arlington, VA: National Science Foundation. Available at: http://www.nsf.gov/pubs/2009/nsb0920/nsb0920.pdf.

National Science Board. 2010. Globalization of Science and Engineering: A Companion to Science and Engineering Indicators 2010. (NSB 10-03). Arlington, VA: National Science Foundation.

National Science Board. 2010. Science and Engineering Indicators. (NSB 10-01). Arlington, VA: National Science Foundation.

National Science Board. 2012. Science and Engineering Indicators. (NSB 12-01). Arlington, VA: National Science Foundation. Available at: http://www.nsf.gov/statistics/seind12/pdf/c08.pdf.

National Science Foundation. 2011. Advisory Committee on Cyberinfrastructure Task Force Reports. March. Available at: http://www.nsf.gov/od/oci/taskforces/index.jsp.

National Science Foundation. NSF Sensational 60. Available at: http://www.nsf.gov/about/history/sensational60.pdf.

National Science Foundation, National Center for Science and Engineering Statistics. Academic Research and Development Expenditures, Fiscal Year 2009. Available at: http://www.nsf.gov/statistics/nsf11313/content.cfm?pub_id=4065&id=2.

National Science Foundation, National Center for Science and Engineering Statistics. 2006. Characteristics of Doctoral Scientists and Engineers in the United States. Available at: http://www.nsf.gov/statistics/nsf09317/content.cfm?pub_id=3920&id=2.

National Science Foundation, National Center for Science and Engineering Statistics. 2009. Doctorate Recipients from U.S. Universities: Summary Report 2007-08 (NSF 10-309). Arlington, VA: National Science Foundation, December.

National Science Foundation, National Center for Science and Engineering Statistics. 2011. Doctorate Recipients from U.S. Universities, 2009 (NSF 11-306). Arlington, VA: National Science Foundation, December. Available at: http://www.nsf.gov/statistics/nsf11306/.

National Science Foundation, National Center for Science and Engineering Statistics. Graduate Students and Postdoctorates in Science and Engineering, Fall 2008. Available at: http://www.nsf.gov/statistics/nsf11311/content.cfm?pub_id=4072&id=2.

National Science Foundation, National Center for Science and Engineering Statistics. National Patterns of R&D Resources, 2008 Data Update. Available at: http://www.nsf.gov/statistics/nsf10314/content.cfm?pub_id=4000&id=2.

National Science Foundation, National Center for Science and Engineering Statistics. 2011. Numbers of Doctorates Awarded in the United States Declined in 2010 (NSF 12-303). November. Available at: http://www.nsf.gov/statistics/infbrief/nsf12303/.

National Science Foundation, National Center for Science and Engineering Statistics. Science and Engineering Degrees, 1966-2006. Available at: http://www.nsf.gov/statistics/nsf08321/.

National Science Foundation, National Center for Science and Engineering Statistics. Survey of Graduate Students and Postdoctorates in Science and Engineering. Available at: http://nsf.gov/statistics/srvygradpostdoc/surveys/srvygradpostdoc_2009.pdf.

National Science Foundation, National Center for Science and Engineering Statistics. Women, Minorities, and Persons with Disabilities in Science and Engineering (NSF11-309). Available at: http://www.nsf.gov/statistics/wmpd/.

National Venture Capital Association, Stuart Anderson (National Foundation for American Policy), and Michaela Platzer (Content First, LLC). American Made: The Impact of Immigrant Entrepreneurs and Professionals on U.S. Competitiveness. Available at: http://www.nvca.org/index.php?option=com_content&view=article&id=254&Itemid=103.

Obama, Barack. 2011. Executive Order 13563: Improving Regulation and Regulatory Review. January 18. Available at: http://www.gpo.gov/fdsys/pkg/FR-2011-01-21/pdf/2011-1385.pdf.

Office of Management and Budget. 2004. Circular A-21: Cost Principles for Educational Institutions. May 10. Available at: http://www.whitehouse.gov/omb/circulars_a021_2004.

Office of Science and Technology Policy. Analysis of Facilities and Administrative Costs at Universities. Washington, DC: July. 2000. Available at: http://clinton4.nara.gov/WH/EOP/OSTP/html/analysis_univ.html .

Organisation for Economic Cooperation and Development. 2011. OECD Science, Technology, and Industry Scoreboard 2011: Highlights. Available at: http://www.oecd.org/data oecd/63/32/48712591.pdf.

Partnership for a New American Economy. The "New American" Fortune 500, A Report by the Partnership for a New American Economy, June 2011. Available at: http://www.renewoureconomy.org/2011_06_15_1.

President's Council of Advisors on Science and Technology. Prepare and Inspire: K–12 Education in Science, Technology, Engineering, and Mathematics (STEM) for America's Future. September 2010. Available at: http://www.whitehouse.gov/sites/default/files/microsites/ostp/pcast-stemed-report.pdf.

President's Council of Advisors on Science and Technology. 2010. Report to the President on Accelerating the Pace of Change in Energy Technologies Through an Integrated Federal Energy Policy. November. Available at: http://www.whitehouse.gov/sites/default/files/microsites/ostp/pcast-energy-tech-report.pdf.

President's Council of Advisors on Science and Technology. 2012. Engage to Excel: Producing One Million Additional College Graduates with Degrees in Science, Technology, Engineering, and Mathematics. February. Available at: http://www.whitehouse.gov/sites/default/files/microsites/ostp/pcast-engage-to-excel-final_feb.pdf.

Shanghai Jiao Tong University. Academic Rankings of World Universities—2010. Available at: http://www.arwu.org/ARWU2010.jsp.

Sharer, Michael, and Timothy L. Faley. The strategic management of the technology transfer function—Aligning goals with strategies, objectives, and tactics, les Nouvelles, September 2008.

Singapore Government, Ministry of Education. 2010. International Academic Advisory Panel, press release, November 12. Available at: http://www.moe.gov.sg/media/press/2010/11/advisory-panel-endorses-continuing-investments-in-higher-education.php.

Solow, Robert M. 1957. Technical change and the aggregate production function. The Review of Economics and Statistics, 39(3):312-320(August).

State Higher Education Executive Officers. 2012. Commentary on FY 2012 state appropriations for higher education. January 23. Available at: http://grapevine.illinoisstate.edu/tables/FY12/SHEEO%20Commentary%20(2).pdf.

State Higher Education Executive Officers. State Higher Education Finance, FY 2010. Available at: http://www.sheeo.org/finance/shef_fy10.pdf.

Talman, William T. 2011. Letter from the President of the Federation of American Societies for Experimental Biology to Charles O. Holliday, Jr., Chair of the National Research Council Committee on Research Universities. March 14.

The Science Coalition. 2010. Sparking Economic Growth: How federally funded university research creates innovation, new companies, and jobs. April. Available at: www.sciencecoalition.org/successstories.

The White House. President Obama Signs America Invents Act, Overhauling the Patent System to Stimulate Economic Growth, and Announces New Steps to Help Entrepreneurs Create Jobs. September 16, 2011. Available at: http://www.whitehouse.gov/the-press-office/2011/09/16/president-obama-signs-america-invents-act-overhauling-patent-system-stim.

Umbach, Tripp. 2010. The Economic Impact of UAB: Current and Projected Economic, Employment, and Government Revenue Impacts. Final Executive Report. November 9.

U.S. Department of Commerce, Economic and Statistics Administration. Education Supports Racial and Ethnic Equality in STEM. ESA Issue Brief, No. 05-11, September 2011. Available at http://www.esa.doc.gov/sites/default/files/reports/documents/educationsupportsracialandethnicequalityinstem_0.pdf

U.S Department of Education, 2008. National Center for Education Statistics. Digest of Education Statistics.

University of California Los Angeles, Higher Education Research Institute. 2010. Degrees of Success: Bachelor's Degree Completion Rates among Initial STEM Majors. January. Available at: http://www.heri.ucla.edu/nih/downloads/2010%20-%20Hurtado,%20Eagan,%20Chang%20-%20Degrees%20of%20Success.pdf.

Vest, Charles M., Harvey V. Fineberg, and Cherry M. Murray. 2011. Remarks in "Making America More Competitive, Innovative, and Healthy," Bulletin of the American Academy of Arts and Sciences, Summer. Available at: http://amacad.org/publications/bulletin/summer 2011.pdf.

Wadhwa, Vivek, AnnaLee Saxenian, Ben Rissing, and Gary Gereffi. 2007. America's new immigrant entrepreneurs: Part I, Duke Science, Technology & Innovation Paper No. 23. January 4. Available at: http://ssrn.com/abstract=990152.

White House. 2011. A Strategy for American Innovation: Securing Our Economic Growth and Prosperity, February.

Wilensky, Joe. Update on budget crisis and "Reimagining Cornell" stresses that all options are on the table, Cornell University Chronicle Online, July 23, 2009.

Winters, L. Alan, and Shahid Yusuf, eds. 2007. Dancing with Giants: China, India, and the Global Economy. Washington, DC: The World Bank.

Appendixes

A

Letter of Request from Congress

Congress of the United States
Washington, DC 20515

June 22, 2009

Dr. Ralph J. Cicerone   Dr. Charles M. Vest
President   President
National Academy of Sciences   National Academy of Engineering
500 Fifth Street, NW   500 Fifth Street, NW
Washington, D.C. 20001   Washington, D.C. 20001

Dr. Harvey V. Fineberg
President
Institute of Medicine
500 Fifth Street, NW
Washington, D.C. 20001

Dear Dr. Cicerone, Dr. Vest, and Dr. Fineberg:

America's research universities are admired throughout the world, and they have contributed immeasurably to our social and economic well-being. Our universities, to an extent unparalleled in other countries, are our Nation's primary source of long-term scientific, engineering, and medical research. We are concerned that they are at risk.

We are writing to ask that the National Academy of Sciences, the National Academy of Engineering, and the Institute of Medicine assemble a distinguished group of individuals to assess the competitive position of American research universities, both public and private, and respond to the following question:

> What are the top ten actions that Congress, state governments, research
> universities, and others could take to assure the ability of the American
> research university to maintain the excellence in research and doctoral
> education needed to help the United States compete, prosper, and achieve
> national goals for health, energy, the environment, and security in the
> global community of the 21st century?

American research universities have been critical assets that have laid the groundwork—through research and doctoral education—for the development of many of the competitive advantages that make possible the high American standard of living. But today research universities are under stress, even as other countries are measurably improving the quality of their research institutions. We ask that your report assess the organizational, intellectual, and financial capacity of public and private American research universities relative to research universities internationally.

We believe that the Academies' report should include an assessment of the relationship, or lack of relationship, of our research universities with other parts of our national research enterprise, including the federally-funded National Laboratories and other federally funded research and development centers. We also believe that the report should take into account the collaborations between universities and privately funded corporate research laboratories and assess what contribution those relationships might make to the Nation's future. And while this report should not focus on the challenges of healthcare reform, this report should address the difficulties faced by medical schools and medical centers that are affiliated with research universities, and the relationships of both with the National Institutes of Health.

This request is a follow-up to the request that a bipartisan group of us made in 2005 when we asked the Academies to identify the key steps needed to ensure a science and technology enterprise that would enable the United States to compete in the global economy of the 21st century. The Academies responded to that request by assembling a distinguished panel, headed by Norman R. Augustine, that quickly produced a list of 20 recommendations along with strategies in the report, "Rising Above the Gathering Storm." Congress enacted and the President signed the "America COMPETES Act" in 2007, incorporating many of the Academies' recommendations and establishing a blueprint for maintaining America's competitive position.

Science and engineering in the last 60 years have fundamentally improved the lives of every person on this globe. The contributions of our research universities cannot be overstated. But many frontiers remain to be explored, and for our children and grandchildren's sake, we cannot let our constellation of universities dim. We are convinced that this report will provide essential guidance for the federal government, states and the universities themselves.

Sincerely,

Barbara Mikulski
United States Senate

Bart Gordon
U.S. House of Representatives

Lamar Alexander
United States Senate

Ralph Hall
U.S. House of Representatives

B
Committee Biographies

CHARLES O. "CHAD" HOLLIDAY [NAE] is former chairman and chief executive officer of DuPont. He became chief executive officer in 1998 and chairman. He started at DuPont in 1970 at DuPont's Old Hickory site after receiving a B.S. in industrial engineering from the University of Tennessee. He is a licensed professional engineer. Mr. Holliday is an elected member of the National Academy of Engineering, and he is past chairman of the Business Roundtable's Task Force for Environment, Technology, and Economy; the World Business Council for Sustainable Development; The Business Council; and the Society of Chemical Industry—American Section. Mr. Holliday serves on the board of directors of Deere & Co. and is chair of the board of directors of Catalyst. In addition, he is chairman emeritus of the Council on Competitiveness and is a founding member of the International Business Council. He is currently a member of the NRC Committee on America's Climate Choices and was a member of the Committee on Prospering in the Global Economy of the 21st Century which authored *Rising Above the Gathering Storm*.

PETER C. AGRE [NAS/IOM] is professor, Johns Hopkins Bloomberg School of Public Health, and director of the Johns Hopkins Malaria Research Institute. In 1970, Dr. Agre earned his bachelor's degree in chemistry from Augsburg College. He received his medical doctorate from Johns Hopkins in 1974. From 1975 to 1978 he completed his clinical training in internal medicine at Case Western University's Case Medical Center. In 1981, after post-graduate medical training and then a fellowship at the University of North Carolina at Chapel Hill, Dr. Agre returned to

Hopkins, where he progressed through the ranks of the departments of medicine and cell biology. In 1993, he was recruited by then-department director Daniel Lane, Ph.D., to become a professor in the department of biological chemistry. He then served as the vice chancellor for science and technology at Duke University Medical Center where he guided the development of Duke's biomedical research. In 2008, he took his current position at Johns Hopkins. Dr. Agre was elected to membership in the National Academy of Sciences in 2000, to the American Academy of Arts and Sciences in 2003, and to the Institute of Medicine in 2005. He holds two U.S. patents on the isolation, cloning and expression of aquaporins 1 and 5, and he is the principal investigator on four current National Institutes of Health grants. Dr. Agre was awarded the 2003 Nobel Prize in Chemistry by the Royal Swedish Academy of Sciences. The Academy recognized him for his laboratory's 1991 discovery of the long-sought "channels" that regulate and facilitate water molecule transport through cell membranes, a process essential to all living organisms. He is a member of the Committee on Human Rights of the National Academy of Sciences, National Academy of Engineering, and Institute of Medicine. In February 2009, Dr. Agre was inducted as the 169th President of the American Association for the Advancement of Science (AAAS).

ENRIQUETA BOND [IOM] served, from 1994 to 2008, as the first full-time president of the Burroughs Wellcome Fund (BWF), a private, independent foundation dedicated to advancing the medical sciences by supporting research and other scientific and educational activities. During her presidency, Dr. Bond guided BWF in its transition from a corporate to a private independent foundation and its endowment grew from $400 million to $800 million. Prior to joining the BWF, Dr. Bond served as the chief executive officer for the Institute of Medicine. In 1997, Dr. Bond was elected as a full member to the Institute of Medicine. In 2004, she was elected as a fellow to the American Association for the Advancement of Science for her distinguished contributions to the study and analysis of policy for the advancement of the health sciences. Dr. Bond is chairman of the National Research Council's Board on African Science Academy Development and a member of the Forum on Microbial Threats. She is a past member of the Report Review Committee as well as numerous other study committees. Dr. Bond is the recipient of numerous honors, including the 2008 Order of the Long Leaf Pine award from the state of North Carolina. This is the highest honor the governor can bestow on a citizen and was awarded to Dr. Bond for her efforts to improve science education for children of North Carolina. She has also received the Institute of Medicine Walsh McDermott Medal, in recognition of distinguished service to the National Academies, and the National Academy of Sciences

Professional Staff Award. She received her bachelor's degree from Welles-ley College, her M.A. from the University of Virginia, and her Ph.D. in molecular biology and biochemical genetics from Georgetown University.

C.W. "PAUL" CHU [NAS] is T.L.L. Temple Chair of Science and profes-sor of physics at the University of Houston and served from 2001 to 2009 as president of the Hong Kong University of Science and Technology. Dr. Chu was born in Hunan, China, and received his bachelor of science from Cheng-Kung University in Taiwan. After service with the Nationalist Chi-nese Air Force, he earned his master of science from Fordham University and his doctorate at the University of California at San Diego. All three degrees were in physics. He is a pioneer in the field of high-temperature superconductivity whose groundbreaking research has earned him global recognition. After 2 years of industrial research with Bell Laboratories, Dr. Chu took an academic appointment at Cleveland State University. He stayed there for 9 years. He assumed his appointment at the University of Houston in 1979. At various times, he has served as a consultant and a visiting staff member at Bell Labs, Los Alamos National Lab, the Marshall Space Flight Center, Argonne National Lab, and DuPont. He is the found-ing director of the Texas Center for Superconductivity at the University of Houston and serves as the center's senior science adviser. Dr. Chu is a member of the U.S. National Academy of Sciences, the American Acad-emy of Arts and Sciences, the Chinese Academy of Sciences, the Academia Sinica, and the Academy of Sciences for the Developing World. He also was elected a foreign member of the Russian Academy of Engineering. Dr. Chu has received numerous awards, including the 1988 National Medal of Science, the highest honor possible for a scientist in the United States, for his work on high-temperature superconductivity. The White House ap-pointed Dr. Chu to be among 12 distinguished scientists who will evaluate National Medal of Science nominees. He also has been awarded the Bernd Matthias Prize and the John Fritz Medal, which he holds with science and engineering icons such as Alexander Graham Bell and Thomas Edison.

FRANCISCO G. CIGARROA [IOM] was appointed the 10th chancellor of The University of Texas (UT) System by the UT System Board of Re-gents on January 9, 2009. He began his service as the UT System's chief administrative officer on February 2, 2009. As chancellor, Dr. Cigarroa oversees one of the largest public systems of higher education in the na-tion, with nine universities and six health institutions, an annual operat-ing budget of $11.5 billion (FY 2009), including $2.5 billion in sponsored programs funded by federal, state, local and private sources, and more than 194,000 students and 84,000 employees. Dr. Cigarroa also serves as vice chairman for policy on the Board of Directors of The University of

Texas Investment Management Co. (UTIMCO). A nationally renowned pediatric and transplant surgeon, Dr. Cigarroa served as president of the UT Health Science Center at San Antonio from 2000 until his appointment as chancellor. A native of Laredo, Dr. Cigarroa earned a bachelor's degree from Yale in 1979 and received his medical degree with highest honors from UT Southwestern Medical Center at Dallas in 1983. He has completed 12 years of postgraduate training. He was chief resident at Harvard's teaching hospital, Massachusetts General in Boston, and completed a fellowship at Johns Hopkins Hospital in Baltimore. In 1995, he joined the UT Health Science Center faculty in San Antonio. Dr. Cigarroa was on the surgical team that in 1997 split a donor liver for transplant into two recipients; it was the first operation of its type in Texas. In 2000, he headed the team that performed South Texas' first successful pediatric small bowel transplant. Immediately prior to his appointment as president, he served as director of pediatric surgery. He serves on the medical staffs of University Hospital, CHRISTUS Santa Rosa Hospital-Downtown, CHRISTUS Santa Rosa Children's Hospital, CHRISTUS Santa Rosa Hospital-Medical Center and the Baptist Health System, and as a consultant at Methodist Children's Hospital. A member of the Institute of Medicine of The National Academies, Dr. Cigarroa is a fellow of the American College of Surgery and a Diplomate of the American Board of Surgery and has received a certificate in pediatric surgery from the American Board of Surgery. He is an accomplished researcher who has published scientific papers on principles of surgery in infants and children. His many professional affiliations include the American Medical Association, Texas Medical Association and Bexar County Medical Society. He is also a member of the Board of Directors of the Greater San Antonio Chamber of Commerce, the San Antonio Hispanic Chamber of Commerce and United Way of San Antonio and Bexar County.

JAMES DUDERSTADT [NAE] is president emeritus and University Professor of Science and Engineering at the University of Michigan. After a year as an Atomic Energy Commission Postdoctoral Fellow at Caltech, he joined the faculty of the University of Michigan in 1968 in the Department of Nuclear Engineering, rising through the ranks to full professor in 1975. In 1981, Dr. Duderstadt became dean of the College of Engineering and, in 1986, provost and vice president for Academic Affairs in 1986. He was elected president of the University of Michigan in 1988 and served in this role until July 1996. He currently holds a university-wide faculty appointment as University Professor of Science and Engineering, co-chairing the University's program in Science, Technology, and Public Policy and directing the Millennium Project, a research center exploring the impact of over-the-horizon technologies on society. During his career,

Dr. Duderstadt has received numerous national awards for his research, teaching, and service activities, including the E. O. Lawrence Award for excellence in nuclear research, the Arthur Holly Compton Prize for outstanding teaching, the Reginald Wilson Award for national leadership in achieving diversity, and the National Medal of Technology for exemplary service to the nation. He has been elected to numerous honorific societies including the National Academy of Engineering, the American Academy of Arts and Sciences, Phi Beta Kappa, and Tau Beta Pi. Dr. Duderstadt is a past chair of the National Science Board and was a member of the National Commission on the Future of Higher Education (The "Spellings Commission"). He is chair of the NRC's Policy and Global Affairs Committee and a former member of Committee on Science, Engineering, and Public Policy (COSEPUP). He chaired a series of COSEPUP studies providing observations on the President's annual federal science and technology budgets and chaired or served on numerous other Academies' committees. Dr. Duderstadt received a B.Eng. in electrical engineering with highest honors from Yale University in 1964 and a M.S. and Ph.D. in engineering science and physics from the California Institute of Technology in 1967.

RONALD G. EHRENBERG is the Irving M. Ives Professor of Industrial and Labor Relations and Economics at Cornell University and a Stephen H. Weiss Presidential Fellow, the highest award for undergraduate teaching that exists, at Cornell. He also is Director of the Cornell Higher Education Research Institute. He was an elected member of the Cornell Board of Trustees from July 2006 to June 2010 and currently serves as a member of the Board of Trustees for the State University of New York (SUNY). From July 1, 1995 to June 30, 1998 he also served as Cornell's Vice President for Academic Programs, Planning, and Budgeting. Ehrenberg is a founding member of the National Academy of Social Insurance (Unemployment Insurance section), a National Associate of the National Academies, a member of the National Academy of Education, a fellow of the Society of Labor Economists, a fellow of the TIAA-CREF Institute, and a fellow of the American Education Research Association. He is a research associate at the National Bureau of Economic Research, a research fellow at IZA (Berlin), was a member of the Executive Committee of the American Economic Association, chaired the AAUP Committees on Retirement and the Economic Status of the Profession, and is past president of the Society of Labor Economists. He also chaired the NRC's Board of Higher Education and Workforce, served on its committee on Gender Differences in the Careers of Science, Engineering and Mathematics Faculty, and serves on its committee studying the measurement of productivity in higher education. He is the author of Tuition Rising: Why College Costs So Much (Harvard

University Press, 2002); a coauthor of Educating Scholars: Doctoral Education in the Humanities (Princeton University Press, (2010), the editor of American University: National Treasure or Endangered Species (Cornell University Press, 1997), Governing Academia (Cornell University Press, 2004), What's Happening to Public Higher Education? (Johns Hopkins University Press, 2007), and the co-editor of Science and the University (University of Wisconsin Press, 2007) and Doctoral Education and the Faculty of the Future (Cornell University Press, 2008). Dr. Ehrenberg has supervised the dissertations of 44 Ph.D. students and served on committees for countless more. He is also passionate about undergraduate education, involves undergraduate students in his research, and has co-authored papers with a number of these undergraduates. In 2003, ILR-Cornell awarded him the General Mills Foundation Award for Exemplary Undergraduate Teaching. Dr. Ehrenberg received a B.A. in mathematics from Harpur College (State University of New York-Binghamton) in 1966, M.A. and Ph.D. in economics from Northwestern University in 1970, an Honorary Doctor of Science from SUNY in 2008, and an Honorary Doctorate of Humane Letters from Pennsylvania State University in 2011.

WILLIAM FRIST, JR., is both a nationally recognized heart and lung transplant surgeon and former U.S. Senate Majority Leader. He is currently University Distinguished Professor of Health Care at Vanderbilt University and a partner at Cressey & Company LP, a private investment firm focused on the healthcare industry. He recently served as the Frederick H. Schultz Class of 1951 Visiting Professor of International Economic Policy at Princeton University's Woodrow Wilson School of Public and International Affairs. Dr. Frist majored in health policy as an undergraduate at Princeton University's Woodrow Wilson School of Public and International Affairs before graduating with honors from Harvard Medical School and completing surgical training at Massachusetts General Hospital and Stanford. As the founder and director of the Vanderbilt Multi-Organ Transplant Center, he has performed more than 150 heart and lung transplants. He has authored more than 100 peer-reviewed medical articles and chapters, over 400 newspaper articles, and 7 books on topics such as bioterrorism, transplantation, and leadership. He is board certified in both general and heart surgery. Dr. Frist represented Tennessee in the U.S. Senate for 12 years where he served on both committees responsible for writing health legislation (Health and Finance). He was elected Majority Leader of the Senate, having served fewer total years in Congress than any person chosen to lead that body in history. His leadership was instrumental in passage of prescription drug legislation and funding to fight HIV in the United States and globally.

WILLIAM GREEN is chairman and chief executive officer of Accenture, a U.S. $21.6 billion global management consulting technology services and outsourcing company. In addition to chairing the board of directors, Mr. Green is responsible for managing the company, formulating and executing long-term strategies and for all interactions with clients, employees, investors and other stakeholders. Mr. Green is Accenture's primary decision maker and policy maker, setting the tone for the company's values, ethics, and culture. He has served on Accenture's board of directors since its inception in 2001. Mr. Green joined Accenture in 1977 and became a partner in 1986. Mr. Green represents Accenture in a number of external venues, including the Business Roundtable, where he serves as chairman of its Education, Innovation and Workforce Initiative, and as chairman of The Springboard Project, an independent commission on workforce issues. He is a member of the Business Higher Education Forum. He attended Dean College and is a member of its Board of Trustees. He received a bachelor of science degree in economics and a master of business administration from Babson College, as well as an honorary doctor of laws.

JOHN L. HENNESSY [NAS/NAE] is president of Stanford University. He joined Stanford's faculty in 1977 as an assistant professor of electrical engineering. He rose through the academic ranks to full professorship in 1986 and was the inaugural Willard R. and Inez Kerr Bell Professor of Electrical Engineering and Computer Science from 1987 to 2004. From 1983 to 1993, Dr. Hennessy was director of the Computer Systems Laboratory, a research and teaching center operated by the Departments of Electrical Engineering and Computer Science that fosters research in computer systems design. A pioneer in computer architecture, in 1981 Dr. Hennessy drew together researchers to focus on a computer architecture known as RISC (Reduced Instruction Set Computer), a technology that has revolutionized the computer industry by increasing performance while reducing costs. In addition to his role in basic research, Dr. Hennessy helped transfer this technology to industry. In 1984, he cofounded MIPS Computer Systems, now MIPS Technologies, which designs microprocessors. In recent years, his research has focused on the architecture of high-performance computers. He served as chair of computer science from 1994 to 1996 and, in 1996, was named dean of the School of Engineering. In 1999, he was named provost, the university's chief academic and financial officer. As provost, he continued his efforts to foster interdisciplinary activities in the biosciences and bioengineering and oversaw improvements in faculty and staff compensation. In October 2000, he was inaugurated as Stanford University's 10th president. In 2005, he became the inaugural holder of the Bing Presidential Professorship. Dr. Hennessy is a recipient of the 2000 IEEE John von Neumann Medal, the 2000 ASEE Benjamin Garver Lamme Award, the 2001 ACM Eckert-Mauchly Award, the 2001 Seymour Cray Computer Engineering Award, a 2004 NEC C&C Prize for lifetime achievement in computer science and engineering and a 2005 Founders Award from the American Academy of Arts and Sciences. He is a member of the National Academy of Engineering and the National Academy of Sciences, and he is a fellow of the American Academy of Arts and Sciences, the Association for Computing Machinery, and the Institute of Electrical and Electronics Engineers. He is currently a member of the NRC's Board on Global Science and Technology and the Co-Chair of the Committee on Scientific Communication and National Security. Dr. Hennessy earned his bachelor's degree in electrical engineering from Villanova University and his master's and doctoral degrees in computer science from the State University of New York at Stony Brook.

WALTER E. MASSEY is president of the School of the Art Institute of Chicago, the former president of Morehouse College, and recently retired chairman of the board of Bank of America. Immediately prior to Morehouse, Massey was provost and senior vice president for academic affairs at the University of California. In this position, the second most senior position in the UC system, he was responsible for academic and research planning and policy, budget planning and allocations, and programmatic oversight of the three national laboratories the University manages for the Department of Energy: Lawrence Livermore National Laboratory, Los Alamos National Laboratory and Lawrence Berkeley Laboratory. Earlier, Massey held a range of administrative and academic positions. He is former director of the National Science Foundation, a position to which he was appointed by former President George H.W. Bush. Massey also served as vice president for research and professor of physics at the University of Chicago, as director of the Argonne National Laboratory, dean of the College and professor of physics at Brown University and as assistant professor of physics at the University of Illinois. Massey is a past chair of the Secretary of Energy Advisory Board (SEAB) and a former member of the President's Council of Advisors on Science and Technology. He is a fellow and past president of the American Association for the Advancement of Science, a fellow and past vice president of the American Physical Society, and a member of the American Academy of Arts and Sciences, the American Philosophical Society and the Council on Foreign Relations. Massey's research has involved the study of quantum liquids and solids. His written work has also addressed science and math education, the role of science in a democratic society, and university-industry interactions and technology transfer in national and international settings.

He is the recipient of more than 30 honorary degrees from institutions such as Yale University, Northwestern University, Amherst, and the Ohio State University. Dr. Massey holds a bachelor of science in physics and mathematics in 1958 from Morehouse and a master's and doctorate in physics in 1966 from Washington University in St. Louis, Missouri.

BURTON J. MCMURTRY has been a Silicon Valley venture capital investor since 1969. He co-founded several venture capital partnerships, including Technology Venture Investors (TVI) and Institutional Venture Associates. Portfolio companies included Adaptec, Altera, Compaq, Intuit, KLA-Tencor, Linear Technology Corporation, Microsoft, NBI, Nellcor, PMC Sierra, Quantum, ROLM Corporation, SpectraLink, Sun Microsystems, Synopsys, Triad Systems Corporation, VeriFone, and Visio. Mr. McMurtry formerly chaired the board of trustees of Stanford University and served as a trustee of Rice University and of the Carnegie Institution of Washington. He served as chairman of the National Venture Capital Association and of the Western Association of Venture Capitalists. From 1957 until 1969 he worked for GTE-Sylvania in microwave and laser research and engineering. A native of Houston, Texas, he holds B.A. and BSEE degrees from Rice University and M.S. and Ph.D. degrees in electrical engineering from Stanford University.

ERNEST MONIZ is the Cecil and Ida Green Professor of Physics and Engineering Systems, director of the Energy Initiative, and director of the Laboratory for Energy and the Environment at the Massachusetts Institute of Technology, where he has served on the faculty since 1973. Dr. Moniz served as Under Secretary of the Department of Energy from 1997 until January 2001 and, from 1995 to 1997, as associate director for Science in the Office of Science and Technology Policy in the Executive Office of the President. At DOE, he had oversight of the science and energy programs, led a comprehensive review of nuclear weapons stockpile stewardship, and served as the Secretary's special negotiator for Russian nuclear materials disposition programs. He is a member of the Council on Foreign Relations and received the 1998 Seymour Cray HPCC Industry Recognition Award for vision and leadership in advancing scientific simulation. He has served on several NRC committees, including the Committee on Evaluation of Quantification of Margins and Uncertainty (QMU) Methodology Applied to the Certification of the Nation's Nuclear Weapons Stockpile and the Committee on Transportation of Radioactive Waste. Dr. Moniz received a Bachelor of Science degree summa cum laude in physics from Boston College, a doctorate in theoretical physics from Stanford University, and honorary doctorates from the University of Athens, the University of Erlangen-Nurenberg, and Michigan State University.

HEATHER MUNROE-BLUM became 16th principal (president) and vice-chancellor and senior officer of McGill University in 2003. An accomplished scholar in the fields of epidemiology and public policy and a distinguished administrator, Professor Munroe-Blum is a member of McGill's Faculty of Medicine and a professor in the Department of Epidemiology, Biostatistics and Occupational Health. She is the author of the report "Growing Ontario's Innovation System: The Strategic Role of University Research" that led to the creation of a new framework of science policies and programs in Ontario. Among her main objectives as principal of McGill is a commitment to strengthen the university's leadership at the world level with respect to research, graduate education, student experience, and positive societal contribution. Professor Munroe-Blum serves on numerous not-for-profit and private boards. Prior to assuming the position of principal at McGill, she served at the University of Toronto as a professor, a governor, dean of Social Work, and as vice-president of Research and International Relations (1994-2002). She has also been a professor at York University and McMaster University. She serves on the board and the Internationalization Committee of the Association of American Universities, and chairs the Association of Universities and Colleges of Canada's Standing Advisory Committee on University Research (SACUR). She is a member of the Science, Technology, and Innovation Council (STIC) of Canada, Canada Foundation for Innovation, Trilateral Commission, and is the co-chair of the Private Sector Advisory Committee of the Ontario-Quebec Trade and Co-operation Agreement. She serves on the boards of the Sir Mortimer B. Davis Jewish General Hospital, Trudeau Foundation, Canada Pension Plan Investment Board (CPPIB), Conférence de Montréal, and the Yellow Media Inc. She is the past president of the Conférence des recteurs et des principaux des universités du Québec (CREPUQ) and was a founding director of the Medical and Related Sciences Discovery District (MARS) and Genome Canada, where she also served as vice-chair of the Board. She has served on the boards of the Council of Canadian Academies, the former Medical Research Council of Canada, Neurosciences Canada, Conference Board of Canada, Montreal Chamber of Commerce, Alcan, Canada Forum of Rio Tinto Alcan, Four Seasons Hotel, and Hydro One, among others. Named an Officer of the Order of Canada for her outstanding record of achievements in science, innovation and higher education policy, Professor Munroe-Blum holds numerous honorary degrees from Canadian and international universities and is a Specially Elected Fellow of the Royal Society of Canada. She is a senior fellow of Massey College. In 2008, she was named a Grande Montréalaise, Montréal's highest honor and in June 2009 was named an officer of the National Order of Quebec. Professor Munroe-Blum holds a Ph.D. with distinction in epidemiology from the University of North

Carolina at Chapel Hill, in addition to M.S.W. (Wilfrid Laurier University) and B.A. and B.S.W. degrees (McMaster University).

CHERRY MURRAY [NAS/NAE] is dean of Harvard University's School of Engineering and Applied Sciences (SEAS) a position to which she was appointed on July 1, 2009. She also holds the John A. and Elizabeth S. Armstrong Professorship of Engineering and Applied Sciences. Previously, Dr. Murray served as principal associate director for science and technology at Lawrence Livermore National Laboratory in Livermore, California, where she led 3,500 employees in providing core science and technology support for Lawrence Livermore's major programs. Before joining Lawrence Livermore in 2004, Murray had a long and distinguished career at the famed Bell Laboratories, home to creative researchers who went on to win numerous Nobel Prizes, garner tens of thousands of patents, and invent revolutionary technologies such as the laser and the transistor. She joined Bell Labs in 1978 as a staff scientist, marking the beginning of a career that culminated in her position as senior vice president for physical sciences and wireless research. Dr. Murray is the current president of the American Physical Society (APS). She was elected to the National Academy of Sciences in 1999, to the American Academy of Arts and Sciences in 2001, and to the National Academy of Engineering in 2002. She has served on more than 80 national and international scientific advisory committees, governing boards, and the visiting committee for Harvard's Department of Physics (from 1993 to 2004.) Dr. Murray serves as chair of the Division Committee on Engineering and Physical Sciences (DEPS) and is a member of the Committee on International Security and Arms Control and the U.S. National Committee on Theoretical and Applied Mechanics (ex officio). She was previously a member of the Committee on Prospering in the Global Economy of the 21st Century that authored *Rising Above the Gathering Storm*.

HUNTER R. RAWLINGS, a classics scholar, is president of the Association of American Universities. He was appointed Cornell University's 10th president by the Board of Trustees on December 10, 1994. He took office on July 1, 1995, before the start of Cornell's 130th year, prior to that he was president of the University of Iowa from 1988 to 1995. Dr. Rawlings was a 1966 graduate of Haverford College, with honors in classics, and received his Ph.D. degree from Princeton University in 1970. His scholarly publications include a book, The Structure of Thucydides' History (Princeton University Press, 1981). A national spokesperson for higher education, he has served as chair of the Ivy Council of Presidents and of the Association of American Universities, and was a member of the American Council on Education board. He is a member of the American

Academy of Arts and Sciences and serves on the board of managers of his alma mater, Haverford College, and on the National Advisory Committee of the Woodrow Wilson National Fellowship Foundation. He also serves on the boards of the National Humanities Center and the American School of Classical Studies at Athens.

JOHN S. REED was born in Chicago, but raised in Argentina and Brazil. He graduated from Washington and Jefferson College and the Massachusetts Institute of Technology in 1961 under a joint degree program earning both a B.A. and a B.S. degree. He served as a Lieutenant in the Corps of Engineers, United States Army, from 1962 to 1964 and then returned to MIT for his M.S. degree. Mr. Reed spent 35 years with Citibank/Citicorp and Citigroup, the last 16 as chairman. He retired in April of 2000. Mr. Reed returned to work as chairman of the New York Stock Exchange from September 2003 until April 2005 and is currently serving as chairman of the Corporation of MIT. Mr. Reed is a Trustee of MDRC, the Isabella Stewart Gardner Museum, and the NBER. He is a fellow of the American Academy of Arts and Sciences and of the American Philosophical Society. He is the former chairman and chief executive officer of Citicorp and Citibank. After Citicorp merged with the Travelers Group Inc., in 1998, Mr. Reed served as chairman and co-chief executive officer of the new company, Citigroup. He retired in 2000 after 35 years with the company. He served as chairman of the New York Stock Exchange from September 2003 until April 2005 and is currently a member of the MIT Corporation, the Institute's governing body, and he is on the board of directors at Altria. He is chairman and a trustee of the Center for Advanced Study in the Behavioral Sciences and he is a trustee of MDRC, a nonprofit, nonpartisan social policy research organization. A fellow of both the American Academy of Arts and Sciences and of the American Philosophical Society, Mr. Reed is also a member of The Presidents' Circle and a former member of the Committee on a Strategic Education Research Plan: Bridging Research and Practice and of the Advisory Board of Issues in Science and Technology. He earned joint S.B. and B.A. degrees from MIT and Washington and Jefferson College. He received his S.M. from the MIT Sloan School of Management. He also spent two years as an officer in the U.S. Army Corps of Engineers.

TERESA A. SULLIVAN was elected eighth president of the University of Virginia, effective August 1, 2010. Ms. Sullivan is currently provost and executive vice president for Academic Affairs at the University of Michigan. She is also Professor of Sociology in the College of Literature, Science, and the Arts. Prior to coming to the University of Michigan, Dr. Sullivan was executive vice chancellor for Academic Affairs for the University of

Texas System, a position she held from 2002 until May 2006. In that role, she was the chief academic officer for the nine academic campuses within the University of Texas System. Her responsibilities included developing tuition-setting procedures, initiating and supporting educational and research collaborations among the various campuses, and developing external collaborations. Dr. Sullivan first joined the University of Texas at Austin in 1975 as an instructor and then assistant professor in the Department of Sociology. From 1977 to 1981, she was a faculty member at the University of Chicago. She returned to Texas in 1981 as a faculty member in Sociology. In 1986 she was named to the Law School faculty as well. Dr. Sullivan also held several administrative positions at Texas including: vice president and graduate dean (1995-2002), vice provost (1994-1995), chair of the Department of Sociology (1990-1992), and director of Women's Studies (1985-1987). Dr. Sullivan's research focuses on labor force demography, with particular emphasis on economic marginality and consumer debt. The author or co-author of six books and more than 50 scholarly articles, her most recent work explores the question of who files for bankruptcy and why. Ms. Sullivan has served as chair of the U.S. Census Advisory Committee. She is past secretary of the American Sociological Association and a fellow of the American Association for the Advancement of Science. A graduate of James Madison College at Michigan State University, Dr. Sullivan received her doctoral degree in sociology from the University of Chicago.

SIDNEY TAUREL is chairman emeritus of Eli Lilly and Company. Born a Spanish citizen in Casablanca, Morocco, Mr. Taurel became an American citizen in November 1995. After graduating from Ecole des Hautes Etudes Commerciales, in Paris, France in 1969, he received a master of business administration degree from Columbia University in 1971. Mr. Taurel joined Eli Lilly and Company in 1971 as an international marketing associate. His 37-year career included 15 years in Brazil, France, Eastern Europe, and the United Kingdom. He became president of Lilly International in 1986, president of the Pharmaceutical Division in 1993, chief operations officer in 1996, chief executive officer in 1998, and chairman of the board in 1999. He retired as chairman and chief executive officer in 2008. Mr. Taurel is chairman of the Strategic Advisory Committee for Capital Royalty, LLC. He is also a member of the boards of IBM Corporation, McGraw-Hill Companies, Inc., and BioCrossroads. He serves on the board of overseers of the Columbia Business School, is a member of the Business Council, and a trustee at the Indianapolis Museum of Art. Mr. Taurel is a past president of Pharmaceutical Research and Manufacturers of America (PhRMA) and a former member of the board of ITT Industries. He received three Presidential appointments: to the Homeland Security

Advisory Council (2002-2004), the President's Export Council (2002-2007), and the Advisory Committee for Trade Policy and Negotiations (2007-2009). He is an officer of the French Legion of Honor. Mr. Taurel is fluent in English, French, Spanish, and Portuguese.

LEE T. TODD, JR. became the 11th president of the University of Kentucky (UK) on July 1, 2001, a post he continued until his retirement on June 30, 2011. He is a native of Earlington, Kentucky and a graduate of UK and the Massachusetts Institute of Technology. Dr. Todd is the sixth UK alumnus to hold the presidency. He is a former UK engineering professor; a successful businessman who launched two worldwide technology companies, both based in Kentucky; and a public advocate for research, technology, and an entrepreneurial economy in the Commonwealth. Dr. Todd serves as chair of the Advisory Board for the National Science Foundation's Directorate for Education and Human Resources Committee. He is immediate past chair of the Board of Directors for the Association of Public and Land-Grant Universities and is presently chair of the APLU Science Math Teacher Imperative. He is president of the Southeastern Conference (SEC) Executive Committee and represents the SEC as a member of the NCAA Division I Board of Directors as well as on the Bowl Championship Series Committee. Dr. Todd is a member of the Executive Committee of the Business Higher Education Forum. He serves on the Equitable Resources Board of Directors and is chair of the Kentucky Council on Postsecondary Education's STEM (Science, Technology, Engineering, and Mathematics) Task Force. He is chair of the National Consortium for Continuous Improvement in Higher Education's Leveraging Excellence Award selection panel.

LAURA D'ANDREA TYSON is the S.K. and Angela Chan Professor of Global Management at the Haas School of Business, at the University of California, Berkeley. She served as dean of London Business School from 2002 to 2006, and as dean of the Haas School of Business, University of California, Berkeley from 1998 to 2001. Since 2007, Dr. Tyson has served as a senior adviser to the McKinsey Global Institute and the Center for American Progress. She is a member of the Brookings Institution Hamilton Project Advisory Council and a member of the Massachusetts Institute of Technology Corporation. Dr. Tyson is an advisory board member of Newman's Own Advisory Board; Generation Investment Management; The Rock Creek Group; and H&Q Asia Pacific. She is a director at LECG (Law and Economics Consulting Group) and she serves on the Board of Directors of Eastman Kodak Company; Morgan Stanley; AT&T, Inc.; the Peter G. Peterson Institute of International Economics; the New America Foundation; and Silver Spring Networks. Dr. Tyson is a member of President Obama's Economic Recovery Advisory Board (PERAB). She served in the Clinton Administration from January 1993 to December 1996. Between March 1995 and December 1996 she served as President Clinton's National Economic Adviser. Prior to her appointment as National Economic Adviser, Dr. Tyson served as the sixteenth chairman of the White House Council of Economic Advisers, the first woman to hold that post since the Council's establishment in 1946. She was responsible for providing the President with advice and analysis on all economic policy matters, for preparing the Administration's economic forecasts and for the annual Economic Report of the President. In January 2003, the United Kingdom's Department of Trade and Industry appointed Dr. Tyson chair of a special Task Force on Non-Executive Directors, and in June 2003, The Tyson Report on the Recruitment and Development of Non-Executive Directors was submitted to the United Kingdom government. Dr. Tyson has written opinion columns for many publications including The New York Times, The Wall Street Journal, The Washington Post, and the Financial Times. She was a monthly columnist for Business Week between 1998 and 2005 and has made numerous television appearances on economic issues. She is the author of numerous reports, academic papers and books on competitiveness, industrial policy and international trade, including the influential book Who's Bashing Whom? Trade Conflict in High Technology Industries. Dr. Tyson has a summa cum laude undergraduate degree from Smith College and a Ph.D. in economics from the Massachusetts Institute of Technology.

PADMASREE WARRIOR is Cisco Systems' Chief Technology Officer. As CTO, she is responsible for helping drive the company's technological innovations and strategy and works closely with its senior executive team and board of directors to align these efforts with Cisco's corporate goals. Dr. Warrior joined Cisco in 2007. Prior to that, she was the CTO at Motorola, where she led a team of 26,000 engineers and directed Motorola Labs, with an annual R&D budget of $3.7 billion. Over the course of her 23 years at that company, she served in a broad range of roles, including as corporate vice president and general manager of Motorola's Energy Systems Group, and as corporate vice president and chief technology officer for its Semiconductor Products Sector. Under Dr. Warrior's leadership, Motorola was awarded the 2004 National Medal of Technology by the President of the United States, the first time the company had received this honor. Recently, the Economic Times ranked her as the 11th Most Influential Global Indian, and the United States Pan Asian American Chamber of Commerce recognized her with its prestigious Excellence Award. Warrior is also a strong and vocal advocate for women and minorities in math, science and engineering. In 2007, she was inducted into the Women in Information Technology International Hall of Fame, and received the YWCA Metropolitan Chicago Outstanding Woman of Achievement Award. She has been recognized as a role model by many organizations, including the Girl Scouts Illinois Crossroads Council, Notre Dame Girls High School, the South Asian Women Leadership Forum and as a Science Spectrum Trailblazer. In 2001 she was one of six women nationwide selected to receive the "Women Elevating Science and Technology" award from *Working Woman* magazine. Dr. Warrior has served on the boards of Chicago's Joffrey Ballet and Museum of Science and Industry, the Singapore Agency for Science, Technology and Research (ASTAR), the Chicago Mayor's Technology Council, Cornell University Engineering Council, and advisory council of Indian Institute of Technology. She previously served on the Texas Governor's Council for Digital Economy, the White House Fellowships Selection Board, and the Technology Advisory Council for the FCC and on the Advisory Committee for the Computing and Information Science and Engineering of the National Science Foundation (NSF). Dr. Warrior holds a M.S. degree in chemical engineering from Cornell University and a B.S. degree in chemical engineering from the Indian Institute of Technology (IIT) in New Delhi, India. In 2007 she was awarded an honorary Doctorate of Engineering from New York's Polytechnic University.

C

Work of the Committee

The National Research Council empanelled a committee to carry out this study that was deliberately composed of individuals who are or who have recently been leaders in academia, industry, government, and national laboratories. The NRC sought this sectoral balance and also diversity among academic institutions, balance across fields, and wide geographic distribution, including individuals with significant international experience.[1]

The committee was organized in July 2010, and began its work through a series of conference calls to discuss its charge, plan its work, and organize its first meeting. That first meeting, held September 21-22, 2010, featured presentations from:

Robert Berdahl, President, Association of American Universities (AAU), and
Peter McPherson, President, Association of Public and Land-grant Universities (APLU)

A second meeting, held November 22-24, 2010, featured additional speakers and three focus groups sessions.[2] Speakers included:

Lamar Alexander, United States Senator
Cora Marrett, Deputy Director, National Science Foundation

---

[1] See Appendix B for committee member biographies.
[2] See Appendix D for agendas of the first two committee meetings.

Sally Rockey, Deputy Director for Extramural Research, National
Institutes of Health

Steven Koonin, Undersecretary of Energy for Science

Jonathan Cole, John Mitchell Mason Professor of the University
and Provost and Dean of the Faculties Emeritus, Columbia
University, and author of *The Great American University: Its Rise
to Preeminence, Its Indispensable National Role, Why It Must Be
Protected*

Anthony DeCrappeo, President, Council on Governmental Relations
(COGR)

Debra Stewart, President, Council of Graduate Schools (CGS)

William Russel, Arthur W. Marks '19 Professor of Chemical and
Biological Engineering, Dean of the Graduate School, Princeton
University, and Chair, Commission on the Future of Graduate
Education in the United States

Stacy Gelhaus, Chair, Board of Directors, National Postdoctoral
Association (NPA), and Research Associate, Center for Cancer
Pharmacology, University of Pennsylvania

Robert Cook-Deegan, Director, Center for Genome Ethics, Law
and Policy, Institute for Genome Sciences and Policy, Duke
University; Member, National Research Council Study
Committee for *Managing University Intellectual Property in the
Public Interest*

Daniel Atkins, Associate Vice-President for Research
Cyberinfrastructure and W.K. Kellogg Professor of Community
Informatics, University of Michigan

This second meeting also included three "focus group sessions" on:

Institutional Environment: Research University Finance and
Administration

Knowledge Capital: Academic Research Agendas, Resources,
Organization, and Commercialization

Human Capital: Doctoral Education, Postdoctoral Training, Labor
Markets, and Careers

Each group included committee members along with about 10 invited guests nominated by AAU, APLU, COGR, CGS, and NPA. These
sessions were designed to ask probing questions about these three areas
of inquiry in order to elicit input for the committee's deliberation. The
sessions began with each invited guest speaking for up to five minutes

each on questions provided them in advance and then continued with open discussion. A summary of each discussion was later provided by staff to the full committee.[3]

Information gathering, then, drew on the speakers in the committee's public sessions, the three focus group sessions, comments provided to the committee by outside groups, comments provided by individuals to the committee through the study Web site, a review of the literature, and data analysis by staff.

---

[3] See Appendix D for a list of questions and participants for each of the three sessions.

D

Meeting Agendas

Meeting 1:
September 21-22, 2010
Tuesday, September 21

OPEN SESSION

1:00   Welcome, Introductions, and Review of Agenda
        Chad Holliday, Committee Chair

1:15   Review of Charge
        Chad Holliday, Committee Chair

1:30   Policy Context
        Charles M. Vest, President, National Academy of Engineering

2:15   Break

CLOSED SESSION

2:30   Issue Identification (summary of calls and table)
        Peter Henderson, Study Director

3:15   Committee Discussion
        Chad Holliday, Committee Chair

OPEN SESSION

4:30   Reception with Stakeholders

5:15   Q&A Led by Chad Holliday, Committee Chair

CLOSED SESSION

6:30   Committee Working Dinner

Wednesday, September 22

CLOSED SESSION

8:00   Breakfast

8:30   NRC Discussion of Committee Balance and Bias
        Charlotte Kuh, Deputy Executive Director, Policy and Global Affairs

OPEN SESSION

9:30   Panel Discussion of Health and Future of U.S. Research
        Universities
        Robert Berdahl, President, Association of American Universities
        Peter McPherson, President, Association of Public and Land-Grant
        Universities

10:30   Break

CLOSED SESSION

10:45   Committee Discussion: Identify and prioritize key issues

12:30   Lunch

OPEN SESSION

1:30   Next Steps

3:00   Adjourn

Meeting 2:
November 22-24, 2010
Monday, November 22, 2010

CLOSED SESSION

8:30   Continental Breakfast

8:30   Welcome and Introductions
       Chad Holliday, Committee Chair
       Committee members

8:40   Committee Discussion of Balance and Conflict of Interest
       Richard Bissell, Executive Director, Policy and Global Affairs

OPEN SESSION

9:30   Welcome to Open Session and Discussion of Meeting Agenda
       Chad Holliday, Committee Chair

10:00 Focus Groups

       Institutional Environment: Research University Finance and
       Administration (Meeting Room A)
       Knowledge Capital: Academic Research Agendas, Resources,
       Organization, and Commercialization (Meeting Room B)
       Human Capital: Doctoral Education, Postdoctoral Training, Labor
       Markets, and Careers (Board Room)

12:20 Break

12:30 Lunch

1:00   Congressional Request
       Lamar Alexander, United States Senator (via teleconference)

1:30   Federal Agency Perspectives
       Cora Marrett, Deputy Director, National Science Foundation
       *Sally Rockey, Deputy Director for Extramural Research, National
       Institutes of Health*

3:00   The Great American University: Its Rise to Preeminence, Its
        Indispensable National Role, Why It Must Be Protected
        *Jonathan Cole, John Mitchell Mason Professor of the University and
        Provost and Dean of the Faculties Emeritus, Columbia University*

4:00   Break

4:15   Issues in Academic Research:

        Finance and Administration
        Tony DeCrappeo, President, Council on Government Relations

        Managing University Intellectual Property in the Public Interest
        *Robert Cook-Deegan, Director, Center for Genome Ethics, Law and
        Policy, Institute for Genome Sciences and Policy, Duke University;
        Member, Study Committee, Managing University Intellectual Property*

5:30   Adjourn

CLOSED SESSION

6:30   Committee Dinner

Tuesday, November 23, 2010

OPEN SESSION

8:00   Committee Gathers

8:00   Continental Breakfast

8:30   Federal Agency Perspectives (continued)
        Steven Koonin, Undersecretary of Energy for Science

9:15   Technology and the Future of the U.S. Research University
        *Daniel Atkins, Associate Vice President for Research
        Cyberinfrastructure and Kellogg Professor of Community Information,
        University of Michigan (via teleconference)*

10:00   Break

10:15   Postdoctoral Training and Doctoral Careers
        Stacy Gelhaus, Chair, Board of Directors, National Postdoctoral
        Association, and Research Associate, Center for Cancer Pharmacology,
        University of Pennsylvania

11:00   The Path Forward: The Future of Graduate Education in the
        United States
        Debra Stewart, President, Council of Graduate Schools
        William Russel, Arthur W. Marks '19 Professor of Chemical and
        Biological Engineering, Dean of the Graduate School, Princeton
        University

12:00   Lunch (Meal ticket for cafeteria provided to each committee
        member)

12:30   Sponsor Perspectives
        Michael S. Teitelbaum, Program Director, Alfred P. Sloan Foundation

CLOSED SESSION

1:00   Committee Business
        Discussion of Project Timeline
        Continuation of Committee Discussion of Balance and Conflict of
        Interest

1:15   *Senator William Frist*: Discussion of working with Congress

1:45   SWOT Analysis: Presentations and Discussion
        Focus Groups: Report Back and Discussion

3:00   Break

3:15   Breakout groups (Rooms 104, 106, 109)

6:00   Committee Working Dinner

Wednesday, November 24, 2010, Keck 109

CLOSED SESSION

7:30   Continental Breakfast

8:00   Report Back from Breakout Groups

8:30   Report Outline and Key Messages

10:30 Schedule and Assignments

11:00 Adjourn

E

Focus Group Sessions: Questions and Participants

Institutional Environment Focus Group:
Financial and Organizational Capacity of Research Universities

In their letter requesting this study, Senators Alexander and Mikulski and Representatives Gordon and Hall asked the National Academies to examine the financial, organizational, and intellectual health of U.S. research universities. In this focus group session, we focus on the organizational capacity and financial health of public and private research universities in the United States. The following questions developed by National Research Council staff will provide helpful input to committee members as they deliberate their findings and recommendations. They do not in any way indicate what those findings and recommendations may be:

> How strong are U.S. research universities, individually and collectively?

> What are the current and possible future threats to the financial health of U.S. research universities? What are the current impacts of federal and state policies on research universities?

> What are the strengths and weaknesses of U.S. research universities in responding to those threats? How can U.S. research universities—individually and collectively—respond to these threats?

How can U.S. research universities strengthen their financial positions by improving management or capitalizing on new revenue opportunities?

Of the following, what are the most important issues that the committee should consider in its deliberations and why?

Changes or instability in revenue streams

Changes in operating costs

Planning for and managing capital costs

Indirect cost recovery

Managing academic, administrative, and other workforce needs and costs

Managing university operations

Managing procurement

Regulatory and reporting requirements for higher education institutions

Efficiently harnessing technology for management, education, and research

Positioning institutions in the evolving ecosystem of U.S. research universities

Competition between public and private universities that harm institutions and drive up costs

Globalization of higher education and research

Public understanding of the value of research universities

Something else?

In what ways will U.S. research universities—individually or collectively—need to change over the next two decades? What might the "game changers" be? How does the enterprise need to evolve? How can public policy facilitate this evolution?

What are the top actions to assure the strong financial and organizational capacity of U.S. research universities that the study committee could recommend to Congress, the federal government, state governments, research universities, and others that are supported by evidence and will have traction in the current fiscal and political environment?

Participants

Committee Members
    James Duderstadt
    William Greene
    Paul Chu

Walter Massey
Hunter Rawlings

NRC Staff
Peter Henderson
Laura DeFeo, Science and Technology Policy Fellow

Invited Guests
Peter Lange, Duke University
Albert Horvath, Pennsylvania State University
Tim Slottow, University of Michigan
Kim Wilcox, Michigan State University
Sally Mason, University of Iowa
Diana Natalicio, University of Texas at El Paso (Tentative)
David Frohnmayer, University of Oregon
V'Ella Warren, University of Washington
Steven Beckwith, University of California System
Arthur Bienenstock, Stanford University

Association Staff
Robert Berdahl, Association of American Universities
David Shulenburger, Association of Public and Land-Grant
    Universities
David Kennedy, Council on Government Relations Knowledge
    Capital Focus Group
Academic Research: Agendas, Resources, Organization, and
    Commercialization

In their letter requesting this study, Senators Alexander and Mikulski and Representatives Gordon and Hall asked the National Academies to examine the financial, organizational, and intellectual health of U.S. research universities. In this focus group session, we focus on key issues in the funding and organization of academic research. The following questions developed by NRC staff will provide helpful input to committee members as they deliberate their findings and recommendations. They do not in any way indicate what those findings and recommendations may be:

> How strong is U.S. academic research? What are the most important challenges we must address to ensure its strength and ability to address national goals going forward? What are the strengths and weaknesses of U.S. research universities in responding to those challenges? Are there differences by field?

Are current federal and state research policies—and by extension the academic research enterprise—aligned with national needs? What emerging needs require changes in research funding or agendas?

What is the proper role of academic research in the larger U.S. research and innovation ecosystem relative to other components (industry labs, national labs, FFRDCs, etc.)?

Of the following, what are the most important issues that the committee should consider in its deliberations and why?
  Implications of trends in federal, state, industry, and philanthropic funding and policies for research agendas, organization, and quality
  Balance in the academic research enterprise across disciplines and types (basic, applied, development)
  Organization or structure of research teams
  Regulatory and reporting requirements
  Quality of or access to research facilities
  Demands on faculty
  Disciplinary organization, interdisciplinarity, emerging fields
  Collaboration (across disciplines, institutions, sectors, nations)
  Managing and commercializing university intellectual property
  Managing conflicts of interest
  Globalization of the academic research enterprise
  The role of information and communications technology in research
  Public understanding of the value of research
  Something else?

What major changes in the U.S. or global academic research enterprise are possible over the next two decades? What might the "game changers" be? How does the enterprise need to evolve? How can public policy facilitate this evolution?

What are the top actions to assure the strength of the U.S. academic research enterprise and its ability to contribute to national goals that the study committee could recommend to Congress, the federal government, state governments, research universities, and others that are supported by evidence and will have traction in the current fiscal and political environment?

Participants

Committee Members
  Chad Holliday, Bank of America
  Teresa Sullivan, University of Virginia
  Peter Agre, Johns Hopkins Bloomberg School of Public Health
  Cherry Murray, Harvard University
  Charles M. Vest, National Academy of Engineering (ex officio)

NRC Staff
  Charlotte Kuh, Policy and Global Affairs
  Michelle Crosby-Nagy, Policy and Global Affairs

Invited Guests
  David Wynes, Emory University
  Richard Marchase, University of Alabama, Birmingham
  Anita Jones, University of Virginia
  Robert Zemsky, University of Pennsylvania (Learning Alliance)
  David Korn, Harvard Medical School
  Luis Proenza, University of Akron
  Marvin Parnes, University of Michigan
  Molly Jahn, University of Wisconsin
  Kelvin Droegemeier, University of Oklahoma
  Leslie Tolbert, University of Arizona
  Randolph Hall, University of Southern California

Association Staff
  Tobin Smith, Association of American Universities
  Howard Gobstein, Association of Public and Land-Grant Universities
  Anthony DeCrappeo, Council on Government Relations

Human Capital Focus Group:
Doctoral Education, Postdoctoral Training, Labor Markets, and Careers

   In their letter requesting this study, Senators Alexander and Mikulski and Representatives Gordon and Hall asked the National Academies to examine the financial, organizational, and intellectual health of U.S. research universities. In this focus group session, we focus on key human capital issues, including doctoral education, postdoctoral training, and the careers of doctorates in academic and non-academic sectors. The following questions developed by NRC staff will provide helpful input to committee members as they deliberate their findings and recommendations. They do not in any way indicate what those findings and recommendations may be:

What are the strengths of our system of doctoral education and postdoctoral training?

What are the most critical challenges the nation faces in ensuring the strength of doctoral education and postdoctoral training? Are there differences by field?

What are the strengths and weaknesses of U.S. research universities in responding to those challenges? Are there differences by field?

Of the following, what are the most important issues/challenges that the committee should consider in its deliberations and why?
> Training doctoral students in the knowledge of their field
> Reflecting the increasing interdisciplinarity in research in doctoral education
> Aligning doctoral training with career paths in and out of academia
> Balancing the demand for and supply of new doctorates
> Funding mechanisms and packages for doctoral students
> Time-to-degree and time-to-first-job for doctoral students
> Attrition and completion in doctoral education
> Enhancing the postdoctoral experience: stipends, benefits, training, length, career counseling, attaining independent positions and research grants, and other issues
> Labor markets and career options for doctorates
> The changing nature of faculty positions in academia
> Ability to attract high-quality domestic students to U.S. doctoral education
> Ability to attract high-quality international students to U.S. doctoral education
> Globalization of the research enterprise
> Using technology for education and research
> Something else?

What major changes in doctoral education, postdoctoral training, and careers of U.S. doctorates are possible over the next two decades? What might the "game changers" be? How does the enterprise need to evolve? How can public policy facilitate this evolution?

What are the top actions to assure the strength of doctoral education and postdoctoral training in the U.S. that the study committee could recommend to Congress, the federal government, state governments, research universities, and others that are supported by evidence and will have traction in the current fiscal and political environment?

Is it time for a "Flexner Report" on doctoral education that would examine doctoral education in a comprehensive manner, taking into account important differences by field?

Participants

Committee Members
    John Hennessy, Stanford University
    Burt McMurty, Former Venture Capitalist
    Enriqueta Bond, Former President, Burroughs Wellcome Fund
    Francisco Cigarroa, University of Texas System
    William Pinkston (On behalf of Dr. William Frist), Vanderbilt University

NRC Staff
    James Voytuk, Policy and Global Affairs
    Mark Regets, Policy and Global Affairs

Invited Guests (confirmed)
    Stacy Gelhaus, University of Pennsylvania
    Victoria McGovern, Burroughs Wellcome Fund
    Howard H. Garrison, Federation of American Societies for
        Experimental Biology
    Timothy Barbari, Georgetown University
    Lisa M. Kozlowski, AAMC GREAT GROUP
    James Wimbush, Indiana University
    Garth A. Fowler, Northwestern University
    Janet Weiss, Dean, University of Michigan
    Andrew Comrie, University of Arizona
    Jeffery Gibeling, University of California, Davis

Association Staff
    Mollie Benz Flounlacker, Association of American Universities
    Peter McPherson, Association of Public and Land-Grant Universities
    Patricia McAllister, Council of Graduate Schools
    Cathee Phillips, National Postdoctoral Association